What Your Colleagues Are S

"Like an amazing orchestra conductor, Janiel Wagstaff makes reading and writing instruction symphonic. She shows teachers how to lead their young learners each day, with teaching strategies and routines that develop students' oral language, comprehension, and writing skills. Teachers and coaches in the primary grades have been waiting for a big book of lessons like this, and whew, here it is: proof that K–2 literacy instruction can be developmentally appropriate and potent at the same time."

—Sharon Taberski
Author of *The Common Core Companion: The Standards
Decoded, Grades K–2* and *Comprehension From the Ground Up*

"I love this book almost as much as I love Janiel Wagstaff herself. What a treasure trove of daily lessons! Wagstaff provides a blueprint for teachers that will definitely make their lives easier. Any reading teacher interested in inspiring students to become more passionate and adamant readers needs this book."

—Dr. Danny Brassell
Author of *75+ Reading Strategies*

"With personal insights and energy, Janiel Wagstaff provides effective and powerful demonstrations for how to link reading and writing instruction. She discusses ways to make writing more personal and provides clear mini-lessons that work. Whether you are an experienced educator or new to the profession, you will appreciate these daily lessons that are certain to boost your students' reading and writing abilities."

—Jan Richardson
Author of *The Next Step in Guided Reading*

"If you're a K–2 teacher looking for a professional book to guide you in seamlessly integrating reading and writing instruction, this is the one! Janiel has packed this resource with ready-to-teach literacy lessons that target the Common Core State Standards and support young learners as they read, write, think, and talk about mentor texts. My copy is already filled with sticky notes!"

—Maria Walther
Author of *Transforming Literacy Teaching in the Era of Higher Standards*

"Janiel thinks of everything! The reading and writing lessons are classroom-tested, engaging, and you can practically see and hear the young learners 'getting it.' The 'goods' that make it workable in any classroom include mentor texts, student writing samples, master teacher tips, If/Then support for a range of learning outcomes, lesson extensions, and suggestions for differentiation. A welcome resource, providing a step-by-step method for introducing the Common Core standards to primary grade students."

—Wiley Blevins
Author of *Phonics From A–Z*

Booster Lessons
At a Glance

Teachers see from the get-go the writing task students can be working toward in the course of the week.

Each lesson sequence begins with an overview of how teachers guide students through the lessons.

Lesson Sequence 1

Integrating Writing Personal Narratives With Identifying Sensory Words in Text

In this lesson sequence, students read realistic, fictional narratives as a lead in to writing personal narratives. We focus on the temporal order of stories in our reading and retellings and use a first-next-then-last framework to recall the events and details of our own stories. Students learn to add onomatopoetic elements to their writing by studying its use and effect in stories and poetry.

Although this sequence is designed for first grade, many of the instructional elements are suited for kindergarten and second grade; only small tweaks are necessary (see grade level adaptations on pages 31 and 32).

This sequence is intended as an introduction to narrative writing. Though students may eventually write a variety of narratives that venture into fiction (e.g., fantasy stories), we focus here on personal narratives. Young writers are generally successful at recalling events that have actually happened to them, so I find this a good place to start. Since this may be students' first attempts at writing personal narratives, we keep things simple, with most of our focus on retelling the events in our stories in sequential order. We use the temporal words suggested in the standard, *first, next, then,* and *last*, to talk out and plan. As we move through the sequence, we add in onomatopoeia as a simple craft element to liven up our compositions.

Naturally, we immerse ourselves in reading the genre we're writing. We read several realistic stories containing real-lifelike characters and situations. We mine these models for topic ideas and study how the authors sequence their events and use onomatopoeia.

The teacher models throughout and makes use of student volunteers to make the steps in the process explicit. Students constantly talk out their stories, share their thinking, and receive feedback from one another. They draft a bit, then rereading, making any changes needed, talking it out a bit more, then continuing to draft.

This sequence was written with first grade in mind, but can easily be adjusted up or down by eliminating the focus on onomatopoeia or adding an additional focus (several are noted in Extending the Work on page 47).

Young writers get so much out of peer feedback!

Core Connection

Focus Writing Standard 3 integrated with **Reading Literature Standard 4**

Reading Literature Standards 1, 2, 4, 7, and 10

Writing Standards 5

Speaking and Listening Standards 1, 2, 4, 5, and 6

Task

Write a story about something that has happened to you. Tell your story in order: what happened first, next, then, and last. We'll share our stories with friends and family.

Integrating Writing Personal Narratives With Identifying Sensory Words in Text   1

ELA/CCSS standards are highlighted at the outset— and strategically throughout the sequence.

What Teachers Guide Across the Week

LESSONS	READING Speaking and Listening	WRITING Speaking and Listening
1	**Lesson 1:** *Narrative Reading* • Review the task. • Identify purposes for reading. • Read *Knuffle Bunny.* • Orally retell story using the *words first, next, then,* and *last*.	**Lesson 1:** *Quick Sketch Retelling* • Have students sketch the events from *Knuffle Bunny* in four boxes labeled *First, Next, Then,* and *Last*. • Have students label and jot in the boxes. • Share.
2	**Lesson 2:** *Narrative Reading, Brainstorm Topics, Tell Stories* • Identify purposes for reading. • Read *Stella Tells Her Story.* • Start Topics List with class. • Model telling a story. • Have volunteers tell their stories (additions are made to the topics list). • Study *First, Next, Then,* and *Last* illustrations. • Have students talk out their stories in temporal order.	**Lesson 2:** *Story Planning* • Plan stories in boxes labeled *First, Next, Then,* and *Last* using pictures and labels and jottings. • Model. • Have student volunteer model. • Have all students plan in boxes.
3	**Lesson 3:** *Narrative Reading* • Identify purposes for reading. • Read *Shortcut.* • Identify onomatopoetic elements and discuss their effects on the story. • Record words on chart. • Revisit other texts from the week to identify the onomatopoeia. • Make connections for future personal narrative writing.	**Lesson 3:** *Review Story Plan, Add Onomatopoetic Element(s), Begin Drafting* • Model reviewing story plan and adding onomatopoetic words. • Have students do the same. • Retell stories emphasizing the onomatopoeia. • Discuss effect on stories. • Make other additions to story plans. • Begin to draft.
4	**Lesson 4:** *Compare Narrative Readings* • Identify purpose for reading. • Read *Bedhead.* • Have collaborative conversation about how this story is like the other stories we've read. • Begin to create a personal narrative anchor chart. • Discuss how observations relate to our own personal narrative writing.	**Lesson 4:** *Continue Drafting, Connect Anchor Chart to Our Own Writing* • Model drafting using story plan. • Debrief about strategies observed during modeling. • Have students continue drafting their stories. • Have students connect their writing to our fledgling anchor chart.
5	**Lesson 5:** *Poetry Reading* • Read selected poems from *Noisy Poems.* • Read twice chorally emphasizing sounds. • Add words to onomatopoeia chart. • Read third time, eliminating the onomatopoeia. • Discuss effects.	**Lesson 5:** *Quick Write Noisy Poems, Finish Stories, Share, Celebrate* (This may take more than one session.) • Brainstorm subjects and onomatopoetic words for noisy poems. • Model writing a noisy poem. • Have students quick write and share. • Have students finish writing their personal narratives. • Share in small groups. • Decide outside audience for personal narratives. • Debrief.

2   Lesson Sequence 1

There are *five* reading lessons in each sequence and *five* writing lessons that build on one another throughout the week.

Teach them in sequence to gain a surefire way to move back and forth between reading and writing each day and to stay focused on a decided goal week to week. The speedometer image is a reminder that each lesson is designed to "rev up" your instruction.

What Students Do Across the Week

Students read realistic narratives to get ideas for writing their own personal narratives. We focus on how stories are told in temporal order and model our writing after the mentor texts. Students walk away with a completed draft of a personal narrative that they are proud to share!

While reading a variety of realistic narratives, students pay close attention to how stories unfold in a logical sequence. In other sequences and other narrative reading, we've focused on basic story elements and structure: setting, characters, problem, events, and solution. Given our focus here, students practice retelling the stories they read using the words *first, next, then,* and *last*. This becomes the structure they use when preparing to write their own personal narratives.

We begin a class topics list to keep track of our story ideas. Students talk out their ideas with one another, often spending about five minutes on this step. In Grades K–2, oral rehearsal before writing is critical, as many children can access their narrative abilities verbally more easily than when writing. Once students settle on a topic, they plan their stories using sketches and words in four boxes labeled *First, Next, Then,* and *Last*. The intent is to get the bones of their stories recorded so they can go back and add more details later. Using their plans, they talk out their stories again as a rehearsal for writing. I model the processes all along the way, and confer with students as I circulate to respond to their efforts.

Additionally, we add some flair to our writing by adding onomatopoetic elements. We study stories and poetry to help us understand and incorporate these elements. Students add an onomatopoetic word or two to their story plan and talk it out again, emphasizing (and relishing!) these fun words. Onomatopoeia is a clear-cut device, which lays the foundation for then introducing alliteration and other craft elements.

The intent of the sequence is to give students a solid first experience with personal narrative writing. Their writing is not "formally published." It is not revised and edited, though revision and editing do occur when students plan their stories, talk them out, add onomatopoetic elements, share and talk with peers while writing, and when I confer with them.

To culminate the sequence, we share our stories with each other and students are invited to take them home to share with their families. When we debrief, we focus on new possibilities for personal narrative writing and extending into other types of narratives.

Literacy Moves

- Widely read the genre
- Focus study of craft element
- Sketch, label, jot
- Begin an anchor chart for the genre
- Modeled writing
- Independent writing
- Talk it out
- Discuss

Notes

_____

Teachers get an overview of the standards, literacy moves, and activities students will encounter in the course of the sequence.

1 Booster Reading Lesson

Core Connections

Grade 1

Reading Literature Standard 1
Ask and answer questions about key details in a text.

Reading Literature Standard 2
Retell stories, including key details.

Reading Literature Standard 7
Use illustrations and details in a text to describe its characters, setting, or events.

Reading Literature Standard 10
With prompting and support, read prose and poetry of appropriate complexity for grade 1.

Speaking and Listening Standard 1
Participate in collaborative conversations with diverse partners about grade 1 topics and texts with peers and adults in small and larger groups.

Speaking and Listening Standard 2
Ask and answer questions about key details in a text read aloud.

Speaking and Listening Standard 6
Produce complete sentences when appropriate to task and situation.

Narrative Reading

Getting Ready

The materials:

- Copy of the task (page 1) to display
- *Knuffle Bunny* by Mo Willems
- The words *First, Next, Then,* and *Last* written on a chart

Context of the Lesson

After discussing our task, we read a fun, realistic story about an event most students can relate to. We then have an open-ended conversation. Though we are accustomed to pointing out story elements and thinking about narrative structure in terms of setting, characters, problem, events, and solution, we reread looking for story highlights that stand out first, next, then, and last. We retell the story using those temporal order words.

The Lesson

"As you can see, (*pointing to the task*) we will be working this week toward writing a story about something that has happened to us. These are called *personal narratives.* We know narratives are stories. Personal narrative means they are true stories about us. They don't have to be about big events or happenings in our lives, they can be about something small. We'll come up with lots of examples together so you get the idea.

"We'll start out by reading a narrative about a child who, though younger than you, goes through something I bet you can relate to. I'll read the story aloud to you. Let's just enjoy it. If you have any questions or observations that come up, keep them in your head, so we can come back to them after reading."

(*After reading aloud*) "Did anyone have a question or observation about the book?" (*Discuss these with the students, encouraging peers to respond to one another.*) Examples:

S: I didn't know what a laundromat was, but then I saw what it was in the pictures.

S: Me, too! I figured it out in the pictures, too!

T: Great observations. Yes, often by reading on, we can figure out words we're not sure about. And, we can't forget how useful illustrations can be. Study them carefully!

S: Why didn't the dad understand Trixie? I knew what she wanted right away!

S: I did, too! She was so upset because they left the bunny at the laundromat!

Each companion lesson has been crafted to complement and intensify the instruction introduced in the previous lesson.

2 Companion Writing Lesson

Story Planning

Getting Ready

The materials:

- Think pads or scratch paper
- First-Next-Then-Last poster
- Document camera

Core Connections

Grade 1

Writing Standard 5
With guidance and support from adults, focus on a topic, respond to questions and suggestion from peers, and add details to strengthen writing as needed.

Speaking and Listening Standard 4
Describe people, places, things, and events with relevant details, expressing ideas and feelings clearly.

Speaking and Listening Standard 5
Add drawings or other visual displays to descriptions when appropriate to clarify ideas, thoughts, and feelings.

Speaking and Listening Standard 6
Produce complete sentences when appropriate to task and situation.

Core Practices

- Modeling
- Guided Practice
- Sketch, Jot, Label to Prewrite
- Sharing
- Discussion

Context of the Lesson

Students are ready to move from oral rehearsal to sketching, jotting, and labeling the major events of their personal narratives on paper. Just as they've practiced, they'll do this in sequential order: first, next, then, last, adding details they'd like to remember when they write their stories.

The Lesson

"We're ready to record the bones of our stories. From what I've been hearing as I walk around, most of you can remember the major events in order for your personal narratives. This is really important because you have to have the main ideas down and know where your story is going. Knowing the basic story from beginning to end makes it easier to then go back and add the details you want to remember."

"I'll model this for you as I retell my story, this time with a bit more detail. Each time I retell it, I'm remembering more and getting clearer about what I want to write." (*Working under the document camera, I fold a paper into four squares and label them first, next, then, and last. I remind students that sketches are quick, stick-figure drawings without a lot of detail. Our purpose is to remember and organize our stories—the real artistic part comes later if students choose to illustrate their stories!*)

"First, my grandma, mom, sister, and I were going on a road trip. That's the first event. Now, I have to think, what details are important here? We were driving to Seattle for the World's Fair—a kind of carnival or festival. I was only about five years old and my sister was eight. It was going to be a long, long drive. (*As I talk, I sketch stick figures of the people in my story and label them. I also sketch a car and road with a sign Seattle and a note World's Fair. I record my age and my sister's age under our stick figures. I write long, long drive on the road.*) The sketch will help me remember the main idea for the beginning of my story. The notes and labels will help me remember the details I want to include. When I talk out my story one more time, I might even come up with more details. I can add them in later."

"Next, as we were driving along the highway, we saw a sign for an antique shop. Antiques are old things like furniture, decorations, and paintings that people have kept

ELA standards addressed.

These little lists are handy reminders of the research-based practices in action and link to an online glossary providing how-tos about each routine.

A Snapshot of the Talk-It-Out Strategy

Talk-it-out is everywhere in this K–2 volume. That's because it is so critical to supporting young readers and writers. Our K–2 students have been using oral language to communicate for a long time. Most are very comfortable speaking and listening to family, friends, and in class. It's a great advantage when we build upon this strength.

Talk-it-out is different from partner sharing or having a conversation. I have students use it in two ways: to talk out their writing and to talk out (summarize or retell) their understanding of what they've read using some kind of graphic organizer or other visual.

When we talk it out, I ask students to use whole sentences as much as possible,* so that what they are talking out sounds like talking. For example, if students are talking out their understanding of the butterfly life cycle using key words (see the kindergarten example on page 231), I don't want to just say, "First, egg, next, caterpillar . . ." as if they are simply reading a list. Instead, they use their oral language skills to turn these key words into sentences that make sense. I may ask them to record the key words on a graphic organizer and then take it home and talk it out to a family member as a way of solidifying their knowledge. Or, I may ask them to talk it out as oral rehearsal for writing. It is amazing how much easier it is for K–2 students to write when we give them the opportunity to support their thinking through talking first. Remember, too, as you see throughout the lessons, I encourage students to talk it out repeatedly as they write, referring back to their graphic organizers, Thinking Boxes, or other notes—we don't just use the strategy for prewriting. Whenever a student gets stuck, I remind her to try talking it out a few different ways to "tease out her thinking."

You have to model this strategy repeatedly because turning notes into whole sentences is new terrain; many primary age kids need to be reminded what whole sentences are, so I model examples and non-examples.

Another way to ensure success with this strategy is to have student volunteers talk it out for the class or group. When necessary, you can provide guidance and feedback as the volunteer talks so students get another glimpse into the thinking involved in sufficiently talking out their writing or learning.

I use this strategy to help writers in small groups and individually with those who need more support. Sometimes, I give them some words to get them started, providing scaffolding just as we do when we use sentence or paragraph frames.

How do we use this strategy to reinforce reading? I might ask students to summarize a story or information we've learned using a graphic organizer we've filled in together. Again, I emphasize that they talk it out using full sentences. When I work with small groups, taking notes or filling out a graphic organizer as we read, we'll practice talking it out together, then with a partner, and finally, students take their notes home and talk it out again. This way, we're strengthening oral language skills, reinforcing text structure (if the graphic organizer or notes reflect a structure), and solidifying content or story knowledge.

*Note: Speaking and Listening Standard 6 asks students to "produce complete sentences when appropriate to task and situation." When you have students talk it out as described above, they are practicing the skills needed to meet this standard.

Current research has underscored how crucial oral language is for young learners' development as readers, writers, and thinkers. Janiel Wagstaff builds in opportunities for peer-to-peer conversation throughout the week, and here, she zooms in for a close-up look at some aspect of language development—a giant step toward addressing the vocabulary, language, and speaking and listening standards, too.

Here, Janiel takes the guesswork (and hard work!) out of adapting the sequence for the grade you teach. So if you are a teacher in kindergarten and Grades 1 and 2, you know you can count on grade-specific how-tos.

In kindergarten, I've had success with planning stories using story boxes like we do in this sequence, however, that has generally been after students have retold many more stories with the quick sketch retelling technique we use in Companion Writing Lesson 1. If this is your kindergartners' first attempts at writing personal narratives, I recommend using a different planning strategy. They fold a paper into two columns. I model as we write *First, Next, Then, Last* in the first column. Students leave the second column blank. After they talk out their stories, they add a key word or phrase in the second column to match what happened first, next, then, and last (see a kindergarten informative example of this on page 231). They may need to talk it out several times to get their key words down. I model the whole time and provide guidance as needed. Once students have their simple plan, I ask them to "tell me more" about each part of their story to stretch their thinking during their oral rehearsals.

Sentence frames can be very useful in helping kindergartners "provide a reaction" as they are asked to do for their narrative ending. Here are some possibilities:

I felt _____.

After it was over, we felt _____.

I'd like to _____.

That was _____.

The amount of writing kindergartners complete is often very different from that of first graders, so it typically takes fewer days to actually write the narratives. We use the same technique as described in this sequence, referring back to our two-column plans and talking it out again and again as we write our stories. As I circulate, I often ask students to "tell me more" in their writing, just as they did in their oral rehearsals. Sometimes this involves cutting their paper and taping it to a new one to make space for more writing. We showcase examples of this on the document camera, so students get the idea how to extend their stories. We continually look at peer models throughout the drafting process to help guide and push the thinking of all our writers.

I eliminate the focus on adding onomatopoeia, especially if this is the first time the kindergartners have written personal narratives. Our main focus is telling our stories in order. This means I also eliminate the poetry and quick writes for now.

I also adjust the mentor texts I use with kindergartners. *Bedhead* is a bit complex for this grade level. I might substitute an Ezra Jack Keats story like *The Snowy Day* or *Whistle for Willie*. There are also two other *Knuffle Bunny* books that follow Trixie and Knuffle Bunny's continued adventures. Kindergartners love these.

Since the standard allows for a combination of "drawing, dictating, and writing," you can support those who aren't as skilled with letters and sounds yet by having them sketch their events in the second column (this then becomes very much like the story planning boxes).

Kindergarten Adaptation

Core Connections

**Kindergarten
Writing Standard 3**
Use a combination of drawing, dictating, and writing to narrate a single event or several loosely linked events, tell about the events in the order in which they occurred, and provide a reaction to what happened.

Second-Grade Adaptation

In adapting this sequence for second grade, given the way the standard is written, you might devote more time to specifically modeling how to accurately and artfully describe actions, thoughts, and feelings. Though the use of onomatopoeia helps, more might be done with external and internal dialogue especially when working on thoughts and feelings.* Digging into mentor texts for examples, modeling how to add these kinds of details in the story plan boxes, and celebrating students' efforts toward these goals will move your writers forward. However, consider this aspect of the standard a long-term goal. It takes a lot of specific modeling and teaching and student-writing practice and play before young writers get a real handle on describing actions, thoughts, and feelings with skill.

*Note: See Extending the Work on page 47. I describe working with students to add dialogue to their narratives. Using internal dialogue is a more advanced skill, but you may have some students who, after writing many narratives, are ready to experiment with this element.

Time might also be spent extending the study of mentor texts to help second graders understand a variety of ways to "provide a sense of closure." (No more, "The End!")* Though students are certainly planning their endings as they work in the box labeled *last* in their plans, that final sentence or two can make all the difference in the overall strength of the story. Keep an ongoing chart labeled something like, *Artful Endings*, where you jot the last few sentences of stories with particularly impactful closings. Be sure to include examples from your own students (even if they aren't *outstanding* examples; if they can push your writers' thinking forward, it's a good idea to include them). Labeling or naming the examples, when possible, will also help give students direction. For example, when one second grader ended her story with, "The party was over, but we knew our friendships would go on and on," we added it to our chart and labeled it as a "wise thought about life." When seeking an idea for a perfect ending, students might now consider, "Is there a 'wise thought about life' that I might include?" or "Could my story lead to a 'wise thought about life'?"

*Note: Though I describe working on effective endings in Extending the Work on page 47, I decided to pay additional special attention to it here. Second graders who've been immersed in writing across genres since kindergarten should be ready to delve into a much deeper study of how authors end their narratives and other genres, as well. If students can learn to be thoughtful about how they're pulling their whole pieces together at the end, this can impact how they conceptualize a piece overall: how it is organized and what their central point or theme is. This is big thinking, but working on the hows and whys of skillful endings can help move students along.

Core Connections

**Grade 2
Writing Standard**
Write narratives in which they recount a well-elaborated event or short sequence of events, include details to describe actions, thoughts, and feelings, use temporal words to signal event order, and provide a sense of closure.

FYI

Here's a little trick I came up with when trying to manage charts. Rather than making charts for everything, we keep a Writers' Craft Notebook. We create labels for sections like: *Great Beginnings, Descriptive Language, Setting the Scene, Effective Dialogue, Artful Endings,* for example, and record the lines we'd like to refer back to here. When we find something noteworthy in our reading or writing work, I simply ask for a volunteer to grab our notebook, find the right section (or start a new one), and write it down for us. Then, I model using the notebook and encourage students to do the same. This saves time and space and is easier to manage than a deluge of charts.

How did the instruction go? Here, teachers begin a section devoted to evaluating students' learning. Janiel shares an example of how a student approached the writing task within the sequence.

What Do I See?
A Kindergarten Opinion Sample

During Companion Writing Lesson 2's independent writing, Hatee wrote, "The most important rule is to be kind." As you can see, she also included a speech bubble, "Thank you!"

If I was to conference with Hatee, I'd ask her to reread her sentence to see if she could identify and fill in the missing word. Depending on how easily she accomplished that, I'd demonstrate using a finger to help space between words.

Hatee is already a skilled writer upon entering kindergarten. Though she basically copied what I did during my modeled writing (remember, though, I had removed my models from view), she clearly communicates which rule she thinks is most important. I don't need to ask Hatee to decipher her writing for me, which is a hallmark of writing growth. Given the skills she demonstrates already, I'm sure she'll quickly feel more confident expressing her own ideas in her writing.

Hatee's work is right on topic. She knows it's important to indicate the topic of what she's writing since she wrote, "The most important (omitted) rule is . . ." or at least she demonstrates an awareness of the purpose of the piece.* She added detail to her drawing (particularly notable are the tears in one student's eyes). She also knows how to use speech bubbles. Hatee obviously has a lot of prior experience as a writer!

*Note: Naming the topic is part of the kindergarten opinion standard.

Hatee was able to skillfully reference and copy from our interactive writing chart (Topic/Detail) as shown by her correct spelling of rule and kind. She also has mastery over some basic sight words. the, is, to, be, you, and was able to reference our field Words We Know Wall (Word Wall of high frequency words). She is also able to segment words to hear sounds. M-f-s-t is an advanced invented spelling for this time of the year in kindergarten, indicating she can hear and isolate beginning and ending sounds and match them with the correct letters.

Commentary from Janiel lets you see what she notices about the student's reading, writing, and thinking.

Authentic Assessment:
Ideas for Evaluating Students' Learning

Inventories are useful in so many ways. In this sequence, I have first graders complete a Personal Narrative Inventory (below) to ascertain their general feelings and attitudes toward personal narrative writing. I want to know how they regarded the experience, what they would change, and what their thoughts are about future personal narrative writing. This has a very different purpose than when I ask students to complete a self-reflection based on the processes and strategies they used while writing and what they think are the most important things they learned (see an example of this type of reflection completed with second graders in the Authentic Assessment section of Sequence 5, page 237).

I read the questions on the Personal Narrative Inventory aloud to my first graders. Here is an example of a response from Kianna:

Name Kianna

Did you like writing a personal narrative? Why or why not? Yes. Because I like to dio and writh! !!! It was SO fun! I want to be an ather wen I gou up!

Do you feel like you were able to tell your whole story? Yes!

Were you happy with how your story turned out? Yes! My picchers! My mommy liked it too!!!

What would you change about writing a personal narrative now that you can have written one? I wod not have bon the picsher boxs because it didint help me!

Did you like writing a personal narrative? Why or why not?

"Yes. Because I like to draw and write! ☺ It was SO fun! I want to be an author when I grow up! ☺"

Do you feel like you were able to tell your whole story?

"Yes!"

Were you happy with how your story turned out?

"Yes! My pictures! My mommy liked it, too!! ☺"

What would you change about writing a personal narrative now that you have written one?

"I would not have drawn the picture boxes because it didn't help me!"

On this next page, you get a firsthand look at how the student reflected on the writing task. Janiel frames these samples as not the end of learning—*but the beginning of a teacher deciding next instructional steps.*

Next Instructional Steps

Janiel describes just how she would use a student's piece as a mentor text in future lessons, giving you the specifics you need to use the writing to best effect.

Want to consider how to integrate more language and foundational skills into follow-up lessons? Janiel provides a section that is chock-full of ideas.

Peer Power:
Using Student Work as Mentor Texts

First grader, Harlan, wrote his personal narrative about a staying with his family in their hot tub for an extended period of time.

"My hot tub was dirty and it needed to be skimmed so I started to skim. Then it was clean. My family got in. We were talking to each other. We got hot, hot, HOT! Sweat, sweat, SWEAT! We stayed up late! We stayed up later than we have before. I can't wait until we get sooooo hot again!"

Integrating Foundational and Language Standards

Foundational and Language Standards cover critical skills and strategies for our K–2 students. I chose not to cite them specifically in the sequences because they have a place in *all* our lessons (plus, if I had done so, this book would have doubled in size!). The speaking and listening, reading and writing we do are the contexts in which we apply what we're learning during foundational and language lessons. We explicitly teach the skills and strategies contained within these standards then reinforce them across the curriculum every day.

There are many fantastic, research-based instructional books written on the skills and strategies covered in the Foundational and Language Standards, and I'll recommend some of my favorite resources throughout the following section. So without further ado, here is a brief overview of the myriad of ways we can integrate these standards into students' everyday literacy activities.

Foundational Standards

Foundational Standard 1:
Print Concepts (Kindergarten and First Grade)
Teaching concepts of print is best done during shared reading and writing experiences and reinforced during guided and independent reading and writing time. As we read big books, charts, or text that is projected on the screen, we can repeatedly identify and label the directionality of print, word boundaries, spaces, and features of sentences. As students read and write, we prompt them: "begin pointing and reading here," or "remember to leave spaces between the words." Young students love to use pointers and show what they know. Thus, as these concepts are becoming solidified for learners, have volunteers come forward during shared reading and point them out for the class.

Here's an example of using shared reading/writing contexts to teach word boundaries: Before we begin reading a big book, I explain, "You can always tell a word by the spaces in between. Print has a pattern. It goes (*pointing*), 'word, space, word, space' Repeat that with me. (*Students: 'Word, space, word, space, word, space.'*) We use that same pattern when we write. Let's look over at this chart we wrote together. Remember how we clapped and counted the words in our sentence, then had someone come up and hold two finger spaces between the words as we wrote? That's the same thing! If we don't leave spaces between words, our readers can't read what we've written. Look here (*I show a non-example, having rewritten the sentence from the same interactive writing chart without leaving spaces between the words*). Can you read this? (*No*) But, you just read it over here (*pointing to the chart*). What makes the difference? Share with your neighbor. (*After sharing*) See, that's how important

Lesson Planning Tools

A handy chart helps you know what to look for in students' reading, writing, talking, and thinking—then, advice for how to move all students forward.

If/Then Chart

If students are struggling to brainstorm personal events to write about,	• Reread the class's running topics list. Often one student's idea will spark ideas in others. • Ask him or her or the group questions like, "Who is someone you often do things with? Name some things you do together. Tell me more." Or "When was a time you were really angry, happy, or sad? Tell me more." • Have the student walk around and listen in to other students as they talk out their story plans. • Return to mentor texts. What's happening here? Can you connect to the events? What might you write based on these connections? (The things we read often lead us to ideas for our own writing.)
If students have too many ideas to write about and can't pick one,	• Have them keep their own topics list and write all the ideas down. • Encourage them to read the list to a buddy and ask the buddy which story she'd like to hear most. • Ask them to talk out the stories on their list. Which do they have the most to say about? Which is most interesting to them at the moment? • If a student is really stuck, tell him to write about his first idea and see where it goes. He can always change his mind and switch to a different topic if the writing doesn't progress.
If students are having trouble putting their events into sequential order,	• Have them sketch out their story in boxes as suggested in the sequence. Then review the work and help the students talk out the story. If needed, cut the boxes apart, and reorder them, relabeling them at the top (*first, next, then, last*). Tape them to a new piece of paper. Ask the student to talk it out again to make sure she's got it. • Read additional simple narratives. Assist students in locating pages with key events. Use sticky notes to label *first, next, then,* and *last*. Use sentence frames to help students retell the events in order. You can also use the same frames as they move into writing.

(Continued)

Mentor Texts

Back to School Rules by Laurie Friedman: Percy's up to sharing rules again (see *Thanksgiving Rules* by the same author), this time about what NOT to do in school ("No spitballs!" "No running in the halls!"). K–2 students enjoy Percy's point of view and the hilarious illustrations. Very entertaining. Talk to students about ways to restate the rules in positive ways.

How to Lose All Your Friends by Nancy Carlson: This is a great addition to your K–2 Back-to-School read alouds. What could be more important than knowing how to be a friend? You can definitely revisit the idea of the Golden Rule after reading. I've also used it as a mentor text for How-to Books since the how-tos are numbered and simply stated, followed by details.

Know and Follow Rules by Cheri Meiners: Meiners explains in simple terms why rules are important then goes on to detail four basic rules for school. The illustrations are very supportive of the text. Meiners has a series of books focused on behavioral issues like sharing and problem solving, all of which I recommend for kindergarten.

Rules for School by Alec Greven: Eleven-year-old, best-selling author Alec details fifteen rules for school. He gives out plenty of sound advice on many issues second grade and older students are concerned about. Students relate to his genuine and often humorous voice. Break up the reading of this book into several sessions.

What If Everybody Did That? by Ellen Javernick: Though the setting isn't all about school, I like this book for this sequence because it relates to the Golden Rule. The boy in the book throws trash out the window of the car and interrupts the librarian during story time, for instance. Each time he breaks a rule, an adult says, "What if everybody did that?" Kids love the zany illustrations that follow up with the answer. Again, treat others like you want to be treated. What if everybody did that? (This would be a fun book to innovate on and create your own *What If Everybody Did That?* class book, with every student doing one page and using this author's structure and style.)

Mentor Texts Containing Letters

Click, Clack, Moo: Cows That Type by Doreen Cronin: The story is a riot and the letters are interesting examples for students to study as mentors. Who doesn't love letters written by cows and ducks?

Dear Mr. Blueberry by Simon James: In this sweet story, a girl writes letters to her teacher all summer trying to figure out the mystery of the whale living in her pond. The letters are short so they're good for study with our youngest learners.

Dear Mrs. LaRue: Letters from Obedience School by Mark Teague: Poor Ike the dog has been sent to obedience school. He writes a series of letters to his owner, Mrs. LaRue, to try to convince her to bring him home. Hilarious text and pictures!

Dear Peter Rabbit by Alma Flor Ada: Like *The Jolly Postman*, this book is a series of letters written by fairy tale characters. Alma Flor Ada created additional books in the same genre: *Yours Truly, Goldilocks*, and *With Love, Little Red Hen*. Students will enjoy revisiting some favorite characters and will experience a rich study in letter writing with the books in this series.

The Jolly Postman by Allan Ahlberg: Since this book is full of envelopes with tiny letters, the format always engages and delights students. They love catching up on the lives of favorite characters as they read letters from one fairy tale character to another.

Sincerely Yours: Writing Your Own Letter by Nancy Loewen (Picture Window Books, 2009): This is a how-to book with tips and steps students might take in writing letters of all types. Loewen has a series of these books, each detailing how-tos for different types of writing. I suggest them for use with Grades 2 and up, though you could use short, targeted sections to augment your instruction in first grade.

Also see descriptions of *I Wanna Iguana* and *The Day the Crayons Quit* in the mentor texts for Sequence 3 on page 145.

Bring on the books! Each sequence includes a roundup of other great texts to teach with.

Extending the Learning Planning Tools

Extending the Work

After participating in this lesson sequence, students should have a pretty good idea of what a personal narrative is. After all, they've drafted and shared a complete story. Now, as we extend the work, we want to continue to build on this foundation, studying and experimenting with story elements to improve the quality of our work. Along the way, we'll refine and add to our personal narrative anchor chart.

I like to do a series of lessons focused on a particular element of the genre we're working on then allow students to play with that element, emulating the models we study. For example, I begin below with a focus on dialogue. This kind of work can go on and on, so we have to pick which elements we feel are most important to improve the quality of the compositions of the students we have in front of us. Students don't have to compose an entire story to experiment with different elements. They can experiment using quick jots or quick writes focused on just a piece of a story. All in all, I like to have them complete at least three drafts during any genre study, if possible.

Note: When extending the work with kindergarten or first graders, you may wish to choose one or two of the following elements to focus on rather than all three outlined below.

LESSONS	READING Speaking and Listening	WRITING Speaking and Listening
6	**Lesson 6:** *Focus on Dialogue* • Define dialogue and its effects on stories. • Read narratives with an eye and ear for dialogue. • You might reread the narratives in this sequence with this focus or choose new stories to explore. • (A nice example of kid-friendly dialogue can be found in *Goggles* by Ezra Jack Keats.)	**Lesson 6:** *Experiment With Dialogue in Our Stories* • Using students' personal narrative plans from this sequence, ask them to look back to find places where they might add dialogue. • Model this with your own narrative plan. • Talk out what the dialogue might sound like. • Ask a volunteer to come forward and guide her as she finds places where dialogue would fit. • Help her talk it out • Invite all students to do the same and share their thinking.
7	**Lesson 7:** *Revisit Dialogue in Reading* • Revisit texts explored in Lesson 6. • Highlight and reread bits of dialogue that stand out or catch your attention. • Record particularly interesting or effective examples on a chart labeled *Effective Dialogue* (or keep the list in your Writer's Craft Notebook). • What makes these examples rich?	**Lesson 7:** *Jot Dialogue* • Students revisit their narrative plans and identify where they thought dialogue might fit. • Once again, they talk out a bit of dialogue with a neighbor • Teacher models doing the same, this time jotting the dialogue (this might be just a few phrases or sentences) on the back of the story plan paper.

LESSONS	READING Speaking and Listening	WRITING Speaking and Listening
7 (Continued)		• Students do the same. • Share and discuss. • Record some student examples on the Effective Dialogue chart.
8	**Lesson 8:** *Continue Dialogue Study* • Read part of a new story or reread part of a narrative you've previously read. • Read the part again, this time without the dialogue. • Discuss what happens. Do students like the story better with our without the dialogue? Why?	**Lesson 8:** *Brainstorm New Personal Narrative Topics, Play With Dialogue* • Review the covers of the new stories you've read. • Brainstorm ideas for another personal narrative—making connections to the stories you've been reading. • Add topic ideas to the class topics list. • Give students a few minutes to briefly talk out a bit of their stories. • Teacher models starting to draft a new personal narrative, this time starting with dialogue. (Again, this could be just a few phrases or sentences.) • A volunteer comes forward and gives it a try, drafting in front of the class with the teacher's help, if needed. • All students begin their drafts starting with dialogue, as modeled. • Share and discuss.
9	**Lesson 9:** *Repeat Lesson 8 With Another Book* • Add to Personal Narrative anchor chart.	**Lesson 9:** *Plan Personal Narratives in First-Next-Then-Last Boxes* • Students reread their bit of dialogue from Lesson 8. • Students then talk out their personal narratives, focusing on key events that occurred first, next, then, and last. • Teacher models sketching, jotting, and labeling in boxes to record the bones of her story. • Students complete their boxes, talking out their stories as they go and jotting any dialogue they think they may want to include on the back of their paper.
10	**Lesson 10:** *Eyes and Ears Focused on Dialogue: Independent Work* • Continue to search for interesting and effective examples of dialogue. • Invite students to do this in their independent reading, placing sticky notes on pages with rich examples.	**Lesson 10:** *Draft Personal Narratives* • Teacher models talking out her story using her plan, starting with her dialogue from Lesson 8 and incorporating any other dialogue she brainstormed. • Students do the same.

Now, Janiel provides additional lesson ideas if you and students want to keep going into a more comprehensive genre study.

For M & M: Thanks for giving.

THE
COMMON CORE
COMPANION Grades K-2

Booster Lessons

Elevating Instruction Day by Day

Janiel Wagstaff

www.corwin.com/thecommoncorecompanion

CORWIN
LITERACY

FOR INFORMATION:

Corwin
A SAGE Company
2455 Teller Road
Thousand Oaks, California 91320
(800) 233-9936
www.corwin.com

SAGE Publications Ltd.
1 Oliver's Yard
55 City Road
London EC1Y 1SP
United Kingdom

SAGE Publications India Pvt. Ltd.
B 1/I 1 Mohan Cooperative Industrial Area
Mathura Road, New Delhi 110 044
India

SAGE Publications Asia-Pacific Pte. Ltd.
3 Church Street
#10-04 Samsung Hub
Singapore 049483

Publisher: Lisa Luedeke
Editor: Wendy Murray
Editorial Development Manager: Julie Nemer
Assistant Editor: Emeli Warren
Production Editor: Melanie Birdsall
Copy Editor: Diane DiMura
Typesetter: C&M Digitals (P) Ltd.
Proofreader: Alison Syring
Cover and Interior Designer: Rose Storey
Marketing Managers: Maura Sullivan and
                                      Rebecca Eaton

National Governors Association Center for Best Practices, Council of Chief State School Officers, Common Core State Standards, English Language Arts Standards. Publisher: National Governors Association Center for Best Practices, Council of Chief State School Officers, Washington, DC. Copyright 2010. For more information, visit http://www.corestandards.org/ELA-Literacy.

Photographs by Janiel Wagstaff unless otherwise credited.

Printed in the United States of America

ISBN 978-1-5063-1127-2

This book is printed on acid-free paper.

15 16 17 18 19 10 9 8 7 6 5 4 3 2 1

Contents

Janiel Wagstaff

Janiel Wagstaff

Janiel Wagstaff

Lesson Sequence 5: Integrating Informative Writing With Use of Text Features 200

Visit the companion website at
www.corwin.com/thecommoncorecompanion
for a glossary of core literacy practices, graphic organizers, reproducibles, student writing task examples, lists of potential mentor texts, and more downloadable resources.

Introduction

Okay, you hold this book in your hand. You think, jeez, it's heavy as a bag of groceries. You flip ahead and think, *it's almost 300 pages, but I've got only about 5 minutes right now to read it and get a handle on it. . . .*

I know, I know: it's a rare professional book we have the time to read cover to cover. So here's how I'd like you to think about *The Common Core Companion: Booster Lessons, K–2*: It's three parts cookbook, one part self-help book, and 100 percent geared to save you time.

First, skim the table of contents and choose whichever lessons you need. These are recipes, if you will, based on best practices that are sure to nourish your students. Each lesson is connected to another within five learning sequences, but they are eminently "dippable."

Next, turn to the front of the book for an At-a-Glance look at the function of each feature in this resource. This section was designed to give a two-minute tutorial on the deeper layers of the book, and how the booster lessons, when done in sequence, can provide almost a year's worth of comprehensive literacy instruction.

So that's the easy-breezy cookbook part. The one part self-help book? What I mean by this is that it is my sincere hope that the book bolsters both your energy and your expertise. We are teaching K–2 students in a time of unusual pressure. The Common Core State Standards in particular and standards in general can lead to changes to the K–2 curriculum that aren't always what's best for children's development. *That's why each lesson in this book shows you exactly how to meet standards—using research-based practices that are developmentally appropriate.* The surest way to improve the quality of your teaching practices is by staying true to what our young learners are ready to learn; so the best self-help advice I can offer is not only ready-to-go lessons but the reminder to keep checking in with kids to see how the lessons are sticking! Adjust the pace and reteach as necessary.

The Five Learning Sequences

The fifty lessons in this book are organized into lesson sequences—meaning each lesson is arranged in an order that builds students' awareness of reading and writing as reciprocal processes. The sequences cover a week or two of instruction, and they help you routinely integrate a handful of English language arts (ELA) standards each week. As you can see from the list below, the sequences happen to mirror the Common Core Standards, but all focus on literacy skills and strategies that are key for children in Grades K–2:

1. Integrating Writing Personal Narratives With Identifying Sensory Words in Text

2. Integrating Research to Build and Present Knowledge With Identifying Topic and Details

3. Integrating Opinion Writing With Close Reading for Text Evidence

4. Integrating Comparing and Contrasting With Publishing Using Digital Tools

5. Integrating Informative Writing With Use of Text Features

Core Practices

Another important organizing feature of this book is that each sequence lists core practices. These are the literacy practices that get the biggest workout in the course of the teaching and learning, and I chose them carefully as a way of telling you, *it's important to focus*. That is, as teachers we are bombarded with new things to do, try, and account for each year. Counterintuitively, sometimes we actually get closer to doing it all but are really accomplishing less. Instead, we need to lean on the handful of best practices that are most effective in helping our students develop as readers, writers, speakers, listeners, and thinkers. One of my main goals for the book is to demonstrate how to utilize these practices over and over again in expert ways within a joyful, relevant literacy environment.

To that end, the reading and writing instruction is designed for integration. A "booster" reading lesson is followed by a "companion" writing lesson, or vice versa, so that students immediately recognize how complementary these two processes are.

Find definitions of the major core practices at **www.corwin.com/thecommoncore companion**.

Mentor Texts

Funny, poignant, informative, classic, digital, cutting-edge texts abound for K–2 learners. Fiction, nonfiction, poetry, articles, movies, YouTube videos—never before has it been so easy to bring top quality texts into the classroom! Those that I selected for each sequence then are just the tip of the proverbial iceberg! So, keep building your own treasure trove of resources. Your classroom library ought to have 500–1000 titles in order to provide easy access to lots of books for all levels and interests (Allington, 2012)!

Model Student Writing

I've included writing samples from students in each sequence. I hope you'll use them in two ways: First, study them as a way to get to know my thinking about what to look for in student's writing in terms of strengths and needs. Second, download and print them from **www.corwin.com/thecommoncorecompanion** and share them with students as mentor texts. Children find the work of peers incredibly engaging and instructive. Use this book as a springboard to building your own bank of student writing to use as models.

Intentional Teaching

Another through-line for this resource is that it's meant to help you give your students a "booster shot" of intentionality. One of the toughest challenges of planning K–2 instruction is to present learning experiences that work for a vast range of developmental levels. Of course, once planned and delivered, we still must take the time during the school week to pause long enough to consider how's it going. What exactly are my students getting and not getting?

In addition to providing tightly choreographed reading and writing lessons, I provide a writing task in each sequence that helps keep the purpose of the work clear and engaging for students and provides you with a concrete way to assess students' learning.

If/Then Charts at the end of each sequence also help you be incisive about which students are ready for a new challenge and which students need further support. Then, following these charts, you'll find an Extending the Work section that gives you lots of lesson ideas if you want to keep working on the goals at hand.

At the end of the book, you'll find a section on integrating the foundational and language standards. I've included some of my favorite ideas there for teaching and reinforcing K–2 skills and strategies within all our literacy lessons.

Integrating instruction not only saves you time, but it just makes sense. When we integrate reading, writing, speaking, and listening, students see how all the pieces fit together. One process complements another. It's so critical they know why they're learning what they're learning and feel that their work has purpose and value. This was at the forefront of my thinking as I designed every piece of every sequence. Each is meant to build up your readers and writers and leave them wanting more!

My fervent hope is that, as you read this book, you find new ways to conceptualize not only your literacy block, but your whole day, and use the tools provided to make insightful decisions about how to infuse standards into meaningful learning as a way of continually crafting your practice. Happy teaching, happy learning!

Acknowledgments

Thanks so much to the Corwin Literacy Team: Wendy Murray, Lisa Luedeke, Maura Sullivan, Rebecca Eaton, Lisa Shaw, Julie Nemer, Melanie Birdsall, Emeli Warren, Rose Storey, and Diane DiMura.

Special thanks to:

Wendy Murray: my longtime friend and world-class editor.

Leslie Blauman: my new friend and partner in "boostering." Our phone conversations and your e-mails have lifted me up! I'm looking forward to more.

Jim Burke, Sharon Taberski, Leslie Blauman, and Barry Gilmore: for paving the way with the Common Core Companion series.

The teachers and students at my schools: I so enjoy learning alongside you every day—there is no place I'd rather work.

And, finally, the many literacy heroes who research, write, and present in this oh-so-important field. Thank you for striving to improve the literacy lives of students and teachers.

Integrating Writing Personal Narratives With Identifying Sensory Words in Text

In this lesson sequence, students read realistic, fictional narratives as a lead in to writing personal narratives. We focus on the temporal order of stories in our reading and retellings and use a first-next-then-last framework to recall the events and details of our own stories. Students learn to add onomatopoetic elements to their writing by studying its use and effect in stories and poetry.

Although this sequence is designed for first grade, many of the instructional elements are suited for kindergarten and second grade; only small tweaks are necessary (see grade level adaptations on pages 31 and 32).

Young writers get so much out of peer feedback!

This sequence is intended as an introduction to narrative writing. Though students may eventually write a variety of narratives that venture into fiction (e.g., fantasy stories), we focus here on personal narratives. Young writers are generally successful at recalling events that have actually happened to them, so I find this a good place to start. Since this may be students' first attempts at writing personal narratives, we keep things simple, with most of our focus on retelling the events in our stories in sequential order. We use the temporal words suggested in the standard, *first*, *next*, *then*, and *last*, to talk out and plan. As we move through the sequence, we add in onomatopoeia as a simple craft element to liven up our compositions.

Naturally, we immerse ourselves in reading the genre we're writing. We read several realistic stories containing real-lifelike characters and situations. We mine these models for topic ideas and study how the authors sequence their events and use onomatopoeia.

The teacher models throughout and makes use of student volunteers to make the steps in the process explicit. Students constantly talk out their stories, share their thinking, and receive feedback from one another. They draft using a recursive model: writing a bit, then rereading, making any changes needed, talking it out a bit more, then continuing to draft.

This sequence was written with first grade in mind, but can easily be adjusted up or down by eliminating the focus on onomatopoeia or adding an additional focus (several are noted in Extending the Work on page 47).

Core Connections

Focus Writing Standard 3 integrated with Reading Literature Standard 4
Reading Literature Standards 1, 2, 4, 7, and 10
Writing Standards 5
Speaking and Listening Standards 1, 2, 4, 5, and 6

Task

Write a story about something that has happened to you. Tell your story in order: what happened first, next, then, and last. We'll share our stories with friends and family.

What Teachers Guide Across the Week

LESSONS	**READING** *Speaking and Listening*	**WRITING** *Speaking and Listening*
1	**Lesson 1:** *Narrative Reading* • Review the task. • Identify purposes for reading. • Read *Knuffle Bunny.* • Orally retell story using the *words first, next, then,* and *last.*	**Lesson 1:** *Quick Sketch Retelling* • Have students sketch the events from *Knuffle Bunny* in four boxes labeled *First, Next, Then,* and *Last.* • Have students label and jot in the boxes. • Share.
2	**Lesson 2:** *Narrative Reading, Brainstorm Topics, Tell Stories* • Identify purposes for reading. • Read *Stella Tells Her Story.* • Start Topics List with class. • Model telling a story. • Have volunteers tell their stories (additions are made to the topics list). • Study *First, Next, Then,* and *Last* illustrations. • Have students talk out their stories in temporal order.	**Lesson 2:** *Story Planning* • Plan stories in boxes labeled *First, Next, Then,* and *Last* using pictures and labels and jottings. • Model. • Have student volunteer model. • Have all students plan in boxes.
3	**Lesson 3:** *Narrative Reading* • Identify purposes for reading. • Read *Shortcut.* • Identify onomatopoetic elements and discuss their effects on the story. • Record words on chart. • Revisit other texts from the week to identify the onomatopoeia. • Make connections for future personal narrative writing.	**Lesson 3:** *Review Story Plan, Add Onomatopoetic Element(s), Begin Drafting* • Model reviewing story plan and adding onomatopoetic words. • Have students do the same. • Retell stories emphasizing the onomatopoeia. • Discuss effect on stories. • Make other additions to story plans. • Begin to draft.
4	**Lesson 4:** *Compare Narrative Readings* • Identify purpose for reading. • Read *Bedhead.* • Have collaborative conversation about how this story is like the other stories we've read. • Begin to create a personal narrative anchor chart. • Discuss how observations relate to our own personal narrative writing.	**Lesson 4:** *Continue Drafting, Connect Anchor Chart to Our Own Writing* • Model drafting using story plan. • Debrief about strategies observed during modeling. • Have students continue drafting their stories. • Have students connect their writing to our fledgling anchor chart.
5	**Lesson 5:** *Poetry Reading* • Read selected poems from *Noisy Poems.* • Read twice chorally emphasizing sounds. • Add words to onomatopoeia chart. • Read third time, eliminating the onomatopoeia. • Discuss effects.	**Lesson 5:** *Quick Write Noisy Poems, Finish Stories, Share, Celebrate* (This may take more than one session.) • Brainstorm subjects and onomatopoetic words for noisy poems. • Model writing a noisy poem. • Have students quick write and share. • Have students finish writing their personal narratives. • Share in small groups. • Decide outside audience for personal narratives. • Debrief.

What Students Do Across the Week

Students read realistic narratives to get ideas for writing their own personal narratives. We focus on how stories are told in temporal order and model our writing after the mentor texts. Students walk away with a completed draft of a personal narrative that they are proud to share!

While reading a variety of realistic narratives, students pay close attention to how stories unfold in a logical sequence. In other sequences and other narrative reading, we've focused on basic story elements and structure: setting, characters, problem, events, and solution. Given our focus here, students practice retelling the stories they read using the words *first, next, then,* and *last.* This becomes the structure they use when preparing to write their own personal narratives.

Literacy Moves

- Widely read the genre
- Focus study of craft element
- Sketch, label, jot
- Begin an anchor chart for the genre
- Modeled writing
- Independent writing
- Talk it out
- Discuss

We begin a class topics list to keep track of our story ideas. Students talk out their ideas with one another, often spending about five minutes on this step. In Grades K–2, oral rehearsal before writing is critical, as many children can access their narrative abilities verbally more easily than when writing. Once students settle on a topic, they plan their stories using sketches and words in four boxes labeled *First, Next, Then,* and *Last.* The intent is to get the bones of their stories recorded so they can go back and add more details later. Using their plans, they talk out their stories again as a rehearsal for writing. I model the processes all along the way, and confer with students as I circulate to respond to their efforts.

Additionally, we add some flair to our writing by adding onomatopoetic elements. We study stories and poetry to help us understand and incorporate these elements. Students add an onomatopoetic word or two to their story plan and talk it out again, emphasizing (and relishing!) these fun words. Onomatopoeia is a clear-cut device, which lays the foundation for then introducing alliteration and other craft elements.

The intent of the sequence is to give students a solid first experience with personal narrative writing. Their writing is not "formally published." It is not revised and edited, though revision and editing do occur when students plan their stories, talk them out, add onomatopoetic elements, share and talk with peers while writing, and when I confer with them.

To culminate the sequence, we share our stories with each other and students are invited to take them home to share with their families. When we debrief, we focus on new possibilities for personal narrative writing and extending into other types of narratives.

Notes

_____

_____

_____

_____

_____

_____

_____

_____

Narrative Reading

Getting Ready

The materials:

- Copy of the task (page 1) to display
- *Knuffle Bunny* by Mo Willems
- The words *First*, *Next*, *Then*, and *Last* written on a chart

Context of the Lesson

After discussing our task, we read a fun, realistic story about an event most students can relate to. We then have an open-ended conversation. Though we are accustomed to pointing out story elements and thinking about narrative structure in terms of setting, characters, problem, events, and solution, we reread looking for story highlights that stand out first, next, then, and last. We retell the story using those temporal order words.

The Lesson

"As you can see, (*pointing to the task*) we will be working this week toward writing a story about something that has happened to us. These are called *personal narratives*. We know narratives are stories. Personal narrative means they are true stories about us. They don't have to be about big events or happenings in our lives, they can be about something small. We'll come up with lots of examples together so you get the idea.

"We'll start out by reading a narrative about a child who, though younger than you, goes through something I bet you can relate to. I'll read the story aloud to you. Let's just enjoy it. If you have any questions or observations that come up, keep them in your head, so we can come back to them after reading."

(*After reading aloud*) "Did anyone have a question or observation about the book?" (*Discuss these with the students, encouraging peers to respond to one another*.) Examples:

S: I didn't know what a laundromat was, but then I saw what it was in the pictures.

S: Me, too! I figured it out in the pictures, too!

T: Great observations. Yes, often by reading on, we can figure out words we're not sure about. And, we can't forget how useful illustrations can be. Study them carefully!

S: Why didn't the dad understand Trixie? I knew what she wanted right away!

S: I did, too! She was so upset because they left the bunny at the laundromat!

S: Yeah, I saw the bunny was missing in the picture as soon as they left.

T: Okay, so does anyone have an idea why Trixie's dad didn't understand?

S: He didn't see the bunny was missing. And, she couldn't talk right. She was making all those sounds and throwing a fit. My mom and dad get mad at my little brother when he throws a fit.

S: It was good that Trixie's mom saw Knuffle Bunny was missing.

T: How do you think Dad felt then? Let's look back for clues in the illustrations.

Continue . . .

This kind of open-ended collaborative conversation is a perfect way to get students involved in asking their own questions about the story elements and details. The questions and answers they model for one another push everyone's thinking.

"Thank you so much for your insightful questions and comments! We're going to switch gears now and reread the text. Our purpose for rereading will be to identify the high points in the events. If you were going to tell someone about this book, and could only tell briefly about what happened first, next, then, and last, what would you tell them? Basically, we'll work together to create a short, sequential summary using those key words (*I list the words* first, next, then, *and* last *on a poster for students to reference*). As we go, we'll put sticky notes in the book to help us remember where these important points are (the sticky notes are labeled with the key words *first, next, then, last*)."

We reread and stop to talk about key events, referring to our First-Next-Then-Last poster. We put the *First* sticky note on the page where Trixie and Dad leave for the errand, we put *Next* on the two-page spread where Trixie puts money into the washing machine at the laundromat and they leave Knuffle Bunny in a machine, we put *Then* on one of the pages where Trixie is throwing a fit, and we put *Last* on the page where Mom, Dad, and Trixie return to the laundromat and find Knuffle Bunny.

"We've taken time to identify first, next, then, and last because authors can use these key words and the idea of sequential order to plan their stories. We will be using this strategy when we plan our personal narratives. It's good to practice with stories we read aloud first.

"Now, I'd like you to turn to your neighbor and retell what happened in the story using the key words on the poster. I will turn to the pages we marked in the book, and you can look up here and use them as hints to help you if you need them. One partner takes a turn then it's the other partner's turn. I'll page through a second time, in case the other partner needs help."

Students retell the story using the words *first, next, then*, and *last*. If they have trouble, I model it for them, emphasizing use of the temporal words and talking it out in whole sentences as I retell.

Core Practices

- Define the Task
- Define the Writing Genre
- Read First for Enjoyment and Gist, Then Again to Highlight Key Events in Order
- Question the Text
- Collaborative Conversation
- Retell the Story

FYI

An open-ended conversation like this, which is prefaced by students being asked to watch for questions or observations during the reading (they can also be invited to jot notations in their think pads [a notebook for students to record informal notes or thoughts] or on scratch paper), can be insightful formative assessment. What kinds of observations are children making? Hence, what type of think alouds may you need to instigate to ratchet up the level of their thinking? What kinds of questions are they asking? Are they only surface level questions or inferential, deeper questions? Again, these observations will lead you to teaching points for your think alouds. Open-ended, collaborative conversations are one of my favorite teaching and learning tools!

Recap: Key Lesson Steps

1. Study the task

2. Define personal narrative

3. Read narrative story for enjoyment

4. Have an open-ended discussion

5. Reread the story, tagging the most important events for first, next, then, and last

6. Have students retell the story to a partner using the key words *first, next, then,* and *last*

Wrap Up

End by reminding students of where and why they are focusing their efforts. "Next, we'll go a bit further with the idea of focusing on the key story events that happened first, next, then, and last. This will help prepare you for planning your own story."

Notes

Quick Sketch Retelling

Getting Ready

The materials:

- Copy of *Knuffle Bunny* by Mo Willems (with sticky notes inside)
- Think pads or scratch paper
- First-Then-Next-Last poster, available on the companion website
- Document camera

Context of the Lesson

Students will practice the concept of temporal order using the words *first, next, then,* and *last* through another modality: sketching. They fold a paper into four boxes, then sketch, jot, and label about the key events we identified in *Knuffle Bunny*.

The Lesson

"Now we'll practice the structure of this simple story one more way using the words on our poster, *first, next, then, last*. The author, Mo Willems, may have actually planned his story out just like this. Fold your paper into fours. Label each box in order: first, next, then, last (*I model under the document camera*). Now draw a quick sketch of the most important happening that occurred first, next, then, and last. Also add jottings and labels, if you can. This way, we're showing the *bones* of the story—the highlights of what happened in the order that things took place. Watch me. (*I model sketching, jotting, and labeling in the first box, looking back at our first sticky note in the book*)."

Next, I differentiate: "If you'd like to continue to stay up here on the rug to work with me, you can. We will work through each box together and look at the book if we need to. If you feel ready, you can return to your desk and work on your other three boxes yourself. We'll share afterwards."

When students finish, they find a peer to share. Their comments and work in boxes is useful formative assessment. I can quickly see who understands the concept of temporal order and who might need more support.

Core Connections

Grade 1
Reading Literature Standard 2
Retell stories, including key details.

Reading Literature Standard 7
Use the illustrations and details in a text to describe its key ideas.

Speaking and Listening Standard 5
Add drawings or other visual displays to descriptions when appropriate to clarify ideas, thoughts, and feelings.

Core Practices

- Revisit Text
- Modeling
- Guided Practice
- Differentiated Support
- Sketch, Jot Notes, Label
- Discussion

Recap: Key Lesson Steps

1. Model sketching the first key story event, adding jottings and notes
2. Have students complete boxes independently or with teacher guidance
3. Revisit the book as needed
4. Have students share

Wrap Up

"Think about how Mo Willems might have used this strategy to plan his story. How would sketching, jotting, and labeling in the first, next, then, and last boxes help someone prepare to write? (*Discuss.*) We will use this same strategy to plan our own stories. Once we decide our topics, or what we'll be writing about, thinking about first, next, then, and last will challenge us to remember what happened in what order. We'll also sketch and jot. Then, we'll have the bones or basics of our stories and we can fill in details from there."

Companion Website Resource

Available for download at www.corwin .com/thecommoncorecompanion

Notes

Narrative Reading, Brainstorm Topics, Tell Stories

Getting Ready

The materials:

- Copy of *Stella Tells Her Story* by Janiel Wagstaff or alternative mentor text(s)*
- First-Next-Then-Last poster
- Chart paper
- Document camera

*Note: If you don't have a copy of *Stella Tells Her Story*, you can use any of the mentor texts listed on page 45. As you read the book, ask students what connections they are making that might lead to their own personal stories. Or, you might preview several mentor texts, reading parts of the stories to stimulate your students' topic brainstorming. Allow them to share parts of their own stories. Create a topics list and record some of the ideas. Then, have them work to talk out the main events of their personal narratives using first, next, then, and last.

Context of the Lesson

We read another narrative: *Stella Tells Her Story*. This book depicts a second grader writing her own personal narrative including the processes she goes through and the strategies she uses. We examine the text to discover the strategies we can use as we prepare to write our own personal narratives.

The Lesson

"I am so excited to share another narrative with you today. Again, I think you'll find you can relate to the story this character, Stella, is telling. Plus, this book's setting is the classroom. We will see the many things the teacher, other students, and Stella do to write their personal narratives, just like we are about to do. Then, we'll use some of the same ideas!

"As we read, think about the stories Stella and her classmates are telling. They are all personal narratives. I'm sure their stories will give you ideas for our own!"

I read the book aloud until we come to the part where the children are sharing their stories and the teacher is starting their class topics list. "So, is anyone thinking of a personal story they could tell?" Just like in the book, we stop and listen as students tell just a bit of their stories. I jot their ideas on a chart we label *Topics List*. I also model telling a bit of my own story.

"Okay, now let's read on to see what story Stella chooses to write about and how she does it."

Core Connections

Grade 1

Reading Literature Standard 1
Ask and answer questions about key details in a text.

Reading Literature Standard 7
Use illustrations and details in a text to describe its characters, setting, or events.

Reading Literature Standard 10
With prompting and support, read prose and poetry of appropriate complexity for grade 1.

Speaking and Listening Standard 4
Describe people, places, things, and events with relevant details, expressing ideas and feelings clearly.

Speaking and Listening Standard 6
Produce complete sentences when appropriate to task and situation.

Writing Standard 5
With guidance and support from adults, focus on a topic, respond to questions and suggestions from peers, and add details to strengthen writing as needed.

Ms. M. went back to the board. Under TOPICS and Max's Puppy she wrote Tineka's Catfish. She could tell we all wanted a chance to talk, so she let us turn to our neighbors and share our story ideas. Kids who couldn't think of anything yet just listened in; maybe hearing our ideas will help them get started.

Source: *Stella Tells Her Story* by Janiel Wagstaff (Peterborough, NH: SDE Professional Development Resources, 2015).

Core Practices

- Identify Purposes for Reading
- Make Connections and Brainstorm Our Own Stories
- Modeling
- Revisit Text for Details: First, Next, Then, Last Illustrations
- Talk It Out in Temporal Order
- Pair-Share
- Differentiated Support

We finish the book so students are able to hear the whole of Stella's story. "For those of you who didn't come up with a topic when we were talking before, do you have an idea for a topic now?" (*We listen to a few more friends share and I add short notations to our topics list.*)

"Don't you love how Stella shared her story with her grandma at the end? (*Discuss.*) You will be able to share your stories here at school and take them home to share with family and friends. Sharing is one of the best things about writing stories!

"Now, as we get ready to plan our stories, let's use another idea we saw in the book. (*I turn back to the page where Max is sharing his new puppy story and the illustrations show picture bubbles up top labeled* First, Next, Then, *and* Last.) What do you see is happening here? Tell your neighbor." (*I listen in and share.*)

"Yes, you see the illustrator is showing how Max planned his story. He had to think back to the events that happened first, next, then, and last when he got his new puppy. Before we sketch out our events, or the bones of our stories, just as we did with *Knuffle Bunny*, let's make sure we all have topics to write about and can at least recall the main happenings that occurred first, next, then, and last.

"If you shared a topic earlier and are going to stick with that one, see if you can recall and talk out what happened first, next, then, and last. You can work with a partner. If you don't have a topic yet, stay here on the rug with me and I'll help you." Students disperse around the room to tease out their events through talking.

I ask students on the rug questions to help them think of an event they might want to write about for their personal narratives. "Can anyone think of a time when they were really happy (sad, scared, proud, etc.)?" I encourage those who raise their hands to tell us a bit, then go find partners to talk it out further. Often, I'll model piggybacking off of an idea a student shared. This frequently sparks other ideas. I continue to pose questions to the rest of the group. "Think of someone who is important to you. Now think, what is something you have done with that person? Who can share?" Again, I encourage those who come up with an idea to share and then move off the rug to flesh it out more through talking. I continue in this way until all or almost all students have ideas and have left the rug.

Wrap Up

Say something along the lines of, "We've practiced telling the highlights of our stories aloud. Next, we'll get our thinking down on paper so we have a recorded plan for our stories. We'll note the main events that happened first, next, then, and last using sketches, jotting, and labeling, just like we did with *Knuffle Bunny*."

Source: Stella Tells Her Story by Janiel Wagstaff (Peterborough, NH: SDE Professional Development Resources, 2015).

Recap: Key Lesson Steps

1. Read a mentor text, stopping in strategic places

2. Have students brainstorm topics and tell a bit of their stories

3. Model, telling a bit of teacher's story

4. Begin and add to a topics list

5. Revisit story, noting the first, next, then, and last brainstorming bubbles in the illustrations

6. Have students talk out the bones of their stories with partners recalling the most important event, first, next, then, and last

7. Give support through questioning and modeling

FYI

This stay-on-the-rug strategy is one I use repeatedly to provide support for those who need it. We simply linger longer on the rug, talking and sharing. One student's idea often gives another student an idea. Most of these kids just need a bit more time to come up with something. If I have a few that are really stuck, I go ahead and move on. The next step in the process can get these friends moving forward.

2 Companion Writing Lesson

Story Planning

Getting Ready

The materials:

- Think pads or scratch paper
- First-Next-Then-Last poster
- Document camera

Context of the Lesson

Students are ready to move from oral rehearsal to sketching, jotting, and labeling the major events of their personal narratives on paper. Just as they've practiced, they'll do this in sequential order: first, next, then, last, adding details they'd like to remember when they write their stories.

The Lesson

"We're ready to record the bones of our stories. From what I've been hearing as I walk around, most of you can remember the major events in order for your personal narratives. This is really important because you have to have the main ideas down and know where your story is going. Knowing the basic story from beginning to end makes it easier to then go back and add the details you want to remember.

"I'll model this for you as I retell my story, this time with a bit more detail. Each time I retell it, I'm remembering more and getting clearer about what I want to write." (*Working under the document camera, I fold a paper into four squares and label them* first, next, then, *and* last. *I remind students that sketches are quick, stick-figure drawings without a lot of detail. Our purpose is to remember and organize our stories—the real artistic part comes later if students choose to illustrate their stories!*)

"First, my grandma, mom, sister, and I were going on a road trip. That's the first event. Now, I have to think, what details are important here? We were driving to Seattle for the World's Fair—a kind of carnival or festival. I was only about five years old and my sister was eight. It was going to be a long, long drive. (*As I talk, I sketch stick figures of the people in my story and label them. I also sketch a car and road with a sign* Seattle *and a note* World's Fair. *I record my age and my sister's age under our stick figures. I write* long, long drive *on the road.*) The sketch will help me remember the main idea for the beginning of my story. The notes and labels will help me remember the details I want to include. When I talk out my story one more time, I might even come up with more details. I can add them in later.

"Next, as we were driving along the highway, we saw a sign for an antique shop. Antiques are old things like furniture, decorations, and paintings that people have kept

Core Connections

Grade 1

Writing Standard 5

With guidance and support from adults, focus on a topic, respond to questions and suggestion from peers, and add details to strengthen writing as needed.

Speaking and Listening Standard 4

Describe people, places, things, and events with relevant details, expressing ideas and feelings clearly.

Speaking and Listening Standard 5

Add drawings or other visual displays to descriptions when appropriate to clarify ideas, thoughts, and feelings.

Speaking and Listening Standard 6

Produce complete sentences when appropriate to task and situation.

Core Practices

- Modeling
- Guided Practice
- Sketch, Jot, Label to Prewrite
- Sharing
- Discussion

in good condition for a long time. My grandma loves antiques so she said, 'Let's go!' The sign said the shop was three miles off the highway. So, we drove and drove on an old dirt road out to a large open field to the store." (*As I talk, I sketch the car going off the highway into a big field. I add a sign for antiques and label* 3 miles off highway *and* field.)

I continue talking out my story (*taking about 10 minutes to quickly complete all four boxes*), sketching, jotting, and labeling—adding notations for specific words or details I want to remember. Next, I invite a volunteer to come up and try their first box under the document camera, so I can guide his efforts and answer any questions students have about the process.

Then, everyone begins the process of sketch, jot, and label. I remind them our goal is to get the bones of our stories down, not everything we want to remember, but the highlights and perhaps some details. "Don't worry about getting everything down in your boxes. It's most important to note your main events in order with some detail and we can add more from there. We'll come back to our boxes tomorrow, retell our stories, and add even more details. I bet, since you're such good writers, you'll be thinking about your personal narrative overnight, maybe even sharing your story with your family. By the time you come back tomorrow, you'll have even more details to make your stories come to life!"

I circulate and provide help, reminding students to go back to the beginning box and talk it out again to remember where their story is going, if they get stuck.

Recap: Key Lesson Steps

1. Model talking out, sketching, and jotting teacher's story highlights in four boxes: first, next, then, and last

2. Have student volunteer come forward to sketch and jot in his first box; provide feedback and guidance

3. Have all students sketch, jot, and label the main events in their four boxes, adding some details

Wrap Up

Build excitement about the next steps, saying something like, "I am so excited about our stories. How are you feeling about yours? (*Discuss students' reactions.*) Don't forget, you are welcome to continue to think about your story and even share it. Good writers often do this because they know that each time they tell their story, they might remember more details or come up with special, just-right words they want to use. Planning a story can take many days! We'll come back to ours tomorrow!"

Narrative Reading

Getting Ready

The materials:

- Copy of *Shortcut* by Donald Crews
- Copy of *Knuffle Bunny* by Mo Willems
- Copy of *Stella Tells Her Story* by Janiel Wagstaff
- Class topics list
- Chart paper
- Document camera

Context of the Lesson

Donald Crews's *Shortcut* is yet another great story students will relate to. We identify the onomatopoetic elements, talk about their effects on the story, and refer back to *Knuffle Bunny* and *Stella Tells Her Story* to find the onomatopoeia in those texts. We record some examples of onomatopoetic words on a chart.

The Lesson

"Today, we'll enjoy Donald Crews's book *Shortcut*. It's about a group of friends who get into some trouble. You might think of an idea for another personal narrative just by listening!

"During this first reading, I want you to just enjoy the story. As you do, listen for the special words Mr. Crews uses that sound like the noise or action they are describing. These words are called *onomatopoeia*."

I read the story aloud, emphasizing the onomatopoeia with my voice. Students catch on quickly since the onomatopoeia is so prominent and creatively incorporated within the pages. (The "WHOO WHOO" of the approaching train is in all capital letters and yellow font and gets bigger and bigger as the train approaches, then smaller as the train rolls out of sight; the huge, roaring, "Klakity-Klak" is also in a special font, running along the bottom of page after page after page as the train passes, then it too grows smaller when the train moves off the page).

"Okay, everyone, let's go back and notice the onomatopoeia on the pages. Look closely at the pictures. What do you see happening with these words? How do they sound? Why do you think the author included them and illustrated them the way he did?" We page back through the book and notice the characteristics of how the onomatopoeia is printed. We make the sounds (it gets a bit loud!) and discuss how the colors, font, and size signals to us to say the words differently (the way they are written affects our voice).

Core Connections

Grade 1

Reading Literature
   Standard 1
Ask and answer questions about key details in a text.

Reading Literature
   Standard 4
Identify words and phrases in stories or poems that suggest feelings or appeal to the senses.

Reading Literature
   Standard 7
Use illustrations and details in a text to describe its characters, setting, or events.

Reading Literature
   Standard 10
With prompting and support, read prose and poetry of appropriate complexity for grade 1.

Speaking and Listening
   Standard 6
Produce complete sentences when appropriate to task and situation.

Core Practices

- Identify Purposes for Reading
- Read First for Enjoyment and Gist
- Make Connections
- Revisit Text
- Discussion

"Let's start a list of these kinds of words. They can be very useful in our writing. (*I write* WHOO WHOO *and* Klakity-Klak *on chart paper under the heading* Onomatopoeia.) We discuss the following questions: "Why do you think the author included these words? How did they affect the way we read the story?" The goal is for students to articulate that these words help readers feel like they are right there, in the story. Onomatopoeia gives readers a big dose of sensory involvement in the action.

"Now, let's revisit the other narrative texts we've read this week, looking for onomatopoeia. We'll record the words we find on our chart." As we revisit *Knuffle Bunny* and *Stella Tells Her Story*, we record such words as *aggle, flaggle, klabble, snurp,* and *waaaa!* (*Knuffle Bunny*) and *swoosh* and *slam* (*Stella Tells Her Story*).

As I write the words on the chart, we repeat them over and over and discuss how they add life to these stories, just like the onomatopoeia did in *Shortcut*. I ask, "Do you think you might like to look back at your plan for your personal narrative and see if you could add some onomatopoeia?"

Recap: Key Lesson Steps

1. Read *Shortcut* aloud

2. Discuss onomatopoetic words and their effects on the story

3. Record words on a chart

4. Revisit other narrative stories from the week; identify and record onomatopoeia

5. Discuss students' connections to *Shortcut* (see Wrap Up)

6. Have students add ideas to their own topics lists if applicable (see Wrap Up)

Wrap Up

Say something along the lines of, "Next, we'll go back to our story plans and consider adding some onomatopoeia. But first let's consider, as I read *Shortcut*, did any of you make some connections that might lead to other personal narrative writing? (*We discuss students' ideas. I add a few to our class topics list.*) If you have an idea, you'll want to add it to your topics list in your writing workshop folder, so you don't forget it. You may have just discovered your next story! Reading great books often gives us ideas for our own writing."

Notes

_____

_____

_____

_____

_____

_____

3 Companion Writing Lesson

Review Story Plan, Add Onomatopoetic Element(s), Begin Drafting

Core Connections

Grade 1

Reading Literature
   Standard 4

Identify words and phrases in stories or poems that suggest feelings or appeal to the senses.

Writing Standard 3

Write narratives in which they recount two or more appropriately sequenced events, include some details regarding what happened, use temporal words to signal event order, and provide some sense of closure.

Writing Standard 5

With guidance and support from adults, focus on a topic, respond to questions and suggestions from peers, and add details to strengthen writing as needed.

Speaking and Listening
   Standard 4

Describe people, places, things, and events with relevant details, expressing ideas and feelings clearly.

Speaking and Listening
   Standard 5

Add drawings or other visual displays to descriptions when appropriate to clarify ideas, thoughts, and feelings.

Speaking and Listening
   Standard 6

Produce complete sentences when appropriate to task and situation.

Getting Ready

The materials:

- Students' story plans
- First-Then-Next-Last poster
- Onomatopoeia chart
- Document camera

Context of the Lesson

We focus on the use of onomatopoetic elements in our own personal narratives. Students review their story plans and consider making further additions. They talk their stories out one more time for about five minutes, then begin to draft.

The Lesson

"I see you are very excited about these special words (pointing to our Onomatopoeia chart). Let's go back into our story plans and see if there are places we might add some onomatopoeia. Watch me first." I review my story plan under the document camera, retelling my story based on my sketches, jottings, and labels in the four boxes. "I think it makes the most sense for me to add some onomatopoeia in my fourth box (*pointing*). After all, this is when I get left behind at the antique barn out in a field, miles off the highway, in the middle of nowhere! I'm sure when my mom figured out I was missing there was some kind of reaction like, 'Ahhhhhh!' Also, at that moment, I bet she slammed on the brakes of the car, 'SCREEEECH!,' so they could turn around and race back to find me. (*I add these words to my box labeled* last.)

"Let me talk out that part of my personal narrative and see how it sounds. I'm going to talk in whole sentences, really working to figure out how it will sound when I write it." After retelling, incorporating the onomatopoetic words, I ask students for their reactions and we discuss how these types of words can enhance our stories.

"Would someone like to come up and talk out their story, focusing on where they might add one or two onomatopoetic words?" A volunteer comes forward, putting her story plan under the document camera. She talks out her story and we help her think about where some onomatopoeia may have a good fit. I ask her to talk out those story parts, again in whole sentences, emphasizing the onomatopoeia. We discuss how these words affect her story.

"Now it's your turn. Go back, review your plan, and see if you can add one or two of these words." I circulate, providing feedback and guidance. I also stop the class to quickly highlight students who have found logical places to insert onomatopoeia. "Oh, everyone stop and listen. Sammie, will you take your plan up and share it under the document camera? Look, she's found two places to add onomatopoeia. Tell us about your thinking, Sammie." Students share with one another as they make these additions (they can't help it!).

After about ten minutes, "Let's come back together so we can continue. I'm going to take our onomatopoeia chart down and put it on the back table so you can add your words, if you like. We'll also continue to add to the chart as we find these words in other stories we read.

"How many of you thought about your personal narrative or shared your story with someone last night? (*Discuss.*) Before we start to draft our stories, let's talk them out one last time. This gives you the opportunity to add any notes you'd like to remember in your boxes. (*I model under the document camera.*) As I thought about my story last night, I remembered more details about what my sister did when I was left behind. She actually looked out the back window of the car and waved to me as they drove away. Can you believe that? How sad! Of course, I started to cry . . . I was really scared. (*As I talk, I add to my sketches and notes in the last box.*)

"Find a partner, if you like, or talk it out one more time on your own. Are there any other details that come to mind: What people said and did? What something looked like? How you felt? Add to your notes. Remember, to talk it out in whole sentences, playing with the words, stating and restating something you are stuck on, until it sounds the way you want to write it.

"When you feel ready, you may begin drafting your story. Remember to do the things good writers do as they compose: Read and reread as you go, making any changes you feel make sense, and sharing with others when you need feedback or help." (**Note:** If your students have a lot of experience, you may not have to model going from the story plan to drafting. If that is not the case however, you'll need to model and perhaps have a volunteer model moving from his prewrite plan to writing. If you've done the oral rehearsal as I've suggested, though, students generally have a pretty easy time getting their thoughts down. They've had a lot of practice and are usually very eager to start writing!)

Core Practices

- Modeling
- Guided Practice
- Make Additions to Prewriting
- Oral Rehearsal Before Drafting (Talk-It-Out)
- Draft
- Differentiated Support
- Sharing
- Discussion

FYI

Responsive teaching is always key. As you circulate, note how students are doing as they talk out their stories, make additions, or draft. If the majority of the class is experiencing success, you can simply intervene with those who need more support either by working individually or gathering a small group. Instead, if you find many students having trouble, stop the class and pull them back together to provide more explicit modeling. Sometimes, if I see this is happening, I'll say, "I see some of you are having trouble getting started with your draft. If you feel like you're having trouble moving from your story plan to writing, come meet me on the rug and we'll work together." This enables the children to decide what level of support they need. Sometimes a student may appear to be having trouble, but she is just deep in thought.

"Okay, writers, our time is up for today. If you'd like to share your writing with a partner or small group, please do so now."

Recap: Key Lesson Steps

1. Model adding onomatopoeia to teacher's story plan
2. Have student-volunteer add onomatopoeia to the story plan
3. Have students add onomatopoeia to their story plans
4. Model talking out teacher's story one more time, making additions to the plan
5. Have students talk out their stories, making additions to their plans
6. Have students begin to draft their stories
7. Circulate, providing guidance and feedback
8. Share

Wrap Up

Reassure students that you are there, responding to their work and seeing lots of strengths. You might say, "We are off to a good start. As I walked around and listened to those of you who chose to share, I noticed . . . (*describe what you heard and saw, focusing on the good things that are happening*). How do you feel it went today? (*Discuss.*) We'll have more time to work on our stories tomorrow. Again, keep thinking about them. Good writers are always thinking and rethinking about what they are writing. You never know when an idea for revision will come to you!"

Notes

Comparing Narrative Readings

4

Booster
Reading
Lesson

Getting Ready

The materials:

- Copy of *Bedhead* by Margie Palatini
- Copy of *Knuffle Bunny* by Mo Williams
- Copy of *Stella Tells Her Story* by Janiel Wagstaff
- Copy of *Shortcut* by Donald Crews
- Onomatopoeia poster
- Chart paper
- Document camera

Context of the Lesson

As writers of personal narratives, we can never get enough experience reading narratives with the same kind of characteristics. The more reading we do within the genre, the more our writing is informed. In this lesson, we read one more entertaining narrative then compare and contrast the stories we've read. We begin an anchor chart for personal narrative writing.

The Lesson

"I have another fun narrative today. I bet many, if not all of you, have experienced the main problem in this story! As we read, just enjoy the story. Be thinking about how this story connects to the other narratives we've read this week. I have all the books here to reference, if needed. What do they have in common?"

I read *Bedhead* aloud. Students see right away that it is full of onomatopoeia and laugh throughout the entire text given the hilarious scenario (Oliver is having a very bad hair day and though the family tries to help, the situation just gets worse and worse). After reading, we first discuss our general reactions to the story. Then, I ask students to share what they noticed that is the same across the texts we've read.

After discussing students' general reactions to the story, I ask, "What connections did you make between this story and the others we've read?"

S: They all have onomatopoeia!

S: This book has a ton!

T: We can look back and add some of the words to our chart. What reaction do you have as a reader to the onomatopoeia in *Bedhead*?

Core Connections

Grade 1

Reading Literature Standard 1

Ask and answer questions about key details in a text.

Reading Literature Standard 4

Identify words and phrases in stories or poems that suggest feelings or appeal to the senses.

Reading Literature Standard 7

Use illustrations and details in a text to describe its characters, setting, or events.

Reading Literature Standard 9

Compare and contrast the adventures and experiences of characters in stories.

Reading Literature Standard 10

With prompting and support, read prose and poetry of appropriate complexity for grade 1.

Speaking and Listening Standard 1

Participate in collaborative conversations with diverse partners about grade 1 topics and texts.

Core Practices

- Identify Purposes for Reading
- Read First for Enjoyment and Gist
- Make Connections
- Revisit Text
- Collaborative Conversation
- Anchor Chart

S: I was laughing.

S: I loved the "bing, bing, boing" over and over. I kept thinking his hair can't get much worse. But, it just keeps popping out. Bing, bing BBBBBOING!

S: It's like you can hear it. Just like in *Shortcut*. I could hear the train on the tracks!

T: Adding these kinds of words to our stories is a good move. They help the reader better sense, feel, or experience our stories. What else did you notice that is the same?

S: I notice the stories all have people as characters.

S: Yep, this one is about a family just like *Knuffle Bunny* and *Stella Tells Her Story*.

S: *Shortcut* is about family, too. They are all friends, but then they talk about the family at the end.

T: Let's look back and reread that part. Are these kids just friends or are some of them members of the same family? (We reread and reexamine the illustrations to determine what we think.)

S: Our stories are about our families, too!

T: That's a great observation. Personal narratives often involve family members, since they are so important in our lives and we spend so much time with them. They are part of our personal events every day.

Students continue to make connections. My goal is to have them walk away with a sense of the characteristics of personal narratives as they've seen across many stories. We begin to create an anchor chart for personal narrative writing given our connections. (For example, for this lesson sequence we add: *About us and often family, True stories— real events, Have beginning, middle and end—first, next, then, and last, Often include onomatopoeia*). We'll continue to add to the chart as we learn more and reference the chart as we write.

If, during our conversation, students don't make the observations I'd like them to make, I ask a few leading questions:

- Do you think the authors may have planned these stories like we did? Thinking about what happened first, next, then, and last? Why do you think so?
- Where do these stories take place?
- Do all of the stories have a problem?
- What do the writers spend time describing?
- Is there much talking or dialogue in these stories?
- What is your favorite part of the stories? Why?

Time Crunched?

Note: Of course, I wouldn't ask all these questions at once. It's important to start small, as we have in this sequence by focusing on just a few elements of the genre. As we continue to work on personal narratives, we can explore other foci within stories and add to our chart. If there is time, go back and reread *Bedhead* again under the document camera. Invite students to join in reading the onomatopoeia.

Recap: Key Lesson Steps

1. Read *Bedhead* for enjoyment

2. Discuss general reactions to the story

3. Discuss connections between all the narrative stories read

4. Revisit texts as needed

5. Begin to create an anchor chart for personal narrative writing

6. Reread *Bedhead*

7. Have students think about how the characteristics of the stories they've read relate to their own personal narrative writing (see Wrap Up)

Wrap Up

We discuss how our connections and observations might impact our personal narrative writing now and in the future. For example, I model, "I notice the problem in these stories is solved at the end, except for in *Bedhead*. As I think of my own story, the problem is solved at the end, too. It's part of my last section in my story planning. Think about your story. Does it have a problem? Is it solved at the end? We don't want to leave our readers hanging. Talk about this with a partner. (*After sharing time*) You see, the more of these types of narratives we read, the more we will learn about the craft of writing our own personal narratives! Who's excited to get back to their own story?"

Notes

4

Companion
Writing
Lesson

Continue Drafting, Connect
Anchor Chart to Our Own Writing

Getting Ready

The materials:

- Students' story plans
- Students' narrative story drafts
- First-Then-Next-Last poster
- Onomatopoeia chart
- Narrative writing anchor chart
- Document camera

Context of the Lesson

Students need time to continue to draft their personal narratives. We continue to employ the recursive writing process: writing, reading and rereading, revising, editing, and sharing as we go. I ask students to make connections between our fledgling personal narrative anchor chart and our earlier collaborative conversation to their own writing.

The Lesson

"Yippee! It's time to get back to our own stories! I'm going to take just a few minutes, writers, to once again model working from my story plan boxes to my draft. I'll think aloud and you watch for the strategies you see me use as a writer.

"First, I have to reread what I've already written. That is always the first thing I do after I've left my writing for a while. If I just start writing, I might repeat myself or things might not make sense. I have to get my writing brain back into my story and see where I am. (*I model rereading the beginning of my draft, stopping to grapple with some word choices and adding a few descriptive words.*) Okay, I know where I am now. I'll look back at my story plan and talk it out again from where I am. 'We pull off the highway. The road is dirt and very long. It stretches off through a field that seems to go on forever.' I see I noted that the sign said it was three miles away. What might I say about that? Let me try talking it out again. 'The antique sign on the side of the highway says the store is three miles away. We pull off onto a bumpy dirt road that is very long. It stretches off through a field that seems to go on forever.' I like it. I'm going to write that down quickly as best as I can remember (*adding to my draft*) Now that I have it down, I'll reread it to see if I have what I want and it sounds like I want it to sound. I can always add or make changes. (*I reread and add the word* bumpy *to describe the dirt road since I forgot it as I wrote.*) I turn to the students and ask, "Do you have any reactions or comments for me?"

(After a few comments)

Core Connections

Grade 1

Writing Standard 3

Write narratives in which they recount two or more appropriately sequenced events, include some details regarding what happened, use temporal words to signal event order, and provide some sense of closure.

Writing Standard 5

With guidance and support from adults, focus on a topic, respond to questions and suggestions from peers, and add details to strengthen writing as needed.

Core Practices

- Modeling
- Pair-Share
- Oral Rehearsal (Talk-It-Out)
- Draft
- Sharing
- Discussion
- Make Connections

"Okay, writers, just quickly since we've done this many times before, what strategies did you see me use as a writer? First, share with your neighbor." (It is so beneficial to allow students to debrief about the strategies they witnessed during modeled writing and describe them in their own words. I see much more application when I include this step. After partner sharing) "Now, let's share as a group." (I jot their noticings like, "added describing word," "read and reread," and "crossed out" in a different color marker on my draft. This makes the strategies more concrete for everyone and helps us create a reference we can come back to as we continually discuss the strategies good writers use.)

"Okay, writers, off you go. Remember to use the strategies you just watched me use."

As students draft, I circulate, conference, guide, and provide feedback. Again, if several students need similar help, I may call them together into a group. Students are encouraged to share as they write and seek help from other writers in our classroom, as well.

I stop the writing time a bit early today so we can make connections between our writing and the personal narrative anchor chart we've started. "We listed characteristics of personal narratives on our chart. Just because they are listed, doesn't mean you have to have everything exactly as it is on the chart. These are generalizations or things that are commonly part of personal narratives. Writers always have the right to try something else or go a different direction. Remember, too, we are going to add to our chart as we learn more about writing personal narratives. But, for now, with what we have, turn to your neighbor and discuss what characteristics from the chart do you have in your writing." (I listen in and share a few examples with the class.) "Is there anything you think we should add to our anchor chart?" (We discuss student responses and make additions, if appropriate.)

FYI

Before we debrief, wrap up, or have Author's Chair time, I give students three minutes of Everybody Share Time. Why? Young writers need the option to share to keep up the motivation to write. This also encourages them to reflect on what they've done. I simply say, "We are now beginning Everybody Share Time. If you would like to share some of what you've written today, find and partner and share. If you don't want to share, use this time to continue writing." Everybody Share Time is especially important to young writers who often feel "cheated" if they don't get a chance to share aloud.

Recap: Key Lesson Steps

1. Model rereading teacher draft, making revisions or edits, talking out the next section, and making additions

2. Have class debrief about strategies they saw the teacher employ

3. Have students draft

4. Have students discuss connections between their stories and the personal narrative anchor chart

Wrap Up

"Many of you are getting close to finishing or are finished with your stories! Tomorrow, you'll have more time to write and we'll celebrate our work. If you're not done, be sure to think tonight about where you want your story to go and the words you'll use to write it down. Then, you'll come in more than ready to write!"

Time Crunched?

Given two sessions of drafting, some students might be finished. Pair them up to share with others who are finished. Have them check to make sure their writing follows their sequential plan (first, next, then, last). You might have the partner sign off by initialing their partner's plan. Students might start another personal narrative or other writing of their choice.

Poetry Reading

Getting Ready

The materials:

- Copy of *Noisy Poems* by Jill Bennett
- Onomatopoeia poster
- Document camera

Context of the Lesson

We augment our understanding of the use and effects of onomatopoeia by reading select poems from Bennett's collection. We read the poems as written, identifying and emphasizing the onomatopoeia and then read them again without the onomatopoeia (or substituting words when necessary). This helps students better understand the effects of onomatopoeia and increases the likelihood they may use this craft element in the future.

The Lesson

"Today, we'll read some poems from this collection, *Noisy Poems* by Jill Bennett. Let's look at the cover and let me page through some of the poems under the document camera. What do you notice? Talk to your partner." We discuss students' observations. They immediately notice the onomatopoeia since some of the poems set it apart with quotations, capitals, or all capitals. They also notice the onomatopoeia in one poem's illustrations. Additionally, they notice the structure of the poetry, how the words move down the page in short phrases.

"We're going to do an experiment. We'll read the poems the first time to enjoy them and reread them again to emphasize the onomatopoeia. We can add some of our favorites to our onomatopoeia chart. Then, we'll reread a few without the onomatopoeia and decide which version you like best and why."

Note: Depending on the amount of support your readers need, you might want to read each poem aloud the first time while tracking the print, then invite students to chorally read along with you during the second reading.

We start with "Song of the Train." After our first read, students naturally make connections to *Shortcut* since the sounds of the train are emphasized. During our third read, leaving out the onomatopoeia, students notice the poem is much shorter, definitely less interesting, and really doesn't work since the author was trying to write about the "song of the track." There's no song without the onomatopoeia.

Core Connections

Grade 1

Reading Literature
  Standard 4

Identify words and phrases in stories or poems that suggest feelings or appeal to the senses.

Reading Literature
  Standard 10

With prompting and support, read prose and poetry of appropriate complexity for grade 1.

Core Practices

- Identify Purpose for Reading
- Read First for Enjoyment and Gist
- Make Connections
- Reread
- Identify Onomatopoetic Elements
- Identify Craft Element and Its Purpose

We next read "Jazz-Man," which is much less dependent on the onomatopoeia. After our second read, students request to add the words *crash*, *CLANG*, *TOOT*, and *Tingle* to our onomatopoeia chart. After reading the poem a third time, without the onomatopoeia, students comment that they like the beginning much better with the onomatopoeia because you *hear* the jazz-man before you *see* him (without the beginning onomatopoeia, the poem would simply begin, "And up in the road the Jazz-Man came!").

We continue with a few more examples. Students uniformly agree the poems are better with the onomatopoeia because they feel they can hear the words of the noisy subjects.

Recap: Key Lesson Steps

1. Read poems twice

2. Add to onomatopoeia chart

3. Read poems a third time, eliminating the onomatopoeia

4. Discuss the differences in the effects of the poems

Wrap Up

Review the learning by saying something like, "Do you think we have a better understanding of onomatopoeia now that we've done this experiment? Recap for your partner how you think the onomatopoetic words affected the poems, how you read them, how you felt about them. . . . *(After students share)* Next, we're going to try writing our own noisy poems so you can have a bit more experience playing with words like this."

Notes

Quick Write Noisy Poems, Finish Stories, Share, Celebrate

Core Connections

Grade 1

Writing Standard 3

Write narratives in which they recount two or more appropriately sequenced events, include some details regarding what happened, use temporal words to signal event order, and provide some sense of closure.

Writing Standard 5

With guidance and support from adults, focus on a topic, respond to questions and suggestions from peers, and add details to strengthen writing as needed.

Core Practices

- Brainstorm
- Modeling
- Quick Write
- Draft and Check
- Differentiated Support
- Sharing
- Celebrate

Getting Ready

The materials:

- Think pads or paper
- Students' narrative story drafts
- Charts from previous lessons
- Document camera

Context of the Lesson

Students enjoy experimenting with their own noisy poems through a quick write. After sharing and discussion, those who need to finish their personal narratives get to work, while other writers compose additional noisy poems, personal narratives, or choice pieces. We conclude the writing period by celebrating our personal narratives and deciding with whom they'll be shared.

The Lesson

"Now that we've read some noisy poems, let's write our own noisy poems. First, we need to brainstorm some things that make noise. (*Students call out examples and I record them on the board.*) You might pick one of these, or come up with another subject for your poem. Jot down your choice in your think pad. (*I model under the document camera.*) Now, take a few minutes to jot some words to describe the sounds your thing makes. (*I model . . . after a few minutes . . .*) Go ahead and share what you have with a partner. They might be able to help you add some onomatopoeia to your list.

"Look up here at my model. We each have a subject or what our poem will be about and some onomatopoeia. Now, we can play with adding words to make phrases and move our writing down the page like we saw in the poems we read. There's no pressure to come up with something great! Watch me for just a minute and then it will be your turn to experiment during our quick write.

(*I write under the document camera while thinking aloud*) "You can see my subject is my son, Max (*pointing to my paper*). I have these words listed: *SCREAM! whine, whimper, giggle giggle, heeeeeeeee!*

"I'm going to try adding some words around each of these words to give the reader some sensory details about what it sounds like, feels like. Hmmm, I need to think about: When does Max make these sounds? I'll move down the page in brief chunks of words or phrases, like we saw with the poems we read." (*Writing*)

'Max (*"I'll start with my subject"*)

SCREAMS, 'MOM! Mom! Mom!' (*"He's always yelling for me, even when I leave the room for two minutes. I don't want to keep using the same word, SCREAMS. So I'll think about other words. I also want to tell when this happens, so I write:*)

I'm upstairs, but he needs me NOW!

Whiiiiiiiine . . . whimper . . .

Mom isn't coming fast enough!'

"Okay, writers, I'm going to stop there so you can have your quick write time.

Before we start, let's review our rules for a quick write (*review rules poster on page* 29). Have fun!"

After about 7 minutes, I say, "I'll stop you here for now. Don't worry if you're not done. Would anyone like to share what they have so far?"

A few volunteers share and we celebrate their attempts. I might also ask questions and make a suggestion.

"This is a lot of fun, huh? If enough of you are interested and would like to work on your poems a bit more, we could bind them together into our own *Noisy Poems* class book! And now we've had more practice playing with onomatopoeia.

"We need to regroup now though. Some of you are finished with your personal narrative and have shared and checked them with a partner. You might continue to write or rewrite your noisy poem, write another, work on another personal narrative, or a piece of your choice. If this is you, off you go! If you're not done, come meet with me on the rug."

I discuss next steps with the group on the rug: rereading what they've already written, reviewing their plan and talking it out, and finishing their pieces. I ask them to share with a partner when they finish and have their partner sign off on their plan. If some students are not as close to finishing, or need more support, I keep them together in a small group to provide even more assistance.

After 20 to 30 minutes, we come together to celebrate. (The amount of time really depends on how many students still need to finish and where they are in the process. If just a few students need just a bit more time, cut it shorter.) "Everyone stop what you're doing for now and bring your personal narrative to the rug.* We need to celebrate our efforts and what we've learned! Look back at your story. What is your favorite sentence or two and why? Take a minute to look and think. (*Wait time*) Now, share with someone near you. (*I listen in and share a few examples.*) Quite a few of you shared a section with onomatopoeia! I also heard a few share where a problem occurred in their story. Those are emotional moments—great places for onomatopoeia to be plugged in! I heard a few endings, too."

Time Crunched?

Save the small-group sharing and debriefing for your next writing period or another time of the day.

*Note: If some students are still not quite done, I have them come to the rug and participate given what they have. Then, they might finish their pieces during the following week or take them home to finish, if they choose.

"Now, to continue our sharing, learning from each other, and celebrating our efforts, find two people who have NOT heard your story. These should be people you haven't shared with as we've been working on personal narratives. We'll get in groups of three and take turns sharing our stories. One person shares, the other two listen. When the writer is finished reading his or her piece, the audience might make a few comments. Ready, go!" (*Students get into groups and start sharing. I assist those who need help finding partners, then circulate.*)

(*After sharing time*) "I can tell we are all excited about our stories! I am, too! Now, writers, you need to consider who you'd like to share your story with outside of our classroom. Maybe you'd like to share with the family members or friends who are part of your story? I'm sure they'd be very interested! Remember in *Stella Tells Her Story*, Stella shares with her Oma? That is such a sweet moment in the book. Stella is very proud of her writing and Oma remembers the event. Our stories are meaningful!" (*I give students a few minutes to talk with their neighbors about who they would like to share with.*)

Recap: Key Lesson Steps

1. Brainstorm subjects for noisy poems
2. Have students jot subjects and some onomatopoetic words in their think pads
3. Model beginning to write teacher noisy poem
4. Have students quick write then share
5. Have students finish writing their personal narratives
6. Share personal narratives in small groups
7. Decide outside audience
8. Debrief (see Wrap Up)

Wrap Up

Debrief by saying something like, "When we finish something, we always take time to talk about our process. What did we do? Why did we do it? How did we do it? What strategies did we use? What will you remember as you move forward in your writing? Today, I'd like you to complete a written inventory to answer a few questions as you reflect on writing your personal narrative. You'll be able to share your inventory with others, if you wish, then I'll collect and review them. We'll take some time to discuss general opinions after that."

Note: You'll find a copy of the Personal Narrative Inventory on page 40 under Authentic Assessment.

Rules for Quick Writes

- ❖ Everyone writes.

- ❖ Stay on topic.

- ❖ There is no one right answer.

- ❖ If you don't know what to write, write "I'm thinking . . . I'm thinking," to jog your mind into action.

- ❖ Continue writing until time is up. Done early? Reread, add, change, sketch.

- ❖ Would you like to share?

Source: Adapted from *Quick Start to Writing Workshop Success* by Janiel Wagstaff (New York, NY: Scholastic, 2011).

Available for download at www.corwin.com/thecommoncorecompanion

Notes

A Snapshot of the Talk-It-Out Strategy

Talk-it-out is everywhere in this K–2 volume. That's because it is so critical to supporting young readers and writers. Our K–2 students have been using oral language to communicate for a long time. Most are very comfortable speaking and listening to family, friends, and in class. It's a great advantage when we build upon this strength.

Talk-it-out is different from partner sharing or having a conversation. I have students use it in two ways: to talk out their writing and to talk out (summarize or retell) their understanding of what they've read using some kind of graphic organizer or other visual.

When we talk it out, I ask students to use whole sentences as much as possible,* so that what they are talking out sounds like talking. For example, if students are talking out their understanding of the butterfly life cycle using key words (see the kindergarten example on page 231), I don't want them to just say, "First, egg, next, caterpillar . . ." as if they are simply reading a list. Instead, they use their oral language skills to turn these key words into sentences that make sense. I may ask them to record the key words on a graphic organizer and then take it home and talk it out to a family member as a way of solidifying their knowledge. Or, I may ask them to talk it out as oral rehearsal for writing. It is amazing how much easier it is for K–2 students to write when we give them the opportunity to support their thinking through talking first. Remember, too, as you see throughout the lessons, I encourage students to talk it out repeatedly as they write, referring back to their graphic organizers, Thinking Boxes, or other notes—we don't just use the strategy for prewriting. Whenever a student gets stuck, I remind her to try talking it out a few different ways to "tease out her thinking."

You have to model this strategy repeatedly because turning notes into whole sentences is new terrain; many primary age kids need to be reminded what whole sentences are, so I model examples and non-examples.

Another way to ensure success with this strategy is to have student volunteers talk it out for the class or group. When necessary, you can provide guidance and feedback as the volunteer talks so students get another glimpse into the thinking involved in sufficiently talking out their writing or learning.

I use this strategy to help writers in small groups and individually with those who need more support. Sometimes, I give them some words to get them started, providing scaffolding just as we do when we use sentence or paragraph frames.

How do we use this strategy to reinforce reading? I might ask students to summarize a story or information we've learned using a graphic organizer we've filled in together. Again, I emphasize that they talk it out using full sentences. When I work with small groups, taking notes or filling out a graphic organizer as we read, we'll practice talking it out together, then with a partner, and finally, students take their notes home and talk it out again. This way, we're strengthening oral language skills, reinforcing text structure (if the graphic organizer or notes reflect a structure), and solidifying content or story knowledge.

*Note: Speaking and Listening Standard 6 asks students to "produce complete sentences when appropriate to task and situation." When you have students talk it out as described above, they are practicing the skills needed to meet this standard.

In kindergarten, I've had success with planning stories using story boxes like we do in this sequence, however, that has generally been after students have retold many more stories with the quick sketch retelling technique we use in Companion Writing Lesson 1. If this is your kindergartners' first attempts at writing personal narratives, I recommend using a different planning strategy. They fold a paper into two columns. I model as we write *First, Next, Then, Last* in the first column. Students leave the second column blank. After they talk out their stories, they add a key word or phrase in the second column to match what happened first, next, then, and last (see a kindergarten informative example of this on page 231). They may need to talk it out several times to get their key words down. I model the whole time and provide guidance as needed. Once students have their simple plan, I ask them to "tell me more" about each part of their story to stretch their thinking during their oral rehearsals.

Sentence frames can be very useful in helping kindergartners "provide a reaction" as they are asked to do for their narrative ending. Here are some possibilities:

I felt _____.

After it was over, we felt _____.

I'd like to _____.

That was _____.

Core Connections

Kindergarten
Writing Standard 3
Use a combination of drawing, dictating, and writing to narrate a single event or several loosely linked events, tell about the events in the order in which they occurred, and provide a reaction to what happened.

The amount of writing kindergartners complete is often very different from that of first graders, so it typically takes fewer days to actually write the narratives. We use the same technique as described in this sequence, referring back to our two-column plans and talking it out again and again as we write our stories. As I circulate, I often ask students to "tell me more" in their writing, just as they did in their oral rehearsals. Sometimes this involves cutting their paper and taping it to a new one to make space for more writing. We showcase examples of this on the document camera, so students get the idea how to extend their stories. We continually look at peer models throughout the drafting process to help guide and push the thinking of all our writers.

I eliminate the focus on adding onomatopoeia, especially if this is the first time the kindergartners have written personal narratives. Our main focus is telling our stories in order. This means I also eliminate the poetry and quick writes for now.

I also adjust the mentor texts I use with kindergartners. *Bedhead* is a bit complex for this grade level. I might substitute an Ezra Jack Keats story like *The Snowy Day* or *Whistle for Willie*. There are also two other *Knuffle Bunny* books that follow Trixie and Knuffle Bunny's continued adventures. Kindergartners love these.

Since the standard allows for a combination of "drawing, dictating, and writing," you can support those who aren't as skilled with letters and sounds yet by having them sketch their events in the second column (this then becomes very much like the story planning boxes).

Core Connections

Grade 2
Writing Standard

Write narratives in which they recount a well-elaborated event or short sequence of events, include details to describe actions, thoughts, and feelings, use temporal words to signal event order, and provide a sense of closure.

FYI

Here's a little trick I came up with when trying to manage charts. Rather than making charts for everything, we keep a Writers' Craft Notebook. We create labels for sections like: *Great Beginnings, Descriptive Language, Setting the Scene, Effective Dialogue, Artful Endings*, for example, and record the lines we'd like to refer back to here. When we find something noteworthy in our reading or writing work, I simply ask for a volunteer to grab our notebook, find the right section (or start a new one), and write it down for us. Then, I model using the notebook and encourage students to do the same. This saves time and space and is easier to manage than a deluge of charts.

In adapting this sequence for second grade, given the way the standard is written, you might devote more time to specifically modeling how to accurately and artfully describe actions, thoughts, and feelings. Though the use of onomatopoeia helps, more might be done with external and internal dialogue especially when working on thoughts and feelings.* Digging into mentor texts for examples, modeling how to add these kinds of details in the story plan boxes, and celebrating students' efforts toward these goals will move your writers forward. However, consider this aspect of the standard a long-term goal. It takes a lot of specific modeling and teaching and student-writing practice and play before young writers get a real handle on describing actions, thoughts, and feelings with skill.

*Note: See Extending the Work on page 47. I describe working with students to add dialogue to their narratives. Using internal dialogue is a more advanced skill, but you may have some students who, after writing many narratives, are ready to experiment with this element.

Time might also be spent extending the study of mentor texts to help second graders understand a variety of ways to "provide a sense of closure." (No more, "The End!")* Though students are certainly planning their endings as they work in the box labeled *last* in their plans, that final sentence or two can make all the difference in the overall strength of the story. Keep an ongoing chart labeled something like, *Artful Endings*, where you jot the last few sentences of stories with particularly impactful closings. Be sure to include examples from your own students (even if they aren't *outstanding* examples; if they can push your writers' thinking forward, it's a good idea to include them). Labeling or naming the examples, when possible, will also help give students direction. For example, when one second grader ended her story with, "The party was over, but we knew our friendships would go on and on," we added it to our chart and labeled it as a "wise thought about life." When seeking an idea for a perfect ending, students might now consider, "Is there a 'wise thought about life' that I might include?" or "Could my story lead to a 'wise thought about life'?"

*Note: Though I describe working on effective endings in Extending the Work on page 47, I decided to pay additional special attention to it here. Second graders who've been immersed in writing across genres since kindergarten should be ready to delve into a much deeper study of how authors end their narratives and other genres, as well. If students can learn to be thoughtful about how they're pulling their whole pieces together at the end, this can impact how they conceptualize a piece overall: how it is organized and what their central point or theme is. This is big thinking, but working on the hows and whys of skillful endings can help move students along.

Sophia enjoys a reread of one of our narrative mentor texts.

What's ahead:

What Do I See?
A Student Sample of Story Planning

Here's an example of first grader, Isaac's, story plan using *First*, *Next*, *Then*, and *Last*.

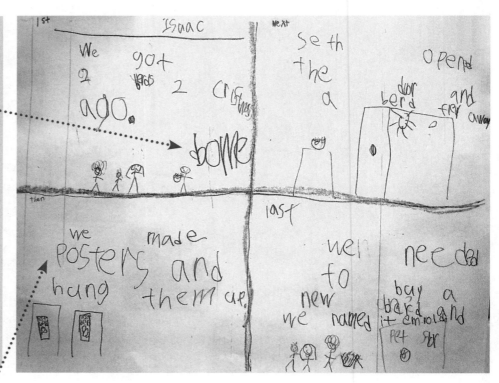

Isaac added onomatopoeia (*boom*) in the box marked *1st*. When I first noticed this, I wondered if he really understood the purpose of onomatopoeia since the word *boom* didn't seem to fit the event depicted. However, as I heard Isaac talk out his story, it made perfect sense with the additional details he stated. Interestingly, he added several more onomatopoetic elements while talking out his story and in his final draft. Though he didn't include all such words in his plan, he felt confident enough to include them in his writing.

When I had a chance to confer with Isaac, I would ask him some questions to spark more detail in his story plan. For example, "In the third box, you say you made posters and hung them up. Why did you do that? Your reader will want to know."

First: "We got 2 birds 2 Christmases ago. Boom"

Next: "Seth opened the door and a bird flew away."

Then: "We made posters and hung them up."

Last: "We needed to buy a new bird and we named it Emerald."

It's easy to see Isaac is skilled at identifying the main events in the order they occurred though he could have added more labels, jottings, and details. Each box depicts a major happening which he was able to detail as he used his plan to talk out his story. Refer to pages 35–38 to see his detailed written story.

Further, I noticed Isaac included a detail in his plan that he omitted in his written story. Under *last*, he noted that his family named the new bird Emerald. Of course, writers do deviate from their plans as they draft, but I would ask him if he did this purposefully or if it was an oversight. I love to hear children explain their thinking, and you never know what their intentions really are until you ask. In this case, if it was an oversight, I'd ask Isaac to reread his ending again, find where the detail fits, and add it in, reminding him to continually refer to his plan as he writes so great details aren't left out in the future!

What Do I See?
A Student Sample of Personal Narrative

Here you see Isaac's completed personal narrative.

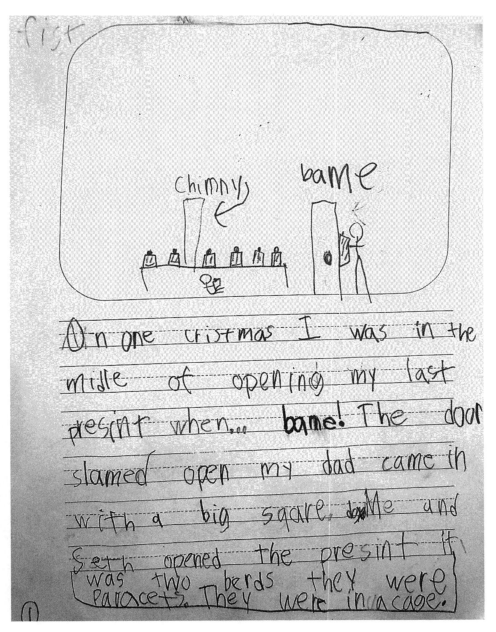

"On one Christmas, I was in the middle of opening my last present when . . .
bam! The door slammed open. My dad came in with a big square box. Me
and Seth opened the present. It was two birds. They were parakeets. They
were in a cage."

"We put the cage in front of a door. A few years later, Seth opened the door. Whoosh! A bird flew away. Seth went to time out."

the
then

After Seth was out of time out I made posters I copyed 100 it took a long time. Then we hung them up the wind blew them awa' ③ WOOSH!

"After Seth was out of time out, I made posters. I copied 100. It took a long time. Then, we hung them up. The wind blew them away. WHOOSH!"

Isaac does a beautiful job meeting the first-grade narrative writing standard. His events are well sequenced. He includes the temporal words *first, next, then,* and *last* at the top of his pages but also signals time order with phrases like "On one Christmas," "After Seth was out of time out," "Then we hung them . . . ," and the words *but* and *so*. He adds details, one of my favorites being, "I made posters. I copied 100. It took a long time." Still, I would push his thinking about details a bit in one place in particular: "I would love to know more about having parakeets as pets. What did they do? How did your family interact with them?"

The artistic way different authors and artists in our narrative mentor texts incorporated onomatopoeia significantly affected the way Isaac used this element in his writing. We can see this given how he wrote these words in bold and some in all capital letters. I'm also impressed with his skillful use of ellipses on page 1, building up anticipation just before the **'boom!'**

His sense of closure is quite poetic, " . . . and they tweet together. **Tweet, tweet!**"

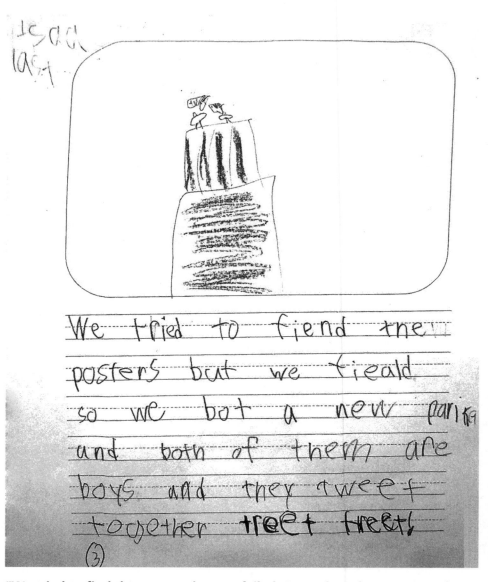

"We tried to find the posters, but we failed. So we bought a new parakeet and both of them are boys and they tweet together. Tweet, tweet!"

In conferencing with Isaac, in addition to congratulating him on the many qualities in his writing, I would push him ahead a bit by asking him to add some dialogue to his narrative (this is where we are headed next as a class). On page 1, I might ask, "What did your dad say when he came in with the big square box?" or "What did Seth say when the bird flew away (page 2)?" If Isaac gets a jump on using dialogue, we can use his writing as a peer model when we move on to study this element.

Authentic Assessment: Ideas for Evaluating Students' Learning

Inventories are useful in so many ways. In this sequence, I have first graders complete a Personal Narrative Inventory (below) to ascertain their general feelings and attitudes toward personal narrative writing. I want to know how they regarded the experience, what they would change, and what their thoughts are about future personal narrative writing. This has a very different purpose than when I ask students to complete a self-reflection based on the processes and strategies they used while writing and what they think are the most important things they learned (see an example of this type of reflection completed with second graders in the Authentic Assessment section of Sequence 5, page 237).

I read the questions on the Personal Narrative Inventory aloud to my first graders. Here is an example of a response from Kianna:

Name Kianna

Did you like writing a personal narrative? Why or why not? Yes. Because I like to dro and writh! ☺ It was SO fun! I want to be an ather wen I gew up!☺

Do you feel like you were able to tell your whole story? Yes!

Were you happy with how your story turned out? Yes! My picchers! My mommy liked it to!!☺

What would you change about writing a personal narrative now that you have written one? I wold not have bon the pisher boxis because it didin't help me

Did you like writing a personal narrative? Why or why not?

"Yes. Because I like to draw and write! ☺ It was SO fun! I want to be an author when I grow up! ☺"

Do you feel like you were able to tell your whole story?

"Yes!"

Were you happy with how your story turned out?

"Yes! My pictures! My mommy liked it, too!! ☺"

What would you change about writing a personal narrative now that you have written one?

"I would not have drawn the picture boxes because it didn't help me!"

Whose personal narrative story was your favorite? Why?

"Harlin and Brinley's. Brinley's was funny because she gets stuck on the slide."

Do you have any other ideas for a personal narrative?

"My family Lagoon Days!"

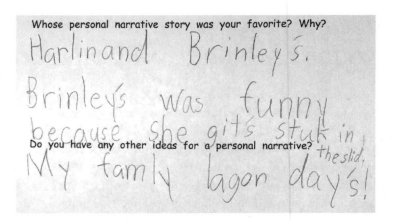

Kiana was invested in her writing, as you can see from her responses. I see that she was motivated by drawing the pictures for her final narrative, and I find it interesting she didn't feel sketching in the first-next-then-last boxes was helpful. She was very excited about this piece and wrote the longest story in the class; perhaps she felt the boxes just slowed down the process, keeping her from the writing she already had planned in her head? I can tell she was tuned in to what the other writers in our class were doing, especially given she was able to name two other personal narratives as favorites. This was not a difficult question for any of the first graders since we shared continuously throughout the sequence. Sharing together as the writing is in process allows everyone to learn from and depend on each other. I'm thrilled Kiana has already identified a topic for another personal narrative (Lagoon is an amusement park about fifteen miles from the school) and was elated to see she wrote, "I want to be an author when I grow up!" (She stated this in class, as well!) Yes!

Note: I *do* refer to the students as *writers* and *authors* all the time. It lends an aura of importance to the work we're doing and I want my students to think of themselves in these terms.

Companion Website Resource

Personal Narrative Inventory

Name _____

Did you like writing a personal narrative? Why or why not?

Were you happy with how your story turned out?

What would you change about writing a personal narrative now that you've written one?

Whose personal narrative story was your favorite? Why?

Do you have any other ideas for a personal narrative?

Retrieved from the companion website for *The Common Core Companion: Booster Lessons, Grades K–2: Elevating Instruction Day by Day* by Janiel Wagstaff. Thousand Oaks, CA: Corwin, www.corwin.com. Copyright © 2016 by Janiel Wagstaff. All rights reserved. Reproduction authorized only for the local school site or nonprofit organization that has purchased this book.

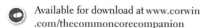 Available for download at www.corwin .com/thecommoncorecompanion

Peer Power:
Using Student Work as Mentor Texts

First grader, Harlan, wrote his personal narrative about a staying with his family in their hot tub for an extended period of time.

"My hot tub was dirty and it needed to be skimmed so I started to skim. Then it was clean. My family got in. We were talking to each other. We got hot, hot, HOT! Sweat, sweat, SWEAT! We stayed up late! We stayed up later than we have before. I can't wait until we get sooooo hot again!"

Though Harlan's story is very short, it has several qualities worth pointing out to peers. I love how he crafted this sentence: "We got hot, hot, HOT!" The repetition is effective and he builds up the heat by writing the last word with all capital letters. He then does the same in his next line with "Sweat, sweat, SWEAT!" Authors often use repitition to add interest and emphasis in their stories. This kind of wordplay certainly catches readers' attention. Harlan takes another risk, playing with the word *so* in his ending sentence, "I can't wait until we get sooooo hot again!" Highlighting his risk-taking for his peers reinforces the word play I model during modeled writing and that we study in mentor texts. Again, it's very powerful if a student thinks, "Harlan did it! I can, too!"

Harlan also shows attention to revision in his piece. He acted on a question a peer asked when he crossed out *we* and replaced it with *My family*. This is big! I'm always encouraging students to ask each other questions as they share. I say, "If anything pops into your mind as your partner is reading, ask about it! You never know when you might help a friend make something more clear or add an important detail, just by asking a simple question." As we're closing writing for the day, we often discuss and look at examples of how students helped other students make changes to their writing. This is a perfect example to show. It's small but signficant.

This may be all we point out in Harlan's piece. But, if there is time and Harlan feels okay about it, we could invite the class to ask more questions or point out places in his writing where he could add detail. Like a public conference, we would talk through the questions and suggestions and Harlan would decide whether or not to make changes. If he decided to make any revisions, he would do so right there, under the document camera, so everyone could benefit from watching and listening to this writer at work!

If/Then Chart

If students are struggling to brainstorm personal events to write about,	• Reread the class's running topics list. Often one student's idea will spark ideas in others.
	• Ask him or her or the group questions like, "Who is someone you often do things with? Name some things you do together. Tell me more." Or "When was a time you were really angry, happy, or sad? Tell me more."
	• Have the student walk around and listen in to other students as they talk out their story plans.
	• Return to mentor texts. What's happening here? Can you connect to the events? What might you write based on these connections? (The things we read often lead us to ideas for our own writing.)
If students have too many ideas to write about and can't pick one,	• Have them keep their own topics list and write all the ideas down.
	• Encourage them to read the list to a buddy and ask the buddy which story she'd like to hear most.
	• Ask them to talk out the stories on their list. Which do they have the most to say about? Which is most interesting to them at the moment?
	• If a student is really stuck, tell him to write about his first idea and see where it goes. He can always change his mind and switch to a different topic if the writing doesn't progress.
If students are having trouble putting their events into sequential order,	• Have them sketch out their story in boxes as suggested in the sequence. Then review the work and help the students talk out the story. If needed, cut the boxes apart, and reorder them, relabeling them at the top (*first, next, then, last*). Tape them to a new piece of paper. Ask the student to talk it out again to make sure she's got it.
	• Read additional simple narratives. Assist students in locating pages with key events. Use sticky notes to label *first, next, then,* and *last*. Use sentence frames to help students retell the events in order. You can also use the same frames as they move into writing.

(Continued)

If/Then Chart (Continued)

If students don't have enough detail,	• Ask questions! Even simple who, what, why, when, where, and how questions can lead to the addition of many important details. • Ask a volunteer if you can use his writing for a public conference. Model asking questions. Allow him to add details right there under the document camera as you work together. Debrief with the class about the process. • Teach students to ask questions of one another as they share. Model this with the class with several volunteers' stories. "Remember, we can help each other greatly if we ask any question that pops into our heads as the writer reads his or her piece." Have a chart with the simple question words above so students can refer to it when they are sharing with one another.
If students are excelling,	• Pull them into a group to share their stories with each other. Interacting with peers who are experimenting with different craft moves can push the work of all the writers in the group. • Encourage them to write multiple personal narratives on different topics. • Give them a few higher-level goals to incorporate into their narratives. Allow them to choose between a couple like *describe the setting in a lot of detail*, *add at least five lines of dialogue*, *find a place to describe a person's feelings in depth*, for example. • Allow them to explore other types of narratives like fictional stories, tall tales, or fantasies. Have them study mentor texts to discover the characteristics of a genre, then experiment with writing in that genre.
If you have English language learners,	• Depending on skill level, have students draw or sketch their narratives then tell them in their native languages. • Again, depending on skill, have students write their narratives in their native languages then use an online translator or speaker of the languages from your school or community to translate. • See Kindergarten Adaptation on page 31 for more ideas.

Bedhead by Margie Palatini: Oliver's bad hair day is hilarious! His whole family tries to help, but in the end, his hair wins the battle. This book is full of craft elements you can bring to students' attention. It has great descriptions, vivid verbs, funny dialogue, and interesting sentence fluency.

Best Friends by Steven Kellogg: Stories about friends will most definitely spark personal narrative writing ideas in your students. In this classic, Kathy and Louise's friendship is tested when Louise goes away for the summer and has a great time. More conflict ensues when a neighbor's dog has puppies. But, these friends work things out in a delightful way!

Come On, Rain! by Karen Hesse: It's been a long time since the last rain, and what a celebration the neighborhood's girls and mammas have when it finally comes! Students can relate to the waiting and ongoing anticipation of something they want. You'll love the poetic nature of the text and gorgeous paintings in this book.

Fireflies by Julie Brinckloe: Every youngster can relate to catching insects and making the decision to let them die or set them free. Brinckloe's beautiful language and illustrations make this another classic for every teacher's personal narrative mentor text collection.

The Girl Who Never Made Mistakes by Mark Pett: Beatrice is well known for not making mistakes. She doesn't realize how she's missing out on taking chances in life until she finally makes a mistake during the school talent show and everything is okay! Your perfectionists will relate to, and hopefully learn from, this story!

Knuffle Bunny by Mo Willems: Young students will relate to Trixie's plight—the loss and recovery of a favorite stuffed animal. Also of interest, watch Trixie grow and have continued adventures with Knuffle Bunny in *Knuffle Bunny Too* and *Knuffle Bunny Free*.

Mitchell's License by Hallie Durand: Though the main character is not quite four, students will relate to his refusal to go to bed. Dad has an imaginative solution; he becomes Mitchell's car so he can "drive" to bed. Riding on dad's shoulders is quite an adventure. Mitchell not only makes it to bed but also gets to drive in his dreams!

The Most Magnificent Thing by Ashley Spires: This story of friendship and perseverance is a keeper. A young, inventive girl decides to make the most magnificent thing, but it doesn't go the way she plans! The text even makes use of the narrative standard's temporal words, *first*, *next*, and *finally* rather than *last*. Spires's use of verbs in threes is a craft move your students might like to try!

My Friend and I by Lisa Clough: Here's one about friendship for our youngest students. A young girl plays alone until a boy moves in next door. They share everything until he gets a new stuffed bear he doesn't want to share. Don't worry—they work it out! This simple story should spark some personal narratives about the trials of friendship!

My Rotten Redheaded Older Brother by Patricia Polacco: In this autobiographical tale, Treesha undergoes the trials and tribulations of having a rotten older brother who's always trying to outdo her. They're friends at the end though, when Rickie comes to her rescue! This is my favorite Polacco narrative to share with students. Most can relate to troubles with siblings and we can always learn so much from Polacco's style.

The Relatives Came by Cynthia Rylant: This classic is another perfect first-next-then-last story line. I'm sure it will get your students talking about times with their relatives! I love the descriptiveness of Rylant's language.

Shortcut by Donald Crews: There's big trouble when this group of friends decides to take a shortcut home over the train tracks! Crews's creative use of onomatopoeia will get your readers really engaged in the story!

The Snowy Day by Ezra Jack Keats: The story of Peter and his adventures in the snow is a perfect example of a first-next-then-last sequence even our youngest students can identify. Though his saved snowball melts, Peter wakes up to a new snowy day and marches off with a friend for another snowy adventure! Keats's *Whistle for Willie, Goggles, Peter's Chair,* and *Pet Show* are also ideal choices as personal narrative mentor texts for our K–2 students!

Stella Tells Her Story by Janiel Wagstaff: Follow Stella and her class as they brainstorm, prewrite, draft, and share their own personal narratives! The strategies depicted will lead your students through the process of creating their own stories to share.

Those Shoes by Maribeth Boelts: Jeremy wants the black tennis shoes with white stripes that so many classmates are showing off. But, his grandma doesn't have enough money. When he is given a pair of toddlerish shoes by the school guidance counselor, one student in his class doesn't laugh. Jeremy surprises this friend, who is equally shoe-challenged, with an incredible gift! This is a story of friendship students will relate to and hopefully, never forget!

Poetry

The following are some of my favorite poetry mentor texts to use with K–2, not necessarily for the onomatopoetic elements but because they are examples that seem achievable to students, thus motivating them to give more poetry a try!

A Stick is an Excellent Thing by Marilyn Singer: Your students will love these poems about playing outside. There's plenty of onomatopoeia and rhyming to get them rereading and reciting these favorites. Many a poem will be inspired by this collection!

Guyku: A Year of Haiku for Boys by Bob Raczka: Who can resist haiku written from boys' perspectives? Included are topics that appeal to boys (and to many girls, alike!).

Kids' Poems series by Regie Routman: Routman includes examples written by students which demonstrate poetry writing on varied topics and at varied proficiency levels. The students' drafts and finished copies are shown. There's a separate book for each grade: kindergarten, first, and second. These are amazing mentor texts for your students!

Little Dog Poems by Kristine O'Connell George: A little girl writes short poems all about her dog. Included are lots of varied styles: shape poems, nonrhyming, for example. Totally doable examples for kindergarten, first, and second graders! Also check out the follow-up volume, *Little Dog and Duncan,* and O'Connell George's many other books of poetry. You won't be disappointed!

Noisy Poems collected by Jill Bennett: Onomatopoeia abounds in this fun rhyming collection on varied topics. Try Bennett's *Tasty Poems* and *Seaside Poems,* too!

Extending the Work

After participating in this lesson sequence, students should have a pretty good idea of what a personal narrative is. After all, they've drafted and shared a complete story. Now, as we extend the work, we want to continue to build on this foundation, studying and experimenting with story elements to improve the quality of our work. Along the way, we'll refine and add to our personal narrative anchor chart.

I like to do a series of lessons focused on a particular element of the genre we're working on then allow students to play with that element, emulating the models we study. For example, I begin below with a focus on dialogue. This kind of work can go on and on, so we have to pick which elements we feel are most important to improve the quality of the compositions of the students we have in front of us. Students don't have to compose an entire story to experiment with different elements. They can experiment using quick jots or quick writes focused on just a piece of a story. All in all, I like to have them complete at least three drafts during any genre study, if possible.

Note: When extending the work with kindergarten or first graders, you may wish to choose one or two of the following elements to focus on rather than all three outlined below.

LESSONS	READING Speaking and Listening	WRITING Speaking and Listening
6	Lesson 6: *Focus on Dialogue* • Define dialogue and its effects on stories. • Read narratives with an eye and ear for dialogue. • You might reread the narratives in this sequence with this focus or choose new stories to explore. • (A nice example of kid-friendly dialogue can be found in *Goggles* by Ezra Jack Keats.)	Lesson 6: *Experiment With Dialogue in Our Stories* • Using students' personal narrative plans from this sequence, ask them to look back to find places where they might add dialogue. • Model this with your own narrative plan. • Talk out what the dialogue might sound like. • Ask a volunteer to come forward and guide her as she finds places where dialogue would fit. • Help her talk it out • Invite all students to do the same and share their thinking.
7	Lesson 7: *Revisit Dialogue in Reading* • Revisit texts explored in Lesson 6. • Highlight and reread bits of dialogue that stand out or catch your attention. • Record particularly interesting or effective examples on a chart labeled *Effective Dialogue* (or keep the list in your Writer's Craft Notebook). • What makes these examples rich?	Lesson 7: *Jot Dialogue* • Students revisit their narrative plans and identify where they thought dialogue might fit. • Once again, they talk out a bit of dialogue with a neighbor • Teacher models doing the same, this time jotting the dialogue (this might be just a few phrases or sentences) on the back of the story plan paper.

LESSONS	READING Speaking and Listening	WRITING Speaking and Listening
7 (Continued)		• Students do the same. • Share and discuss. • Record some student examples on the Effective Dialogue chart.
8	Lesson 8: *Continue Dialogue Study* • Read part of a new story or reread part of a narrative you've previously read. • Read the part again, this time without the dialogue. • Discuss what happens. Do students like the story better with our without the dialogue? Why?	Lesson 8: *Brainstorm New Personal Narrative Topics, Play With Dialogue* • Review the covers of the new stories you've read. • Brainstorm ideas for another personal narrative—making connections to the stories you've been reading. • Add topic ideas to the class topics list. • Give students a few minutes to briefly talk out a bit of their stories. • Teacher models starting to draft a new personal narrative, this time starting with dialogue. (Again, this could be just a few phrases or sentences.) • A volunteer comes forward and gives it a try, drafting in front of the class with the teacher's help, if needed. • All students begin their drafts starting with dialogue, as modeled. • Share and discuss.
9	Lesson 9: *Repeat Lesson 8 With Another Book* • Add to Personal Narrative anchor chart.	Lesson 9: *Plan Personal Narratives in First-Next-Then-Last Boxes* • Students reread their bit of dialogue from Lesson 8. • Students then talk out their personal narratives, focusing on key events that occurred first, next, then, and last. • Teacher models sketching, jotting, and labeling in boxes to record the bones of her story. • Students complete their boxes, talking out their stories as they go and jotting any dialogue they think they may want to include on the back of their paper.
10	Lesson 10: *Eyes and Ears Focused on Dialogue: Independent Work* • Continue to search for interesting and effective examples of dialogue. • Invite students to do this in their independent reading, placing sticky notes on pages with rich examples.	Lesson 10: *Draft Personal Narratives* • Teacher models talking out her story using her plan, starting with her dialogue from Lesson 8 and incorporating any other dialogue she brainstormed. • Students do the same.

LESSONS	READING Speaking and Listening	WRITING Speaking and Listening
10 (Continued)	• They might do this with books they are reading with buddies and in guided reading, too. • Allow students to share and discuss their findings. • Add a few examples to the Effective Dialogue chart.	• Teacher models adding more dialogue and some onomatopoeia, if appropriate. • Students do the same. • Teacher models continuing to draft using her plan, talking it out, and rereading as she proceeds. • Students do the same. • Share and discuss.
11	Lesson 11: *Continue Work of Lesson 10* • Add to Personal Narrative anchor chart.	Lesson 11: *Complete Drafts, Share, and Celebrate* • (This may take more than one session.) • Teacher models continuing to draft, rereading, revising, and editing as she goes. • Students continue to draft and share. • When most students are done, share in small groups and celebrate: Who will you share your new story with? • Also, easily create digital stories students and families can access on any device using Flip Snack (it's free at www.flipsnack.com). Just scan the stories in as pdfs and drag them across to create a swipeable, digital book that can be shared with anyone who has the html address!
12 **13**	Lessons 12 and 13: *Mini-Study: Crafting Settings* • Read narrative stories in which the authors have carefully crafted effective settings. • Study what the authors did to make the settings effective. • List some questions the author may have considered in creating the scene: Where did this happen? When did it happen? What did I see there? What did I hear there? What was it like? What did it remind me of? Begin a chart labeled *Setting the Scene*. • Record some favorites. • Highlight the key words and descriptive phrases that make the examples stand out. • Add to Personal Narrative anchor chart.	Lessons 12 and 13: *Experimenting With Settings* • Teacher models talking out a setting to go along with one of her previously completed personal narrative story plans. As she does this, she refers to the list of questions and the favorite examples recorded earlier. Her example can be brief, so as not to overwhelm students. • A student volunteer comes forward with one of his previous plans. The teacher assists him in talking out the setting by asking questions. • All students give this a try, jotting their ideas on the back of their story plans. • Emphasize that these can be brief, but students should try to use some descriptive words to paint a picture of the setting for their reader.

LESSONS	READING Speaking and Listening	WRITING Speaking and Listening
12 **13** (Continued)	(My favorite example is *Owl Moon* by Jane Yolen. She beautifully describes the setting as it changes throughout the story.)	• If students are having trouble, go back and reread the settings in the stories you visited earlier. Provide some sentence frames: • One _____ _____ (morning/ afternoon/ evening) . . . • Deep (inside/outside) a _____ _____ _____ . . . • Swish! (or other onomatopoetic word) The _____ • _____ . . . • Share. • Record some student examples on the chart.
14 **15**	Lesson 14 and 15: *Mini-Study: Crafting Endings* • Read narrative stories in which the authors have carefully crafted effective endings. • Study what the authors did to make the endings effective. • Begin a chart labeled *Effective Endings*. • Record some favorites. • Highlight the key words or name what the authors did to make the examples stand out.	Lesson 14 and 15: *Experiment With Endings* • Teacher models talking out an alternative ending to go along with one of her previously completed personal narrative story plans. As she does this, she models her work after one of the examples from the Effective Endings chart. • A student volunteer comes forward with one of her previous plans. The teacher assists her in talking out an ending modeled after one of the examples from the chart. • All students give this a try, jotting their ideas on the back of their story plans. • Share. • Record some student examples on the chart.
16 **17** **18**	Lessons 16–18: *Summing Up* • Add to Personal Narrative anchor chart.	Lessons 16–18: *Putting It All Together: Plan, Draft, Share, and Celebrate One More Personal Narrative* • Brainstorm topics (refer to ongoing topics list), talk out stories, and plan in boxes. • Emphasize adding notes in the boxes where onomatopoeia and dialogue may fit. • Take time to carefully craft the setting and ending while referring to charts and models. • Allow students to share and get feedback as they proceed. • Draft. • Share and celebrate! • Debrief and self-evaluate.

Integrating Research to Build and Present Knowledge With Identifying Topic and Details

In this sequence, students engage in a form of action research to gather information about which classroom rules are considered most important to them and to other students in their school. Our goal is to "Research to Build and Present Knowledge" (Writing Standard 7) and do so in a purposeful way. Students collect information, analyze it, write about it, and share their findings with the classes they poll. The sequence is designed to give students experience in moving from media sources to text sources and to engage in discussion and multiple types of writing in the course of this action research.

I had kindergartners partner with fourth-grade peers, but of course, there are many ways to adapt and extend the work for first and second grades (see grade level adaptations on pages 78 and 79). Truly, any grade level will love the processes involved in these lessons!

Rick Harrington Photography

Students are much more motivated when their writing is purposeful!

This sequence is best done at the beginning of the year since it is then that students are most interested in the topic of rules. Students are highly motivated to find out what their peers and other classes think is the most important class rule. The data gathering, analysis, writing, and presenting are lively processes. The rich, respectful conversation about which rule(s) may be most important helps build classroom community and fits right in with the back-to-school curriculum.

Multiple types of reading, viewing, and writing are involved in this experience. If done at the beginning of the year, students get a preview into multiple forms and purposes for writing. Since they share their findings with other classes, they learn researching and writing are useful, important activities!

Task

We will research this question: Which is the most important class rule and why? We will gather data on what our class and other classes think is the most important rule. We'll study the data, decide what it means, and share what we've learned with the other classes.

Core Connections

Focus Writing Standard 7 integrated with Reading Informative Standard 2

Reading Literature Standards 1, 2, 3, 7, and 10

Reading Informational Standards 1, 3, and 9

Writing Standards 1, 2, 5, and 8

Speaking and Listening Standards 1, 2, 3, 5, and 6

What Teachers Guide Across the Week

LESSONS	READING Speaking and Listening	WRITING Speaking and Listening
1	**Lesson 1:** *Viewing Media to Begin Information Gathering and Discussion* • Explain the task. • Watch video on rules. • Identify the topic. • Re-view the video, focusing on details. • Discuss topic and details.	**Lesson 1:** *Jot Topic and Details Using Interactive Writing* • Use interactive writing to record topic and details from the video. • Reread continuously as you write. • Discuss students' thoughts about rules. • Reread the entire chart upon completion. • Have collaborative conversation about additional rules. • Write these ideas in a notebook.
2	**Lesson 2:** *Narrative Reading, Comparing Sources* • Interactively read aloud *Kevin Knows the Rules.* • Identify topic and details of the text. • Find text evidence for why the rules are important. • Compare sources: Which rules are the same in the book, video, and our notebook and which are different? • Have collaborative conversation about what makes a rule important.	**Lesson 2:** *Informal Opinion Drawing and Writing* • Model writing a sample opinion about which rule is most important so far. • Modeling is done at varied proficiency levels. • Have students write their opinions independently. • Share, discuss, and celebrate writing under the document camera.
3	**Lesson 3:** *Narrative Reading to Increase Background Knowledge* • Read aloud *The Golden Rule.* • Define the Golden Rule. • Record student definition. • Revisit text to find examples of why the Golden Rule is important. • Revisit students' independent writing to determine if the rules they wrote about are included in the Golden Rule. • Draw conclusion that the Golden Rule is the most important rule. • Read the class rules for the partnering class • Practice asking research questions aloud.	**Lesson 3:** *Interviewing and Opinion Writing* • Have students interview their buddy (fourth grade). • Have fourth graders write their opinion about which of their class rules is most important and why. • Have kindergartners work with their buddies to collaboratively add a picture to the writing.
4	**Lesson 4:** *Reading and Discussing Our Fourth-Grade Partners' Opinions* • Have students reread their buddies' opinions and tally them on a chart. • Discuss and compare results to our own thinking.	**Lesson 4:** *Interactive Writing to Record Data* • Use interactive writing to create a class data chart. • Have students reread their buddies' opinions and tally them on the chart. • Discuss and compare results to our own thinking.
5	**Lesson 5:** *Reading Mentor Texts for Parts of a Letter* • Read aloud *Click, Clack, Moo: Cows That Type* • Reread the letters. • Identify and record the parts of a letter on a chart. • Give a book talk on another related book. • Invite students to read this and other related books independently.	**Lesson 5:** *Interactive Writing to Inform About and Present Knowledge* • Reread class data chart and analyze results. • Use interactive writing to compose a letter to the partnering class. • Read and reread the letter chorally. • Present the letter to the partnering class. • Celebrate. • Debrief.

What Students Do Across the Week

The week begins with a video and the reading of two narratives to build students' background knowledge about rules and to spark discussion. By midweek, students are ready to interview a partnering class to determine which rule *they* think is most important. Once the data is tallied and analyzed, the kindergartners cooperatively write a letter and present their findings to the other class.

Our study begins with building background knowledge about rules using multiple sources. After students watch a short video, they identify the topic and details presented. The academic words *topic* and *details* are explained and students "share the pen" with me to record the topic and details of the video. We follow up with a narrative, *Kevin Knows the Rules*, again focusing on how to identify the topic and details. As we reread, we use sticky tabs to cite text evidence about why each rule is important.

Ongoing discussion is an integral part of this sequence. We discuss what makes a rule important and I model writing about my opinion. I model writing at a variety of proficiency levels so students feel comfortable writing themselves. Students then write independently about which of the rules discussed thus far is the most important and share their thinking about why with one another. Their writing is discussed and celebrated.

Reading the book *The Golden Rule* is a pivotal experience. Students determine the Golden Rule is the most important rule of all since all the other rules can be included therein.

Next, we examine the rules of a partnering fourth-grade class and prepare to interview them about which of their rules they think is most important and why. We orally rehearse asking the interview questions. When the fourth graders arrive in the kindergarten classroom, the kindergartners interview them and watch as they write their opinion. Working together, they both add an illustration to the page.

With data in hand, the kindergartners are excited to determine the results. Each child rereads his fourth-grade buddy's opinion and we tally the votes on a data chart we've created using interactive writing. We discuss our findings and conclude the other class picked the rule that was closest in meaning to the Golden Rule as the most important!

The book *Click, Clack, Moo: Cows That Type* is an entertaining read, and we study the letters written between the animals and Farmer Brown as mentor texts to determine the parts of a letter. We use interactive writing to compose a letter to the partnering class in order to inform them of the results of our research. We read the letter chorally numerous times to prepare to present in front of our audience. After presenting, students discuss how they felt about the experience, and we celebrate their efforts and debrief about what they learned. Meanwhile, the other class decides to write back to us, setting in motion a series of letters back and forth.

Literacy Moves

- Use multiple sources
- Write across modes
- Research
- Collect and analyze data
- Study mentor texts
- Write about findings
- Present findings
- Discuss

Booster Reading Lesson

Viewing Media to Begin Information Gathering and Discussion

Getting Ready

The materials:

- Copy of the task (page 51) to display
- YouTube video "Understand the Basic School Rules": https://www.youtube .com/watch?v=RyLzsQKFpB0 (Another short video of this type can easily be substituted.)

Context of the Lesson

First, I want students to understand the overall purpose of the sequence, so we discuss our task. Then, we view a short video which details a few school rules. We identify the main topic of the video and the key details.

The Lesson

"This is going to be an exciting week for us. We'll be working on figuring out what we think is the most important classroom rule. After all, we'll be learning together all year, so we want to get along as best we can to make the most of our time together! We'll also be doing research to find out what other kids think is the most important class rule. We'll be busy viewing video, reading, writing, and researching. When we're done, we'll know a lot about getting along as a group of learners and about researching questions."

"We'll start by watching a fun video. It's only 3 minutes long. As you watch, think, 'What is this video about?'"

After viewing: "What was the video about? If you could say it was about just one thing, and everything else told about that one thing, what would it be? That is called a *topic*. (*I write the word* topic *on the board.*) Think for a minute. Tell your neighbor what you think. (*I listen in as students share.*) You've got it! It's about rules.

"The three specific rules are part of the details. (*I write the word* details *on the board.*) Let's look at it this way. What is this? (*I hold up an orange.*)"

S: An orange.

T: So, let's talk all about this orange. That's our topic. Who can tell me more about this orange? (*Students offer: It's orange; it's round; it's a fruit.*)

T: Great! Those are all details or more information about the orange. (*I begin to peel the orange.*) What other details can you tell me? (*You peel it to eat it; it's sweet and juicy are two ideas offered.*)

T: Yes. So details tell us more about our topic. Often we can ask and answer who, what, when, where, why, and how questions to figure out details: What does the orange look like? What kind of food is it? How do you eat it?

Another idea for explicitly teaching topic and details is to have three children stand in front of the class. "Our topic is clothing. Let's focus on details about this topic. Looking at our friends, what details can you share about their clothing?" You could repeat this lesson focusing on all kinds of concrete objects. I've found children in Grades K–2 really catch on to abstract concepts like topic, main idea, and details when I use concrete, familiar objects as props.

T: Now that you understand the words *topic* and *details* more clearly, let's watch the video again. When we're done, see if you can name each of the three rules and share some information or details about each one.

After viewing: "Talk to your neighbor. What were the three rules shown? What did you learn about them?" (*Again, I listen in.*) If this is too difficult for students, divide the viewing into three shorter segments. As you watch, stop to identify and discuss each rule as is it presented.

"You've got it. First, the video showed how students should raise their hands. I heard one of you say that's important so we can hear each other. Then the video showed what? Who'd like to share?" (*I draw out students' recall of what to do about bullying and then move on to the last rule.*)

T: You're doing a good job. What was the last rule that was covered in the video? Talk to your neighbor. (*After talk-time*) Who would like to share? (*Students share that the video talked about using nice words, kind words, and I draw them out, pushing them to tell why it's important.*)

Recap: Key Lesson Steps

1. Explain the task
2. Watch video
3. Identify topic
4. Define *topic* and *details* using concrete objects
5. Re-view the video focusing on details
6. Discuss topic and details

Wrap Up

Recap for students what they've just learned by saying something like, "So the topic of the video, or what it's all about, is rules. The details or specific information about the topic are the three rules and why they are important. Next, we're going to take some time to jot down what we learned. Then, we'll discuss what other rules you think might be important for us."

Jot Topic and Details Using Interactive Writing

Getting Ready

The materials:

- Chart paper

Context of the Lesson

Using interactive writing, we work together to record the topic and details shown in the video. Our chart is used to spark a collaborative conversation about additional rules not shown in the video.

The Lesson

"Now we're going to record what we identified from the video on a chart. That way we can remember what we learned today and reread it later to help us think about and add to our learning. We will write on the chart together.

"We decided the topic of the video is 'rules' (*I write the heading* Topic *at the top of the chart*). Remember, the *topic* is what something is all about. Everything else you learn is details about that one *topic*. Watch me as I stretch the word *rules* to hear the sounds inside the word. I need to be able to hear the sounds and connect them with letters I know to spell the word." (*I model segmenting the word* rules *into sounds. I call volunteers to the chart to record the* r *and* l *using our Name Wall of students' names as a reference* [Wagstaff, 2009].) (See Integrating Foundational and Language Standards on page 251.) I write the other letters in the word. (See Interactive Writing in A Snapshot of the Varied Writing Modes on page 76 for details about the process.)

"Let's write the three rules on our chart. We will label these *Details*. Remember, details tell about or give more information about a topic. (*I write the word* Detail *on the chart*.) Since the topic of the video is rules, we can list *what* rules we learned about." I call on volunteers to once again share a rule that was included in the video. We use interactive writing to record the rule on the chart. After writing each rule, we reread it and briefly discuss what students learned, thought, or wondered about it.

"Now let's go back and reread the entire chart. (*I point and students read along with my voice. If needed, we use echo reading instead, so students can read the chart successfully.*) Our topic is rules (*pointing*). The video detailed these rules: raise your hand, tell if you see bullying, use kind words. Okay! Now we have a record of what we saw and the three rules we've already talked about. What other rules do you think we need as a class in order to best get along with each other? Think about that for a minute, then we'll talk about it together."

After think-time, we hold a collaborative conversation. Students share other rules they think might be important to us as a group. I push them to explain *why* they think a rule is important.

"Instead of writing all your ideas on a chart, I will record them in this notebook as we talk. That way, we'll have a record of them if we need it." I choose to do this to save time since we've already spent time building our writing skills through interactive writing, just as we'll continue to do daily. I also want students to know their ideas are important and worth writing down for further consideration.

Wrap Up

"Thank you for all your thoughts about class rules. We'll do some reading and additional talking over the next few days to help us decide which rules are most important to us. It would be great to make a poster of the most important rules so we can always remember them. We can't write down every rule, so we'll have to decide which key ones will help us the most."

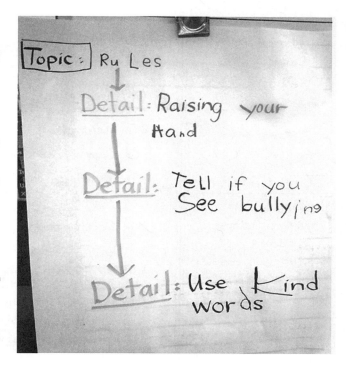

Topic/Detail: One of our first interactive writing charts of the year.

Companion Website Resource

Topic/Detail Chart

Name _____

Topic: _____

⬇

Detail

Detail

Detail

Retrieved from the companion website for *The Common Core Companion: Booster Lessons, Grades K–2: Elevating Instruction Day by Day* by Janiel Wagstaff. Thousand Oaks, CA: Corwin, www.corwin.com. Copyright © 2016 by Janiel Wagstaff. All rights reserved. Reproduction authorized only for the local school site or nonprofit organization that has purchased this book.

Available for download at www.corwin.com/thecommoncorecompanion

Recap:
Key Lesson Steps

1. Use interactive writing to record the topic and details from the video

2. Reread as the writing proceeds

3. Have students share thoughts about the rules

4. Reread the entire chart

5. Collaborative conversation about additional rules

6. Record students' ideas in a notebook

Core Connections

Kindergarten

**Reading Literature
Standard 1**

With prompting and support, ask and answer questions about key details in a text.

**Reading Informative
Standard 9**

With prompting and support, identify basic similarities in and differences between two texts on the same topic.

**Reading Literature
Standard 10**

Actively engage in group reading activities with purpose and understanding.

**Speaking and Listening
Standard 1**

Participate in collaborative conversations with diverse partners about kindergarten topics and texts with peers and adults in small and larger groups.

Core Practices

- Identify Topic and Details
- Identify Purposes
  for Reading
- Choral or Echo Reading
- Find Text Evidence
- Modeling
- Gradual Release
- Pair-Share
- Compare Sources
- Collaborative Conversation

Narrative Reading, Comparing Sources

Getting Ready

The materials:

- Copy of *Kevin Knows the Rules* by Molly Dowd
- Topic/Detail chart from Companion Writing Lesson 1
- Notebook with list of students' ideas for rules
- Document camera

Context of the Lesson

We engage in an interactive read aloud of *Kevin Knows the Rules*. We once again determine the topic and details of the text, focusing on finding text evidence to support our thinking. Students also compare their learning in this text to the video and our prior conversation. They begin to evaluate through conversation: What makes a rule important? Based on what we've studied and talked about, what may be the most important rule for us to follow and why?

The Lesson

I hold up the copy of *Kevin Knows the Rules* and ask, "What do you think this book is about?" As students examine the title and cover illustration, they determine the book is all about classroom rules. "So, this book will be about the same topic as yesterday's video? Let's study the cover picture and a few of the illustrations inside closely: What are the clues that make you think 'rules' is the topic?" We discuss students' observations and add sticky notes to the cover and pages inside to record the evidence they find (e.g., the word *rules* is in the title, the boy is raising his hand, sitting at desk, chalkboard behind him, we see the boy in line with the other students, etc.).

I think aloud: "Another strategy I use when I'm trying to figure out the topic of a book is to watch for what I find the *same* on every (or almost every) page. Here I see the author includes a unique feature. She chose to write some words in bold, or big, dark, blue letters and repeat those words at the bottom of the page. Let's read just those words, after all, they must be really important since they are in bold and repeated, to see if we can determine (or confirm) the topic of this book." Dowd highlights each rule in the bold blue type. Students notice this pattern as we read under the document camera. "So, we can confirm the topic of this book is definitely school rules!"

"We'll read the whole book under the document camera. You can chime in to read the bold blue rules with me. As we read, I want you to think about the following questions: What rules does the author teach us about? What details does she share? We'll stop as we read to talk about these questions. They'll help us as we try to decide what the most important classroom rule might be."

> "When we walk out of the classroom together, we walk in one long line," said Kevin. "There are other classes doing their work, so we must always **walk quietly in the hall**. Today, the teacher chose Grace to be line leader and we all followed her

Source: *Kevin Knows the Rules: Introduces Classroom Rules to Kindergarten Through Third Grade Students* by Molly Dowd (Bloomington, IN: AuthorHouse, 2008). Used with permission.

As we read, I remind students to chime in on the bold words. If support is needed, we use echo reading. As we read about each rule, we discuss details related to why the rule is important. I begin by modeling: "I see here in the bold blue type that the rule is 'sit quietly on the carpet.' In the very next sentence, Kevin shares *why* this rule is important. I see it here (*pointing*), 'If we sit quietly, we can all listen and learn.' It's important to understand why the rules matter so we know why we need to follow them. (*After reading on*) I see the rule is 'clean up after ourselves.' Sure enough, the author shares the same detail of *why* this is important. It's even right here in the same sentence (*pointing*) 'so that we can keep the classroom nice and neat.' And, there's more here at the end of the paragraph, 'This is how we can show we care about our classroom.' Now I understand why this rule is important. Are you noticing the pattern in this book? The rule is shared then there are details about why it is important. Let's try this next one together (*reading on*). We just read about the rule 'walk quietly in the hall.' What are some of the details given for *why* this is important?" Students talk to their neighbors. Volunteers share their thinking and I give feedback. We mark the specific words or illustrative evidence in the text using transparent sticky tabs (see photo below). If volunteers need help, we reread the words around the rule to find the answer.

"Why is walking quietly in the hall important? Other classes are doing their work."

Transparent sticky notes are an engaging way to involve students in finding text or illustrative evidence.

If students are successful, we continue in this fashion throughout the book: Students pair-share on every page: What is the rule the author is detailing here? *Why* is this rule important? I listen in and repeat what I hear students saying to redirect or celebrate their thinking. I also call on a volunteer to come forward and point out the language which indicates why the rule is important, marking it with a transparent sticky tab. (*I only do this last step for a few examples since I know this will be a routine I use throughout the year and students will get plenty of practice over time.*)

Next we make some simple comparisons. "Let's reread our chart from yesterday to review the rules we talked about. (*After rereading*) What rules from the video are the same and different in *Kevin Knows the Rules*? (*Students talk to their neighbors and I listen in and report about what I heard.*) Several of you noticed the rule about raising your hand was in both sources, but the rest of the rules were not. I'll reread the notes

I took yesterday during our conversation about other important rules. Listen carefully as we review our thoughts. (*After reading*) Let's look back through the book, that's something good readers do all the time when they are thinking, to see if any of the rules that came up in our conversation yesterday are also in the book." (*We discuss which are the same.*)

"Looking back we see there are several rules that are the same. If a rule came up more than once, do you think it is more important? (*Some students say yes and some say no. This question helps us clarify what it means for a rule to be important.*) Let's think then, what makes a rule important?"

We hold a collaborative conversation:

S: It keeps people safe.

T: Yes, we definitely want to be safe at school. That's important! What are some rules about safety that you already know? (*Students might offer no running in the hallway, wearing seat belts, no standing while school bus is in motion.*) What other kind of rule did we learn about?

S: Rules that help us get along.

T: Does anyone want to say something more about that?

S: We have to get along. We can't be fighting all the time.

S: I don't like it when someone is mean to me.

T: Good thinking, everyone. Yes, rules that help us get along are important in and out of school. These rules allow everyone to be productive and get things done peacefully. OK, so, we think rules that keep us safe and help us get along are the most important. Anything else?

We continue our conversation if students have more to offer. However, identifying what makes a rule especially important is a complex question. If you find students don't have anything to say about what makes a rule important, ask some leading questions like the following:

"How would you feel if someone hit you? (*Students respond.*) Okay, so rules that keep us safe from harm are pretty important. How would you feel if someone called you a name? (*Students respond.*) So, rules that help us get along and remind us to be kind are important, too. How would you feel if someone talked while we were walking in the hall? (*Students respond.*) So this rule is important, but not as important as the other rules. How would you feel if someone talked without raising her hand? (*Students respond.*) So again, this rule is important, but not as important as keeping us safe or helping us get along and be kind to one another."

Recap: Key Lesson Steps

1. Conduct an interactive read aloud

2. Identify topic and details

3. Find and mark text evidence

4. Model and gradually release responsibility to students, if appropriate

5. Compare book to video and previous conversation: Which rules are the same, which are different?

6. Collaborative conversation: What makes a rule important?

Wrap Up

Let students know that they are about to have a chance to voice their opinion. "We've done a lot of deep thinking about rules and we're not done. This is a big, important topic that will affect us all year long. But, I'm anxious to hear what you are thinking at this point. So, in a minute, we'll all have a chance to write about which rule we think is most important so far. This way, everyone will have a chance to share their thoughts."

Notes

Informal Opinion Drawing and Writing

Getting Ready

The materials:

- Topic/Detail chart
- Think pads or scratch paper
- Document camera

Context of the Lesson

Students are now given the chance to express in writing what they think may be the most important rule we've studied so far. Though we are also interested in *why* they pick a particular rule, they share this orally rather than write it. I model writing at different levels of proficiency so all students feel confident putting their ideas on paper as best they can. We share, celebrate students' efforts, and discuss our thinking.

The Lesson

"Do you think we are all going to agree about which rule is the most important? (*Discuss*) Do you think we've talked about every rule there is? (*Discuss*)

"Think about the rules we talked about so far. Which of these do you think is most important and why? We're all going to have a few minutes to write about what we think. But, first, I want to demonstrate what your writing might look like. (*I model under the document camera, thinking aloud.*) Let's say, I think the most important rule is to use kind words. (*As I talk, I draw stick figures to show one student giving a pencil to another who says, 'Thank you.' I show this only by sketching without any words at this point.*) See writers, if you are not at the point where you're writing words yet, you can sketch to show your thinking. Maybe, though, you know a little bit about listening for sounds in words like we did yesterday when we wrote on our Rules chart. If you do, you might add some letters to go with the sounds for the words you're sharing in your drawing. (*I model segmenting /th/ /ank/ and write the letter* k, *then write the letter* u *for the word* you. *I get a new piece of paper.*) Maybe you've had more experience writing and you know more letter sounds and words. If so, you can use what you know to write. You can also use the charts we have in the room as well as the Name Wall. (*I repeat the same message but show a more advanced stage of writing.*) I think the most important rule is to use kind words." (*As I talk, I sketch and write as shown in the sample on the facing page, modeling segmenting some words into sounds. I also refer to our interactive writing chart from the day before to write the word* rule *and the phrase* use kind words. *Additionally, I use our Name Wall to show how I'm matching letters to sounds as we did in the previous writing lesson.*)

I show each example one more time on the document camera saying, "No matter where you are as a writer, we want to know what you think. Your thoughts are important. Get them down the best you can so you can share them. We will write every day in our class, so don't worry if your writing doesn't look like your neighbor's. We are all going to grow and become better writers all year long!" (*I put my models away, hoping students don't all write about the same rule I just modeled! However, it is natural for students to 'copy' ideas from one another or from your model, especially towards the beginning of the year when they may be feeling nervous about their writing. As their confidence builds through experience, and you show them how you are truly interested in their thinking, you'll see less of this.*)

"Now it's your turn. Think about the rules we've talked about. Which do you think is most important? This is your opinion, your thinking, not mine or your neighbors. Don't be afraid to be different. Which do you think is the most important? Also, think about *why* that rule is most important. You can talk about this when you share your writing."

I circulate as students write, giving feedback and encouragement. We share several examples at different points of completion and at different proficiency levels under the document camera as we go. I celebrate efforts and discuss the writing with the authors in a public way, all to encourage students to write as much as they can.

We debrief to close the lesson (see Wrap Up).

Recap: Key Lesson Steps

1. Model writing at varied proficiency levels while thinking aloud
2. Have students write their opinions independently
3. Discuss and celebrate writing samples under the document camera

Wrap Up

Invite students to work with a partner. "Find a buddy and share your writing. If you've already shared, find someone new to share with. Be sure to tell why the rule you chose is most important. (*After a few minutes*) I love writing! I love how it allows us all to express our thinking!

"Do we all agree that the same rule is the most important? (No.) Is it okay that we have different opinions or ideas? (*Discuss*) Tomorrow, we will read one more book on the topic of rules. It will be interesting to see if this new book changes your thinking. Then, we'll begin to research our question with other students to see what rule they think is most important and why!"

FYI

I might have provided a sentence frame for students to use like: "I think the most important rule is
_____." I chose not to do that for this lesson since I want to see what students can do without such heavy support. Their independent writing then becomes a great formative assessment I can use to ascertain where they may be along the developmental stages of the writing continuum. Naturally, I'll use several independent writing samples and my daily observations to really get a handle on this. Since we write from the first day of school, I already have some knowledge which informs my teaching. For instance, since I have some students who are drawing to write at this point in the year, I honored this stage during my modeling.

Booster Reading Lesson 3

Narrative Reading to Increase Background Knowledge

Getting Ready

The materials:

- Copy of *The Golden Rule* by Ilene Cooper
- Sentence strips
- Chart paper
- Students' independent opinion writing
- Photo or copy of rules poster from partnering class
- Document camera

Context of the Lesson

We read and discuss the book *The Golden Rule*, thinking about what this rule means and why it is important. We decide this rule includes all the others and thus is the most important rule of all. We prepare to begin our research into a fourth-grade class's rules. We read their rule chart and practice asking our research questions.

The Lesson

"Today, we'll enjoy a book called *The Golden Rule* by Ilene Cooper. In it you'll hear a little boy and his grandfather talking about one special rule and why it is important. When we're done reading, we'll discuss what the Golden Rule is and why it is important. So, as I read to you, be thinking about those questions." (*I have them already written on sentence strips posted on the board.*)

(*After reading aloud*) "Let's first answer the questions I posed before we started reading. What is the 'Golden Rule?' Share your thinking with your neighbor. (*I listen in.*) I heard some friends say, 'Treat others like you want to be treated.' I think that's a good way to put it. Should we write that down?"

(We use interactive writing on chart paper to record the rule under the heading *The Golden Rule*. I write a lot of the text, sharing the pen only minimally, since we want to move quickly to get back to the book before students forget what we read.)

"Why is the Golden Rule important? Think for a minute. What examples did we see in the book? (*After think-time*) Share with your neighbor. (*I listen in.*) Let's page back through the book to find some examples of why the Golden Rule is important." (*As I page through, students call out when they see an example based on the illustrations and we discuss it. Additionally, I reread some of the text to help them when the illustration is not as supportive.*)

Core Connections

Kindergarten

Reading Literature Standard 1

With prompting and support, ask and answer questions about key details in a text.

Reading Literature Standard 7

With prompting and support, describe the relationship between illustrations and the story in which they appear.

Speaking and Listening Standard 3

Ask and answer questions in order to . . . get information.

Speaking and Listening Standard 6

Speak audibly and express thoughts, feelings, and ideas clearly.

Core Practices

- Identify Purposes for Reading
- Read Aloud
- Interactive Writing
- Revisit Text
- Echo Reading
- Make Connections
- Pair-Share
- Discussion

For example,

S: There's a bully!

T: What does that have to do with the Golden Rule?

S: He's not treating the boy like he'd want to be treated.

S: The boy feels mad.

S: The boy feels sad.

T: Yep, I see those words right here (*pointing to the text*). And, I see how the boy is feeling in the picture (*pointing*). And, the grandfather says (*pointing*), "Do you like feeling like that?"

S: No!

T: So, there's an example of why the Golden Rule is important. If we remember to treat others like we want to be treated, people won't have hurt feelings. Let's look for another example.

We continue paging through the book, discussing the examples.

"Think about your writing yesterday. Which rule did you say was most important? Share with your neighbor. Remember to tell them why you thought that was the most important rule. (*After sharing time*) Today, you've learned about the Golden Rule. Do you still think the rule you wrote down yesterday is most important or have you changed your mind? Think for a minute. (*After think-time*) Talk to your neighbor about this." After students share, we discuss this as a whole class.

"We can agree, then, that the Golden Rule includes all the other rules, right? Let's make sure that is true. I'm going to reread your opinions from yesterday. Let's see if the rules you picked as most important would be included in the Golden Rule. (*Reading from a student paper*) This one says the most important rule is to use kind words. If you treat others how you want to be treated, will you use kind words? (Students all chime in, 'YES!') Yes, of course, because you don't want someone to speak to you with unkind words!" I continue with more examples.

"To sum up then, we believe the Golden Rule (*pointing to our Golden Rule chart*) is the most important rule because it includes all the others. If we treat others like we want to be treated, we'll be following all the rules.

"Now we're going to switch gears a bit. Remember our task (*pointing to the copy of the task*)? Our plan is to research the question of which is the most important rule and why with other classes and share our results. So, drum roll please . . . I have a photograph of the rules chart Ms. B. has hanging in her fourth-grade classroom. I'll read it to you, then we'll read it together and discuss it (*I enlarge the photo under the document camera and we echo read each rule. We briefly discuss each one and I define the words* respect,

Time Crunched?

If you're out of time for the day, you can save the reading and discussion of a partnering class's rules for the next day.

Ms. B's Class Rules

I will respect myself by making good choices.

I will respect my classmates by treating them kindly.

I will take responsibility for my actions.

Ms. B's Fourth-Grade Class's Rule Poster

responsibility *and* actions.) How are Ms. B's class rules like the rules we've discussed over the past three days? Think about that for a minute. (*Think-time*) Now share what you're thinking with a neighbor." (*I listen in and share some of the students' observations aloud.*)

"In just a few minutes, Ms. B's class is going to come in. Each of you will get a partner from her class. Your job as a researcher is to ask your fourth-grade partner, 'Which of these fourth-grade class rules do you think is most important?' Then ask, 'Why?' (*I have these two questions written on sentence strips. I point to them and read them again.*) Let's practice. Pretend the person next to you is your fourth-grade partner. Go ahead and ask the questions. You don't have to say them exactly like this (*pointing to the sentence strips*), but you want to make sure you speak clearly and the fourth grader understands what you are asking."

Recap: Key Lesson Steps

1. Read *The Golden Rule* aloud

2. Define the Golden Rule and record it in students' language using interactive writing

3. Revisit text to identify examples of why the rule is important

4. Revisit students' independent writing: "Are these rules included in the Golden Rule?"

5. Draw conclusion the Golden Rule is the most important rule

6. Read partnering class's rule poster

7. Practice asking research questions

Wrap Up

"I think you're ready for our fourth-grade buddies. I wonder if they will agree with what we've decided is the most important rule. Be sure not to tell them your opinion. We want to find out what *they* think and why!"

Notes

Interviewing and Opinion Writing

Getting Ready

The materials:

- Photo or copy of partnering class's rules
- Plain paper
- Document camera

Context of the Lesson

Our fourth-grade buddies come to our room to discuss their classroom rules. Kindergartners interview their buddy, asking them our two research questions. The buddies write their opinion about which of their class rules is most important and why. Next, kindergarteners help them add a quick sketch to go along with their opinion.

The Lesson

"Remember, researchers, we want to know which of *their* classrooms rules they think is most important. We're not asking them about *our* rules, or sharing information about the Golden Rule. We want to know their opinions about their rules. Your job is to ask and then listen to their opinions and why they feel the way they do."

As the fourth graders enter, I have them sit with a kindergarten partner. "As soon as we all get settled, our kindergarten researchers will ask you two questions. Please tell them *your* opinion, don't worry about what other people think. Since they'll be asking you about *your* classroom rules, I'm projecting a photo of your rules poster here on the board for you to see."

The kindergartners interview their partner as I circulate, listen in, and provide any guidance needed. As the talk in the room starts to die down, "I'm going to call us all back together in about 30 seconds. Kindergartners, did you thank your fourth-grade buddy for sharing his or her opinion?"

"Now, *fourth graders*, we would like you to each take a minute and write down what you said on a piece of paper so we can tally your opinions and decide what the data shows. Just quickly jot what you think your most important class rule is and why. Tell your kindergartner what you're writing as you write. Kindergartners, you watch closely. Fourth graders, when you're done writing, you and your partner can add a quick sketch at the bottom of the page. Make sure your kindergartner has the opportunity to draw with you."

Core Connections

Kindergarten
Writing Standard 7
Participate in shared research and writing projects.
Speaking and Listening Standard 3
Ask and answer questions in order to . . . get information.
Speaking and Listening Standard 5
Add drawings or other visual displays to descriptions as desired to provide additional detail.
Speaking and Listening Standard 6
Speak audibly and express thoughts, feelings, and ideas clearly.

Core Practices

- Interview
- Observe a More Experienced Writer in Action
- Collaboratively Illustrate

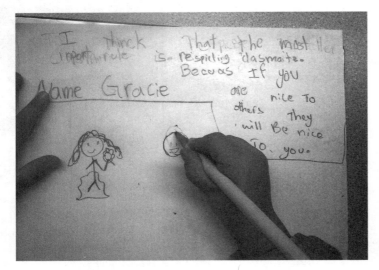

Fourth-grader Domenica answers the interview questions then writes her opinion: "I think that the most important rule is respecting classmates. Because if you are nice to others, they will be nice to you." Here you see her kindergarten buddy, Gracie, adding to the picture.

Again, as the partners work, I circulate, making sure everyone is engaged. I let the group know when there are 5 minutes left so they can finalize their work. I ask them to write both of their names at the top of the paper.

"Thank you so much for sharing your opinions about your class rules with us. We've been working over the past few days to decide what rule is most important to us, too. We will keep your papers so we can read them, tally your votes, and discuss the findings. Then, we'll write to you to let you know the results!"

Recap: Key Lesson Steps

1. Have students interview their fourth-grade partners

2. Have fourth graders write their opinion on paper

3. Have partners collaboratively illustrate the opinion

Wrap Up

Debrief and build excitement about the next day's work by saying something like, "What did you think about interviewing your fourth-grade buddy? (*Discuss*) Do you think interviewing someone is a good way to gather information about a question? (*Discuss*) Tomorrow, our job will be to reread the fourth-graders' opinions and tally the data. Then we can write to them to tell them what we find!"

Notes

Reading and Discussing Our Fourth-Grade Partners' Opinions

Getting Ready

The materials:

- Fourth-graders' opinion writing
- Topic/Detail chart
- Photo or copy of partnering class's rules
- Chart paper
- Document camera

Context of the Lesson

The reading and writing in Lesson 4 are so integrated, we do both lessons in one sitting. In terms of reading, students reread their buddies' opinions aloud so they can be tallied. Additional reading occurs as we reread our completed data chart. Discussion follows.

The Lesson

"It's an exciting day! We've gathered data on our research questions from our fourth-grade friends. Now, we need to have a way to record our data so we can determine the results. Which rule do you think they voted was most important? (*Discuss; I display Ms. B's rules and number them so we have an easy way to tally each vote.*) Let's tally their votes and see!" (This lesson is continued in Companion Writing Lesson 4.)

Core Connections

Kindergarten
Reading Informational Standard 10
Actively engage in group reading activities with purpose and understanding.

Speaking and Listening Standard 1
Participate in collaborative conversations with diverse partners about kindergarten topics and texts with peers and adults in small and larger groups.

Core Practices

- Reread Text
- Draw Conclusions
- Make Connections
- Discussion

Notes

Interactive Writing to Record Data

Getting Ready

The materials:

- Fourth-graders' opinion writing
- Topic/Detail chart
- Photo or copy of partnering class's rules
- Chart paper
- Document camera

Context of the Lesson

Again, this lesson is completely integrated with Booster Reading Lesson 4. We use interactive writing to create a chart for recording our data about our fourth-grade buddies' opinions. We reread their papers and tally the votes for each of their three class rules. Our class is very excited to find out the results and compare them to our own thinking!

The Lesson

(Continued from Booster Reading Lesson 4)

"If we're going to tally our data on a chart, what shall we call this chart or put as the *title*?" (*After discussion, we decide to write our research question at the top. We use interactive writing, segmenting some words into sounds, referring to the Topic/Detail chart we wrote earlier in the sequence, as well as to our Name Wall and the Words We Know Wall [for the words* is *and* the*]; Wagstaff, 1999). (See A Snapshot of the Varied Writing Modes on page 76 and Integrating Foundational and Language Standards on page 251. As we construct the sentence, we constantly reread.*)

"As you can see, I've numbered Ms. B's rules so we can easily keep track of the fourth-graders' votes. The first rule, 'I will respect myself by making good choices,' is Number 1. If we come across a paper in which the student said *that* rule was most important, we'll put a tally here under the box that says Rule 1. (*I point to the correct place on our data chart and explain the same process for Rule 2 and Rule 3.*) If you'd like to keep record of the data yourself as we go along, you can use a whiteboard or a piece of paper. (*I wait for students to get materials. I also pass the fourth-graders' opinion papers back to their kindergarten partner.*) While you're waiting, reread your fourth-graders' opinion to yourself. If you're having a hard time, look at the picture you helped draw to remind you of what they said.

Core Connections

Kindergarten

Writing Standard 2
Use a combination of drawing, dictating, and writing to compose informative/explanatory texts . . . *(We compose an informative chart.)*

Writing Standard 7
Participate in shared research and writing projects.

Writing Standard 8
With guidance and support from adults, recall information from experiences or gather information from provided sources to answer a question.

Core Practices

- Reread Text
- Interactive Writing
- Gather and Record Data
- Draw Conclusions
- Make Connections
- Discussion

"Let's get tallying!" (*As kindergartners share their buddies' papers, they stand next to me up front by the chart so I can help them reread if necessary. As each paper is read, that student makes the tally on our class data chart.*)

"So, we see Rule 2, 'I will respect my classmates by treating them kindly,' got the most votes! Of Ms. B's three rules, which one do you think is most like the Golden Rule? Let's reread all three and you think about it (*We reread, think-time*). Share with your neighbor." (*We discuss how Rule 2 is most like the Golden Rule because when we respect others and treat them kindly, we are treating them how we would like to be treated.*)

"Isn't that interesting? Both our classes seem to agree on which rule is most important."

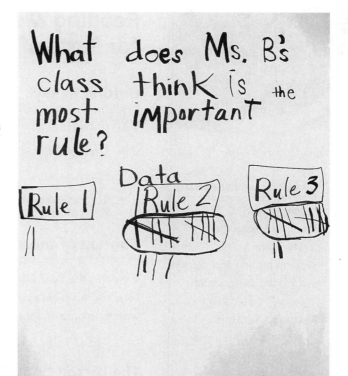

Our Class Data Chart

Recap: Key Lesson Steps

1. Have the class use interactive writing to create a class data chart

2. Have students keep their own data, if desired

3. Have students take turns rereading their buddy's opinion and tally it on the chart

4. Discuss the results and make connections to our own thinking about rules

Wrap Up

Build students' anticipation for the next day's learning by saying something like, "Part of our goal is to present our findings to the other class. Tomorrow, we'll spend some time looking at how to write a letter so we can write our own letter to Ms. B's class to inform them about the findings of our research!"

Notes

Reading Mentor Texts for Parts of a Letter

Core Connections

Kindergarten
Reading Literature
    Standard 1
With prompting and support, ask and answer questions about key details in a text.
Reading Literature
    Standard 10
Actively engage in group reading activities with purpose and understanding.

Core Practices

- Identify Purposes for Reading
- Read for Enjoyment
- Echo Reading
- Reread
- Identify Elements of a Letter
- Shared Writing
- Book Talk
- Independent Reading (by choice)

Getting Ready

The materials:

- Copy of *Click, Clack, Moo: Cows That Type* by Doreen Cronin
- Chart paper
- Document camera

Context of the Lesson

We enjoy the book *Click, Clack, Moo: Cows That Type* and study the letters exchanged back and forth between the animals and Farmer Brown. We study how the letters are written to prepare for writing our letter to our partnering fourth-grade class.

The Lesson

"Since we'll be writing a letter to our fourth-grade buddies today, we need to study how letters are written. One way to do this is to look closely at some sample letters to see what parts they have. In this book (*holding up book*), the cows write letters to Farmer Brown and he writes back. I've studied the letters to make sure they are written correctly and they are! So, first we'll enjoy this silly story together and then go back and study the letters closely."

I read aloud *Click, Clack, Moo: Cows That Type* in big-book format, tracking the print. We then go back and echo read the letters written by the cows, Farmer Brown, and finally the ducks.

"What is the first thing you notice that all of these letters have in common or that is the same?" (*I have a piece of chart paper standing by titled Parts of a Letter.*)

S: They say "Dear somebody."

T: Yes, that is called a *greeting*. We can use different words for a greeting, but *Dear* followed by the name of the person or group is a nice way to start a friendly letter. Let me write that here on our chart so we remember letters start with a greeting. (*I record the words* greeting *and* Dear _____.) Let's go back and examine each of the letters. Do they all start with a greeting? (*After looking back*) What else do you notice that is the same about all the letters?

S: They all say, "Sincerely somebody."

T: Yes. That is called the *closing*. All letters should have a closing so the reader knows who it is from. *Sincerely* is another word for *truthfully*, meaning everything said in the letter is true, and it is a kind way to end a letter. I'll write that on our chart, too, because we want to remember to have a closing. (*I record the words* closing *and* Sincerely, _____.) Let's go back and examine each of the letters. Do they all end with a closing? (*After looking back*) What else do you notice that is the same about all the letters?

S: They have something in the middle.

S: The animals say what they want.

S: Farmer Brown says he wants milk and eggs.

T: OK, so there is a middle to each letter. The middle is called the *body* of the letter and it includes the main message, what the writer wants the reader to know. In our letter, we'll inform Ms. B's class of the results of our interviews. So, not every letter's body is about something somebody wants. We will study more letters in the future so you learn different types and purposes for letters. (*I record the words* body *and* main message *on our chart.*)

"Wow! We've learned a lot about letter writing already. We know the three parts we need to have for now. We will add more information to our chart as we study more letters. I have several copies of *Click, Clack, Moo: Cows That Type* if you'd like to reread it during independent reading time. Also, the author, Doreen Cronin, wrote this book (*holding up the book*) *Giggle, Giggle, Quack*. In it, Farmer Brown goes on vacation and leaves his brother, Bob, in charge. Those clever animals do some more interesting writing you've just got to see. (*I read the first funny note from duck and show the picture, where duck is clearly shown holding a pencil and piece of paper. By now, the students are laughing and chatting about what they think is going on.*) I have several copies of it, and a basket of other books by this author, that you might like to read."

FYI

Book talks are like magic in the classroom. Like so many teachers, this is a strategy I use often to pique students' interest for reading a variety of books. I read just a bit—something funny or intriguing to get their attention, and show a picture or two. This often gets them talking. Some may have read the book and they proceed to tell a bit more and recommend it to their friends. Students are then invited to read the books during independent reading or check them out to take for home reading. Later in the year, I ask students if they'd like to do brief book talks for the class. I have them sign up for dates and intersperse them with my own talks. Their recommendations often have more power than mine!

Recap: Key Lesson Steps

1. Read *Click, Clack, Moo: Cows That Type* aloud for enjoyment
2. Reread the letters
3. Identify and record the parts of a letter on a chart
4. Invite students to read independently
5. Give a quick book talk on another related book

Wrap Up

Provide directions for the next step by saying something like, "We're ready to write our letter to Ms. B's class! I have our charts right here so we can refer to them to make sure we report our results correctly and have all the parts we need in our letter. Let's get to it!"

5
Companion
Writing
Lesson

Interactive Writing to Inform About and Present Knowledge

Getting Ready

The materials:

- Charts from this sequence
- Copy of *Click, Clack, Moo: Cows That Type* by Doreen Cronin
- Chart paper
- White sticky-tape
- Document camera

Core Connections

Kindergarten

Writing Standard 2

Use a combination of drawing, dictating, and writing to compose informative/explanatory texts . . . *(We compose an informative letter.)*

Writing Standard 5

With guidance and support from adults, focus on a topic, respond to questions and suggestions from peers, and add details to strengthen writing as needed.

Writing Standard 7

Participate in shared research and writing projects.

Speaking and Listening Standard 6

Speak audibly and express thoughts, feelings, and ideas clearly.

Context of the Lesson

We review the data from our research and use interactive writing to write a letter to report the results to Ms. B's class. Once the letter is written, all students sign and we visit the fourth-grade class to present it to them through choral reading.

The Lesson

"Before we write, let's review our data. (*We reread our class data chart and talk briefly once again about the results*.) Aren't you excited to present our findings to Ms. B's class? They don't know how the vote turned out! How should we start our letter?" (*We refer to our Parts of a Letter chart*.)

S: A greeting!

S: Dear Ms. B's class.

T: That sounds good. Let's look at our Parts of a Letter chart again as a reference. Who thinks they can come up and write the word *Dear* correctly on our letter?

A volunteer comes forward to write *Dear* as we all spell it aloud referring to our chart. We continue to negotiate what to write together and I remind students of the parts of a letter as we go. We also look back at the letters inside the book *Click, Clack, Moo: Cows That Type* to check on correct punctuation (particularly the commas after the greeting and closing. We add notations about these to our chart). Again, we segment words and refer to Word Walls and other charts to help us record letters and spell whole words. As we write, we reread and reread to make sure everything makes sense and looks right. We make changes as we go, if necessary. If a student comes forward and makes a mistake, we use white sticky-tape (purchased at office supply stores) to cover it up and fix it.

You'll notice we have a few capital letters in the wrong places in our letter. Since it's toward the beginning of the kindergarten year, I don't have students fix these. I'm thrilled they are segmenting words to hear sounds and connecting those sounds to the right letters. However, once students are more automatic with these skills, we do correct

Core Practices

- Reread Reference Charts We've Written
- Interactive Writing
- Choral Reading
- Present to an Audience
- Debrief
- Celebrate

capital letters, especially since knowledge of when to use capitals becomes part of our work as writers (and is included in the language standards).

As we work, we continue to refer to our Parts of a Letter chart and the letters in the book. We negotiate which word we'd like to use for the closing and write examples of other words students share on our Parts of a Letter chart for future reference. Then, all students sign their name.

"Before we visit Ms. B's class to present our findings, let's reread our letter together a few times to make sure we can read it smoothly and easily. We want our audience to be able to hear us clearly and understand what we are saying. When you present something, you often have to practice to make sure you'll do your best job in front of an audience. People often get nervous, so the practice helps them feel more confident."

We chorally read the letter numerous times. Different children take turns tracking the print with a pointer as we read. We pull a name from our "names cup" to determine who will use the pointer to track the print for us as we read to the fourth-grade class.

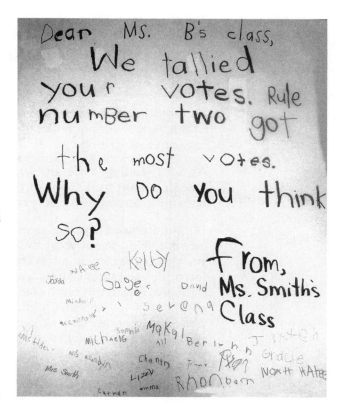

After reading our letter aloud to Ms. B's class, the fourth graders clap and the kindergartners beam with pride! They also ask us some questions and a brief discussion ensues. So many fourth graders have something to say that Ms. B decides her class should write a letter back to us!

When we return to class, we discuss student's reactions to reading in front of an audience. We celebrate our work by congratulating one another and shaking hands!

Time Crunched?

Write part of the letter in one session and then finish it in the next writing session. Just be sure to reread before you make additions.

Recap: Key Lesson Steps

1. Reread data chart
2. Negotiate what will be written in the letter
3. Use interactive writing to write the letter
4. Refer to charts, Word Walls, and the letters in *Click, Clack, Moo: Cows That Type*
5. Practice choral reading
6. Present the letter in the partnering class
7. Celebrate
8. Debrief (see Wrap Up)

Wrap Up

We take a few minutes to debrief. I ask, "What did you like about doing this research? Would you like to do more of this type of research? What have we learned?"

A Snapshot of the Varied Writing Modes

It's essential for K–2 teachers to understand the differences between and the benefits of the varied writing modes: modeled writing, shared writing, interactive writing, and independent writing.

As with reading, different writing modes provide different benefits for students. I wouldn't want to skip any of them because I want to support students' writing development in any way I possibly can.

During **modeled writing,** teachers are the writers. They do all the work. They think aloud, talking about what they are doing as they compose in front of the class under the document camera or on chart paper. Over time, as students listen and watch, they learn the strategies writers use while composing. We model what our students need most. We figure this out by looking closely at their everyday writing. At the beginning of kindergarten and first grade, we often need to model how to express ourselves on paper using nonexistent or very little letter-sound knowledge. So, we sketch, then we sketch and label while segmenting words to hear sounds. We model using the Word Walls and charts we've written together to help us problem solve how to write words. We model talking out what we want to write, rehearsing orally over and over to support what we record on paper. We continue to model at different proficiency levels as students gain skill and focus on the strategies writers use like rereading, playing with word choice, and making revisions to add details, for example. We can't forget the importance of modeling how to spell words at all levels, since poor spelling strategies can severely cripple a writer's ability to make progress.

During modeled writing, teachers work on pieces over time, just as we want our students to do. Students learn the ins and outs of the writing process as they see and hear the thinking and writing develop right in front of them in real time as you, a fellow writer, value, struggle, problem solve, and persevere.

During **shared writing**, we negotiate what will be written together with the students, talking out the content, giving it a try on paper, and making changes as we go. The content is owned by all of us, but the teacher is the one who does the physical writing. Since I have the pen, students can focus all their attention on content without worrying as much about spelling or mechanics. However, I still want to take the opportunity to encourage the use of references for spelling, and I often involve students in segmenting and spelling a few challenging words as we compose. Conventions like punctuation and capitalization are addressed, as well. For example, I might quickly remark as I write, "OK, we're starting a new sentence here so we need a capital . . ."

In contrast, during **interactive writing**, the teacher *and* students do the physical writing. The content is still negotiated jointly, but as students "share the pen," they grapple with spelling and mechanics continuously, thus working on their phonological awareness and phonics skills. (Since interactive writing promotes amazing growth in these areas and does so within the meaningful act of writing, it is a staple in my K–2 classrooms.) We work together to segment words into sounds and volunteers come forward to write corresponding letters. We refer to Word Walls to spell high frequency words correctly or use chunks we know. We use previously written charts as references, too. The teacher leads the students to write what they can but takes the pen when the task is too difficult. For example, when writing the word *shout*, perhaps you've taught and have a reference for /sh/ but haven't taught /ou/ or the *out* chunk. A volunteer could record the letters *s-h* then the teacher models writing the *out* chunk.

We need to keep students engaged during interactive writing sessions, so I often have everyone call out a spelling, make the letter, or spell a word in the air as the volunteer is writing, or I give everyone whiteboards to write on as we record on our chart. If students' attention begins to wane, I stop the interactive writing session and pick it up later that day or the next day. We always begin a new session by rereading what we've written.

In both shared and interactive writing, students have more responsibility for the writing than they do with modeled writing, but scaffolding and support are always available since the teacher is actively involved. In essence, these are forms of guided practice.

Note that any of these modes of writing can take place with the whole class, a small group, or even one-on-one and can be used for various purposes across the curriculum. Modeled, shared, or interactive writing sessions should be kept to 5 or 10 minutes depending on the grade level. Often pieces are worked on over time.

Obviously, students need opportunities to try out all they are learning independently, so having time in the day for Writing Workshop or **independent writing** is critical. Students will approximate the use of the strategies they've seen modeled and have tried during guided experiences. Though the teacher may be available to provide some support, it's important that students grapple with the act of composing on their own or with some assistance from peers. Teachers look closely at what their students are producing to help them determine next steps in their instruction.

Even our youngest, most emergent writers must have daily, independent writing time just as they need daily, independent reading time. If they are not given this time, how will their skills develop? They might begin by drawing and labeling or scribbling down letter-like forms, but the more teachers model and involve them in shared and interactive writing, the more they will grow. Naturally, the instruction they receive in phonological awareness, phonics, spelling, and vocabulary will also push their development as writers, but only if they are given daily opportunities to apply what they are learning!

Two students review our data as we prepare to write about our results.

First-Grade Adaptation

Few adaptations are necessary to make this sequence appropriate for first grade. Preview the video to determine if you feel it's right for your class. If not, you might find a different video on rules to substitute or begin the experience by reading *Kevin Knows the Rules*. If you use the book the first day, choose a book from the mentor texts listed on page 92 for the second day and continue to identify the rules and why they are important, picking out the relevant text evidence. If you choose a book that has several rules, pick just a few to reread and study more closely.

When deciding how you'll model before independent writing in Companion Writing Lesson 2, consider your students' ability levels based on the writing you've already reviewed. Often in first grade, I start my modeling at the same point I do in kindergarten since I tend to have at least a few students who are still figuring out the alphabetic principle. They need to be supported in knowing they can sketch or draw to express their thinking and that what they are able to put on the page will be honored.

Since the sequence is best done at the beginning of the year, I would keep the writing experiences the same, focusing on shared and interactive writing for the charts and the letter to the partnering class. The heavy support these writing modes provide will help your students feel comfortable participating as writers and also remind them of what they already know. Of course, throughout the day, students should have other opportunities to write independently, so they are always getting a bit of this type of practice in, just as you provide daily opportunities for your readers to read independently, no matter their skill level. (For more on this see A Snapshot of the Varied Writing Modes on page 76.)

Core Connections

Grade 1
Writing Standard 7
Participate in shared research and writing projects (e.g., explore a number of how-to books on a given topic and use them to write a sequence of instructions).

Notes

This sequence is perfect for the second-grade standard. Students use action research to get information then write about the results. In second grade, even at the beginning of the year, most students should be able to independently write about the results of their research. However, if you have several emergent writers, differentiate by allowing those who'd like to write their own letter do so independently then use interactive writing with the rest of the group to write a cooperative letter. When you visit the other class to present results, allow those who wrote their own letter to partner up with their buddies and share while the rest of the group meets together to listen to the second graders chorally read their cooperative letter.

I would not show the video to second graders. You might find a different video that is more age appropriate, or instead, begin by reading *Kevin Knows the Rules* as the first text for building background knowledge. You can still create a Topic/Detail chart listing Rules as the topic, recording the specific rules as details, but expand the details to include the reasons why the rules are important. I would also cite text evidence using transparent sticky tabs just as we did in kindergarten. You might want to use shared rather than interactive writing since you'll be recording more on the chart, but be careful not to spend too much time—just record the rules the students feel are most important rather than all of them. Even though it is the first day of the sequence, still allow children to share other rules they brainstorm that are not included in the text and write these in a notebook.

For the second day of reading, I suggest picking one of the mentor texts listed on page 92 and continuing to identify the rules and why they are important, picking out the relevant text evidence. If you choose a book that has several rules, you may want to read the whole text aloud, then pick just a few rules to reread and study more closely.

Naturally, you'll need to adjust the modeled writing you do for Companion Writing Lesson 2 to focus on the needs of your writers. I'd still model at a variety of proficiency levels, but in second grade, I can often start out by thinking aloud while writing with letter-name spelling, then on my next piece of paper, write the same message with within word pattern spelling (spelling with simple chunks) (Bear, Invernizzi, Templeton, & Johnston, 2011).

> **Core Connections**
>
> **Grade 2**
> **Writing Standard 7**
> Participate in shared research and writing projects (e.g., read a number of books on a topic to produce a report; record science observations).

Notes

Working with our fourth-grade buddies was a high point of this lesson sequence!

What's ahead:

What Do I See?
A Kindergarten Opinion Sample

During Companion Writing Lesson 2's independent writing, Hatee wrote, "The most important rule is to be kind." As you can see, she also included a speech bubble, "Thank you!"

If I was to conference with Hatee, I'd ask her to reread her sentence to see if she could identify and fill in the missing word. Depending on how easily she accomplished that, I'd demonstrate using a finger to help space between words.

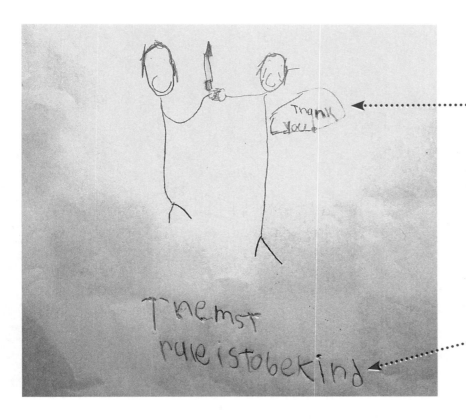

Hatee's work is right on topic. She knows it's important to indicate the topic of what she's writing since she wrote, "The most important (omitted) rule is . . ." or at least she demonstrates an awareness of the purpose of the piece.* She added detail to her drawing (particularly notable are the tears in one student's eyes). She also knows how to use speech bubbles. Hatee obviously has a lot of prior experience as a writer!

***Note:** Naming the topic is part of the kindergarten opinion standard.

Hatee was able to skillfully reference and copy from our interactive writing chart (Topic/Detail) as shown by her correct spelling of *rule* and *kind*. She also has mastery over some basic sight words: *the, is, to, be, you,* and was able to reference our fledgling Words We Know Wall (Word Wall of high frequency words). She is also able to segment words to hear sounds. *M-s-t* is an advanced invented spelling for this time of the year in kindergarten, indicating she can hear and isolate beginning and ending sounds and match them with the correct letters.

Hatee is already a skilled writer upon entering kindergarten. Though she basically copied what I did during my modeled writing (remember, though, I had removed my models from view), she clearly communicates which rule she thinks is most important. I don't need to ask Hatee to decipher her writing for me, which is a hallmark of writing growth. Given the skills she demonstrates already, I'm sure she'll quickly feel more confident expressing her own ideas in her writing.

What Do I See?
Another Kindergarten Opinion Sample

Here is another kindergartner, Cathan, in action, writing independently about which rule he feels is most important: "If you see a bully, go tell."

Cathan shows a good understanding of several conventions like starting a sentence with a capital letter, the correct directionality of the words, and spacing between words. He also spells several sight words correctly (again, either on his own or by referencing our interactive writing chart about rules or one of the Word Walls): *if, you, see, a, go.* He appears to have the ability to segment words into sounds and match those sounds with the correct letters. This is demonstrated in his spelling of *bully* (*b-l-e*) and *tell* (*t-e-l*). As with any other conclusion teachers draw, we need to examine several ongoing writing samples to determine if these are independent skills.

Cathan demonstrates a lot of writing skill. He understands the purpose of the writing and stays on topic, though he doesn't indicate the topic to the reader (The most important rule is . . .). He feels confident enough to write his own thoughts, given the discussions and knowledge we've built from the sources thus far, rather than copying my model.

In conferencing with Cathan, in addition to congratulating him on the many qualities in his writing, I would ask him why he scribbled out the faces in his drawing. Adding details to faces is an effective way to convey meaning and I might show him some other student samples (like Hatee's) to help him understand this point. I also notice the *b/d* reversal, and may point that out. Though, as we kindergarten, first-, and second-grade teachers know, this is a typical error and we always have to directly teach strategies so students can practice *b/d, p/q,* for example, correctly as they write.

Authentic Assessment:
Ideas for Evaluating Students' Learning

Looking at students' independent writing samples is the best way to authentically assess where they are as writers. As I've already mentioned, we have to look at several samples and watch our writers over time to get a true picture of where they are in terms of the strategies they use, the developmental spelling stage they are in, and their attitudinal characteristics. We're also interested in other skills that are important: the craft moves they try, their concepts of print, phonological awareness, conventions, and vocabulary, for example. As I cover each specific area in my teaching, I begin to look for evidence of growth in that particular area in students' writing.

At the beginning of the year in kindergarten, I pay special attention to the strategies a student is using to get his ideas on paper, as well as the concepts of print and the spelling stage.

Sample 1:

In terms of her spelling, the kindergartner above is at the prealphabetic/emergent stage, using letter-like forms as one way to express herself (note the letter-like markings at the bottom of the page). It appears she has some concept of directionality since her writing is moving from left to right and down the page in sentence-like form. Given her drawing, my guess is she is indicating that using kind words is the most important rule. I say this because of all the hearts, smiles, and the flower. Certainly, I would have to check with the writer to see if that is indeed her intent. I might say, "Tell me about your writing." This way, I can ascertain whether or not she wrote on the topic or understood the nature of what she was being asked to do.

Sample 2:

This student's picture is more clear and specific than Sample 1. He chose to write about a rule we had discussed and I recorded in our notebook, "Line up when the whistle blows" (on the playground). His letters at the top look more sophisticated than the forms shown in the first sample, but he is still at the prealphabetic/emergent stage, using random letter strings to write rather than matching sounds to letters. I had to ask him to tell me about his writing, which is how I know with certainty that he is on topic and understood the intent of the piece.

Sample 3:

First, I know exactly what the student is writing. He's writing that the most important rule is to tell if you see bullying. Since I can figure out his message with ease, I know he's on topic and understood the purpose of the writing. He obviously has some phonemic awareness skill and letter-sound knowledge, since he's either located and copied or segmented the words to spell them: *b-u-l-l* for *bully* and *t-e-l-l* for *tell*. I would have to observe him while writing to discern whether he is using references or attempting to segment words to spell or both. However, I can safely say he is in the letter name-alphabetic stage. If he can find the words he needs on a chart with a lot of print, he has some letter-sound knowledge; if he can segment words and even hear and represent the vowel sound, he has sophisticated phonemic awareness and phonics knowledge for this point in the kindergarten school year. I appreciate the bit of detail he included in his picture: the frown on the bullied student's face and the smile on the face of the bully.

Sample 4:

I know with certainty the writer of Sample 4 has advanced phonemic awareness and letter-sound knowledge because the word she wrote, *share,* was not recorded anywhere visible in the classroom. (Now wait a minute? What if this writer received help from another student? Again, that is why we must look at students' writing samples over time. If she's not demonstrating like skills in her other pieces from this same time frame, something else is going on. I'd either need to observe her in action or meet with her and talk or have her spell some words for me.)* Though she has misrepresented the vowel sound, even knowing that a vowel belongs in the middle of the word is sophisticated for this time of year. Also, recording *sh* for the /sh/ sound is impressive and beyond what many kindergarteners can do at this point. Her letters are well formed, which may again indicate she's had more writing experiences than many of our other writers. She's on topic (we talked about the importance of sharing as one of the rules recorded in our notebook) and understands her purpose. In her drawing, the child on the left shows more detail than the child on the right and I'd like to see representation of *what* is being shared. This way, her message would be clearer to the reader.

*Note: In addition to looking at daily writing, many teachers administer the Words Their Way spelling inventory (kindergarten or primary) at the beginning of the year (Bear et al., 2011), and a couple of times during the year, to get a handle on students' spelling skills.

Peer Power:
Using Student Work as Mentor Texts

Honoring the writing of students at varied proficiency levels is of critical importance. We can all learn something from other writers if we look at their writing through a positive lens. (Ask yourself, "What has the writer done well here?") Talking publicly with writers at different stages can shed light on strategies they use that may help push others forward. Making writers feel valued is one other core reason we use student samples as mentors.

Below, kindergartner Gracie writes about the rule we listed on our Topic/Detail chart: *Tell if you see bullying.* When sharing her sample as a powerful model, I point out the following:

"I see a lot of detail in Gracie's picture which helps me understand what she has written. I see the students are outside on the playground because this is clearly a slide (*pointing*). She's spent some time adding details to the children's faces. The girl on the left looks shocked (*pointing*); look at her face. Two others have big frowns. The girl on the ground looks mad or dizzy, like she's been knocked down; see these markings above her head? And her glasses have been knocked off and are on the ground. I see another

child yelling 'bully!' I know this because his mouth is open and there is a speech bubble (*pointing*) with the letters *b-l-e*. Because of all the details, Gracie's picture clearly shows me what she's writing about. Do any of you notice any other details I've missed?" (*Discuss*)

"Another thing I'd like to point out is Gracie didn't stop by just drawing a detailed picture to express her message. She also used letters to write a word. See here (*pointing*) she has the letters *b-l-e*? She must have stretched the word *bully* so she could hear the sounds inside the word and match those sounds with letters. Watch me: (*I model segmenting the word 'bully' into sounds using a strategy I call* stretchy hands. *[See Integrating Foundational and Language Standards on page 251 for more on this strategy.]*) See how she wrote the right letter for each sound?

"I am so impressed with all the amazing things Gracie did to make her message clear. I know she thinks the most important rule is to tell an adult if you see bullying. I am so proud of the effort this writer has put into her piece. Congratulations, Gracie!"

(Of course, you might talk about her sample with Gracie standing alongside you, asking her questions to clarify parts of her piece. Or, you might ask her to make comments at the end. Another idea is to talk to the student about the strategies she's used beforehand to save time when presenting the sample to the class.)

"Everyone take a moment to think about what have you learned from our study of Gracie's piece that might help you as a writer." (*Pair-share, discuss*)

If/Then Chart

If students' attention is waning during modeled writing,	• Remember to keep sessions only 5 to 10 minutes long depending on the grade level.
	• Stop the writing session. Continue writing later in the day, if appropriate, or wait until the following day. Be sure to reread what you had already written before adding to your writing.
	• Involve the students more. Ask them questions like, "Writers, what word would you suggest I use here?" or "What do you think of my piece so far? Does it make sense? Do you have any suggestions?"
	• Think about your purpose for modeled writing. Often we may need to just model a portion of the writing to support our students, not complete a whole piece.
If students' attention is waning during shared writing,	• Remember to keep sessions only 5 to 10 minutes long depending on the grade level.
	• Stop the writing session. Continue writing later in the day, if appropriate, or wait until the following day. Be sure to reread together what you've already written before adding to the piece.
	• Move quickly. When negotiating what to write with students, you can't possibly listen to every idea and vote on each one. Just pick one and move on. You can always revise later. (I explain to students why we must do this but tell them their thinking and ideas are always valued. Their ideas can inform what they produce in their own writing.)
	• Think about your purpose for shared writing. Write only as much as needed to meet your goal. Not every piece of shared writing must be taken to completion.
If students' attention is waning during interactive writing,	• Remember to keep sessions only 5 to 10 minutes long depending on the grade level.
	• Stop the writing session. Continue writing later in the day, if appropriate, or wait until the following day. Be sure to reread together what you've already written before adding to the piece. This is true even if you are writing only one sentence during the session!

(Continued)

If students' attention is waning during interactive writing, *(Continued)*	• Take the pen and quickly finish the writing (if it's just a few words to end a sentence or one additional sentence), thinking aloud as you go. • Engage students more by having them draw or write the word in the air (or trace it on the floor or in the palm of their hands, etc.) as the volunteer comes forward to write on the chart; have them call out the letter, the convention, or the spelling of a word while the volunteer writes; have them write on their own small white boards while the volunteer comes up and writes. • Ask students to write the next letter or word on their own small white boards. They show their boards and you pick someone to come forward to write on the chart.
If students want to pick more than one rule as the most important,	• Tell them to write about just one for their assignment. Then invite them to compose their own book about the many rules they want to write about. (I use this technique often. It's fabulous when students have so many ideas that they are trying to decide which to write about. They can quickly jot all of their ideas down and GO FOR IT! once they've completed the assignment. Remember, though, not all writing should be assigned. There has to be a balance between assigned and self-generated topics, even in kindergarten. See the idea of the Running Topics list on page 9 for more information.)
If students are stuck and can't get started,	• Use the strategy of keeping those who are having difficulty on the rug a bit longer. Ask them questions to get them going. Revisit the sources to remind them of ideas. • Have them talk out what they want to write. Listen and repeat what they say. Then say, "See? You're ready to write! Go write that down!" • Allow them to circulate the classroom and observe what other students are writing. • Help them write the first word or two (sharing the pen or giving them a word on a sticky note).

If/Then Chart

If students don't move beyond just sketching, drawing, or letter-like forms after the first few months,	• If you've been reading and writing every day in varied modes, working directly on phonemic awareness and phonics, and celebrating students' writing work, they should begin to hear and represent the first sounds in words on the page. If they do not, encourage them to draw their picture then help them segment words to hear the first sound and write labels with even just one letter. This will often get students moving. You can work with individuals or small groups.
	• Assess the students' phonological awareness. Can they hear sounds in words? Can they match words with the same beginning and ending sounds? Can they isolate sounds? Segment words into sounds? I like to use Wiley Belvin's Phonemic Awareness Assessment (2006). If results show the students are low, which particular areas do they need to work on? Work with small groups using hands-on materials to help students develop their abilities. They can't move along the developmental continuum in spelling if they can't hear and isolate sounds or segment words into sounds.
	• See Integrating Foundational and Language Standards on page 251.
If you want to push students who are not writing complete sentences,	• Have them talk out what they want to say in whole sentences before they write. If they can't do this, model it for them and have them repeat before writing.
	• Provide sentence frames or sentence starters.
If you have English language learners,	• You are supporting them using the strategies suggested in this sequence.
	• Many additional ideas are included in this If/Then chart.

Mentor Texts

Back to School Rules by Laurie Friedman: Percy's up to sharing rules again (see *Thanksgiving Rules* by the same author), this time about what NOT to do in school ("No spitballs!" "No running in the halls!"). K–2 students enjoy Percy's point of view and the hilarious illustrations. Very entertaining. Talk to students about ways to restate the rules in positive ways.

How to Lose All Your Friends by Nancy Carlson: This is a great addition to your K–2 Back-to-School read alouds. What could be more important than knowing how to be a friend? You can definitely revisit the idea of the Golden Rule after reading. I've also used it as a mentor text for How-to Books since the how-tos are numbered and simply stated, followed by details.

Know and Follow Rules by Cheri Meiners: Meiners explains in simple terms why rules are important then goes on to detail four basic rules for school. The illustrations are very supportive of the text. Meiners has a series of books focused on behavioral issues like sharing and problem solving, all of which I recommend for kindergarten.

Rules for School by Alec Greven: Eleven-year-old, best-selling author Alec details fifteen rules for school. He gives out plenty of sound advice on many issues second grade and older students are concerned about. Students relate to his genuine and often humorous voice. Break up the reading of this book into several sessions.

What If Everybody Did That? by Ellen Javernick: Though the setting isn't all about school, I like this book for this sequence because it relates to the Golden Rule. The boy in the book throws trash out the window of the car and interrupts the librarian during story time, for instance. Each time he breaks a rule, an adult says, "What if everybody did that?" Kids love the zany illustrations that follow up with the answer. Again, treat others like you want to be treated. What if everybody did that? (This would be a fun book to innovate on and create your own *What If Everybody Did That?* class book, with every student doing one page and using this author's structure and style.)

Mentor Texts Containing Letters

Click, Clack, Moo: Cows That Type by Doreen Cronin: The story is a riot and the letters are interesting examples for students to study as mentors. Who doesn't love letters written by cows and ducks?

Dear Mr. Blueberry by Simon James: In this sweet story, a girl writes letters to her teacher all summer trying to figure out the mystery of the whale living in her pond. The letters are short so they're good for study with our youngest learners.

Dear Mrs. LaRue: Letters from Obedience School by Mark Teague: Poor Ike the dog has been sent to obedience school. He writes a series of letters to his owner, Mrs. LaRue, to try to convince her to bring him home. Hilarious text and pictures!

Dear Peter Rabbit by Alma Flor Ada: Like *The Jolly Postman*, this book is a series of letters written by fairy tale characters. Alma Flor Ada created additional books in the same genre: *Yours Truly, Goldilocks,* and *With Love, Little Red Hen.* Students will enjoy revisiting some favorite characters and will experience a rich study in letter writing with the books in this series.

The Jolly Postman by Allan Ahlberg: Since this book is full of envelopes with tiny letters, the format always engages and delights students. They love catching up on the lives of favorite characters as they read letters from one fairy tale character to another.

Sincerely Yours: Writing Your Own Letter by Nancy Loewen (Picture Window Books, 2009): This is a how-to book with tips and steps students might take in writing letters of all types. Loewen has a series of these books, each detailing how-tos for different types of writing. I suggest them for use with Grades 2 and up, though you could use short, targeted sections to augment your instruction in first grade.

Also see descriptions of *I Wanna Iguana* and *The Day the Crayons Quit* in the mentor texts for Sequence 3 on page 145.

Extending the Work

An obvious way to extend this work is to repeat the data collection and analysis with another partnering class. Students can then compare if the new class also had a rule like the Golden Rule and if the students' votes were similar or different from the other class they interviewed. You might have students pursue this work with a variety of grade levels to see if this affects their findings. Keep up all the interactive writing along the way, creating new charts and letters for each class polled. Perhaps a new series of letter exchanges can be ignited! Additional ideas are below.

LESSONS	READING Speaking and Listening	WRITING Speaking and Listening
6 7	Lessons 6 and 7: *Repeat Research With Another Class* • Partner with another class, maybe on a different grade level. • Study their rules. • Interview them, collecting data (buddies write their opinions, and kindergartners cooperatively draw, as before). • Reread buddies' opinions and tally votes. • Discuss results.	Lessons 6 and 7: *Repeat Research and Present Findings With Another Class* • Use interactive writing to create another data chart. • Tally votes. • Use interactive writing to write a letter to the partnering class about the results. • Practice reading the letter fluently. • Present letter through choral reading. • Debrief.
8	Lesson 8: *Big Thinking About Rules* • Read other texts involving school rules suggested in the mentor texts. • Identify the rules and some details using the same strategies presented in the sequence. • Discuss: Do these rules *also* fall under the Golden Rule?	Lesson 8: *Independent Writing/Class Collage* • Have students talk about what the Golden Rule means to them and why it is important. • Record some of their thoughts using shared writing on a chart. • Give them independent writing/art time to write about their thoughts and draw and color an artistic representation of what the Golden Rule means to them. • Teacher-model first. • Post students' work in a collage in your room. Come up with a title for the display together. • Leave it up all year to remind students of their commitment to the rule.

LESSONS	READING Speaking and Listening	WRITING Speaking and Listening

9	**Lesson 9:** *Additional Research Questions*
	
	• Ask students to brainstorm additional questions they might be interested in interviewing other students about.
	
	• Some examples might be asking about something that could make a difference to the school, like one of the following:
	
	  o What suggestion would you make for a school assembly? What would make our library better? Would you like to have a guest reader in your class? Why or why not?
	
	  o (Rather than open-ended questions like these, you could have three answer choices for the interviewees to pick from.)
	
	  o If your students have trouble coming up with questions, brainstorm your own list and present it to the class. Allow them to vote on which question they'd like to find out more about.
		Lesson 9: *Record Our Research Question(s)*
		
		• After students vote on which question they'd like to research, ask them to talk out how they would ask the question(s). What exact wording will they use when interviewing other students?
		
		• After talk time, allow volunteers to share examples.
		
		• Pick one. Write it on a chart using interactive writing.
		
		• Have students read and reread the chart, practicing asking the question(s).

10		**Lesson 10:** *Interview and Collect Data* • Rehearse asking the research question(s). • During lunchtimes, allow your students to interview others in the cafeteria about your research question(s). • Each student should be equipped with a clipboard and several sheets of blank paper. (If students are nervous to do this on their own, they can be given the choice to partner up with another student from your class and they can chorally ask the research questions together.) • Older interviewees can be asked to quickly jot their response on a piece of paper. • If you're working with first and second graders rather than kindergartners, some may be able to record responses independently or with a little help from older interviewees.

LESSONS	READING Speaking and Listening	WRITING Speaking and Listening
11	Lesson 11: *Reading Interviewees' Responses* • Pick some interviewees' responses to show under the document camera. • Read them aloud to the class. • Discuss the responses and how you will manage tallying the data. • Create a data chart using interactive or shared writing.	Lesson 11: *Tally and Analyze Data and Write Letter Informing Stakeholders of Results* • Tally the data, analyze, and discuss the results. • Use interactive writing to write a letter to stakeholder(s). • Deliver the letter. • Encourage stakeholder(s) to respond in writing, even if it is just to explain a policy or rule. • Debrief and celebrate!
12	Lesson 12: *Add to Letter Anchor Chart* • Select a book that contains letters from the mentor texts on page 92. (You might choose to share parts of *Sincerely Yours: Writing Your Own Letter* so you can study different types of letters and their purposes.) • Read and reread some of the letters. • Examine their parts, formats, purposes, and word choices. • What additions can you make to your Parts of a Letter chart?	Lesson 12: *Write Letters* (This may take more than one writing session.) • Students brainstorm reasons to write letters (or refer to the Parts of a Letter chart, if you've added information about this). • Students brainstorm who they'd like to write to and for what purpose. • They share ideas orally, rehearsing before writing. • Students write letters independently. • They analyze their letters in comparison to the Parts of a Letter chart. "Do I have all the parts I need?" • Students share their letters with one another. • Teachers might copy some student examples to use as models for later instruction. • Students deliver their letters.

LESSONS	READING Speaking and Listening	WRITING Speaking and Listening
13	**Lesson 13:** *Revisit Identifying Topic and Details Using Informative Text* • Pick two new informative texts students have not seen. • Choose titles with a clear single topic and sections with headings and great picture support. • Think aloud, modeling identifying the topic using the title and picture on the cover and flipping through the pages. "What do I see that is the same on most pages? Does this help me confirm the topic?" • Model finding the main ideas and details. Use section headings and illustrations, plus other text features, as appropriate for your grade level. • Using the second book, invite students to try the strategies you just demonstrated to cooperatively identify the topic and details. • Have them pair-share their thinking as you go.	**Lesson 13:** *Write an Informative List: Steps to Figure Out the Topic of a Book* • Work cooperatively with students to identify the steps you take to identify the topic of a book. • Keep it simple. • Record ideas in a list format using interactive or shared writing • (You might add picture support to your chart by photocopying a book's cover and a few pages and labeling what you look for.)
14	**Lesson 14:** *Repeat: Identifying Topic and Details Using Informative Text* • Model Lesson 13 again with a new book. • If students are getting the idea, skip the modeling and guide the class to identify the topic and details.	**Lesson 14:** *Add to Informative List: Steps to Figure Out the Details of a Book* • Work cooperatively with students to identify the steps you take to identify the main ideas and details of a book. • Keep it simple. • Record ideas in a list format using interactive or shared writing. • You might add picture support to your chart by photocopying some pages and labeling what you look for and the text features you use. • You could make copies of your chart and share them with other classes: "Let's teach other students how to identify topics and details!" • Refer to your chart repeatedly in a variety of reading contexts!

In this lesson sequence, students learn the ins and outs of opinion writing: what opinions are, why we express them, what forms they may take, and what elements are present in effective spoken and written opinions. With these understandings in place, the emphasis becomes engaging deeply with text to devise opinions that are well supported. Though the sequence is written for second grade, many of the same texts, tools, and techniques can be utilized in kindergarten and first-grade opinion writing (see pages 132–134 for grade level adaptations).

Keegan and Porter listen thoughtfully as Lily shares her writing. Writing sharing circles give students another opportunity to voice their ideas and receive valuable feedback from one another.

This sequence could occur at any time of year as a launching-off point for opinion writing throughout the year. Though the focus of the week is on writing an opinion about a text, similar strategies can be utilized to delve into opinion about topics (these are addressed in A Snapshot of Moving From Opinions About Text to Opinions About Topics on page 130 and the Extending the Work section on page 147). As you model and guide students to mix evidence from texts (or other sources) with their own thinking across numerous experiences, their discussions and writing become richer and richer.

We rely heavily on oral language scaffolds throughout the week. There is plenty of talk as we first try spoken opinions, then build support for our opinions about *Prudence Wants a Pet* by Cathleen Daly through collaborative conversation, sharing and feedback. Additionally, once students organize their opinions using Thinking Boxes (Wagstaff, 2011), they talk them out with a partner as a bridge to drafting on paper. Once the drafts are complete, revisited, shared, and celebrated, we're ready to pass them on to the school librarian, lending real purpose to our work. We debrief about our experience and discuss other possibilities for opinion writing in the future.

In Grades K and 1, we spend even more time on oral language practice, sharing our opinions aloud, before getting into writing. Our first writings will be shared, interactive, or both. The mentor texts listed are still fine choices, though you may want to truncate the reading of some. Once we get to independent writing, Thinking Boxes work nicely, though they'll be less detailed as fewer reasons are required and students' abilities to provide the evidence behind their thinking is not as developed. (We still work on this, though, and it is especially evident in our shared texts. But, in my experience, it's enough for students in Grade K–1 to offer opinions based on reasons that are their own feelings and thoughts. In other words, don't get too hung up on students being able to name reasons based on facts or evidence in a text.) Sentence and paragraph frames provide help as well.

Core Connections

Focus Writing Standard 1, integrated with Reading Literature Standard 1
Reading Literature Standards 1, 3, 5, and 7
Writing Standards 5, and 8
Speaking and Listening Standards 1, 2, and 6

Task

Write an opinion about the book *Prudence Wants a Pet*. Explain whether or not you liked it, and why you think that. Would you recommend it to other readers? Should our librarian buy a copy of this book for our school library?

What Teachers Guide Across the Week

LESSONS	READING Speaking and Listening	WRITING Speaking and Listening
1	**Lesson 1:** *Re-Identify Elements of the Text Type Using a Mentor Text* • Read aloud *Stella Writes an Opinion.* • Re-identify elements of opinion. • Note and chart elements (Effective Opinions . . .). • Discuss why opinions matter.	**Lesson 1:** *What Is an Opinion?* • Define opinion and create context. • Identify basic elements of opinions. • Model forming verbal opinions. • Practice oral language with feedback.
2	**Lesson 2:** *Deeply Understanding a Text to Stimulate Opinion Writing* • Explain the task. • Interactive Read Aloud: *Prudence Wants a Pet.* • Complete Narrative Story Map. • Retell the story.	**Lesson 2:** *Revisiting Text to Quick Jot Opinion Notes* • Revisit sections of the text. • Quick jot notes about opinions, reasons, and evidence. • Have collaborative conversation: Explain your opinion using notes as a reference (build our opinions through talk).

3	**Lesson 3:** *Charting Character Development and Character Traits*
	
	• Further examine character: Graph how the main character responds to events in the story.
	• Chart character traits.
	• Provide evidence for our thinking.
	• What is your overall opinion of the text (Walk to Vote)?
		Lesson 3: *Organizing Our Opinions With Thinking Boxes*
		
		• Plan opinion writing using Thinking Boxes while referring to anchor chart from Companion Reading Lesson 1 or rubric:
		  ○ Opinion statement
		  ○ Reasons (while referring to notes)
		  ○ Elaborate on reasons.

4	**Lesson 4:** *Studying Mentor Texts: Concluding Opinions* • Study conclusions in mentor texts. • Identify elements. • Chart elements.	**Lesson 4:** *Completing Thinking Boxes and Drafting Opinions* • Complete thinking boxes: Conclusion. • Final check of each Thinking Box. • Oral rehearsal with partners. • Begin drafting.

5	**Lesson 5:** *Exploring Multiple Forms and Purposes for Opinion Writing*
	
	• Reading mentor texts to note:
	  ○ Purposes of different opinion texts
	  ○ Forms of different opinion texts
		Lesson 5: *Finish Writing and Celebrate!*
		
		• Complete drafts.
		• Share.
		• Celebrate: deliver opinions to librarian.

What Students Do Across the Week

Using read alouds and shared readings, students read and discuss multiple opinion texts this week. They should walk away with a clear understanding of what an opinion is, what elements comprise written opinions, and why opinions are important. Substantial time is spent revisiting sections of texts to deepen students' understanding of the elements of opinion, as well as to assist them in developing and elaborating on reasons they like or don't like the narrative story *Prudence Wants a Pet*. These experiences culminate in the creation of a written opinion as stated in the task.

As we launch into a study of any genre, it's important to find mentor texts that not only are clear models of the text type but are also very engaging. If students are going to spend a good amount of time revisiting and analyzing, the text should be outstanding on many levels. Students across grade levels love interacting with Daly's *Prudence Wants a Pet,* the main book used in this sequence. There are no moans and groans throughout the week as the text is brought out again and again, since Prudence's antics are fun to think and talk about and the problem in the story is relatable for most students.

Students engage in reading the entire story on Tuesday for both enjoyment and general understanding. They also spend time rereading sections and examining illustrations to detail reasons for their opinion by jotting notes. They bolster their thinking by sharing ideas in collaborative conversation. On Wednesday, they're deep into the book again, analyzing Prudence's character and clarifying reasons and evidence as they organize their opinions in Thinking Boxes and begin to draft. On Thursday, "look backs" are common as they finish up their drafts. On Friday, students are finishing, sharing, and celebrating their work. Reflecting on the week is crucial, since I want to gauge students' understanding of opinion writing and of the processes involved. My ultimate goal is for them to get a sense of how fun engaging and empowering opinion sharing and writing can be as it provides them with an avenue for expressing their thoughts—their voices. I also want them to understand how to study sources carefully so they can clearly back up their opinions whether they are writing about texts or topics. Since we're dealing with second grade (and K–1) students here, we expect that these understandings and abilities are developing, not perfected.

Literacy Moves

- State one's opinion
- Read and reread closely to identify reasons and details for one's opinion
- Quick jot notes during rereadings and discussions
- Organize for writing: Thinking Boxes
- Draft with ongoing revision
- Share, celebrate, and deliver writing to appropriate audience

Notes

Core Connections

Grade 2
Writing Standard 1
Write opinion pieces in which they introduce the topic or book they are writing about, state an opinion, supply reasons that support the opinion, use linking words (e.g., *because*, *and*, *also*) to connect opinion and reasons, and provide a concluding statement or section.
Speaking and Listening Standard 6
Produce complete sentences when appropriate to task and situation in order to provide requested detail or clarification.

Core Practices

- Explicitly Define Examples and Purpose Setting
- Modeling
- Scaffold With Sentence Frames
- Oral Language Practice
- Pair-Share
- Immediate Feedback

What Is an Opinion?

Getting Ready

The materials:

- Kid-friendly opinion definition chart
- Oral language sentence frames (written on a chart or sentence strips)

Context of the Lesson

Students need to understand what opinions are before they are expected to state and write their own. Bolster this understanding by providing an explicit definition of opinion, with lots of examples. Bring in a positive and negative review of a picture book they know; share examples of movie reviews and letters to the editors from children (e.g., emailbag@timeforkids.com). Model verbally forming opinions on everyday topics and be sure to state your reasons for those opinions. Then scaffold students to do the same. Written scaffolds like sentence frames can provide highly supportive explicit models.

The Lesson

"Today we will learn what opinions are. We need to know how to form opinions because we'll be writing and sharing many of our opinions this year. Opinions are important because it's good to be able to express how you feel and our opinions can sometimes change things around us.

"Believe it or not, we are all forming opinions all day, every day! For example, you probably formed an opinion about your breakfast this morning. Maybe you thought the scrambled eggs didn't taste very good because they didn't have enough salt. Or maybe, you were given oatmeal to eat, and in your opinion, oatmeal is not a very good breakfast food because it is mushy and bland. Let me share my opinion about my breakfast today: In my opinion, my breakfast this morning wasn't very good because I only had time to grab a granola bar. I know granola bars taste yummy, but they don't fill me up. So, I'm probably going to be hungry here in a few minutes.

"Maybe you formed an opinion when you walked into class today and saw the schedule. You might have thought something like, 'It's going to be a great day today because we have art. I really like making creative, colorful pictures, so I just love art! Knowing I'm going to do some art later makes me feel happy!'

"Let's look at a definition of *opinion*: An opinion is what *you* believe, your thoughts, and your judgment about something. It is not what your friend thinks, or your mom thinks, or your teacher thinks—it's what you think. It's OK if your opinion is different from someone else's because it is *your own*.

"Did you notice when I shared examples of opinions that I used the word *because* a lot? The scrambled eggs didn't taste very good *because* they needed salt. The oatmeal is not a great breakfast food *because* it is mushy and bland. My breakfast this morning wasn't

> **Opinion . . .**
>
> An opinion is what *you* believe, your thoughts, and your judgment about something. It is not what your friend thinks, or your mom thinks, or your teacher thinks—it's what you think. It's OK if your opinion is different from someone else's because it is *your own.*

I keep this definition up all year.

good *because* it didn't fill me up. I told you why—the reasons why I think or feel as I do. What if I came up to you and said, 'This is my favorite book!' without saying anything else? What would you naturally ask?

"Yes, you would ask 'WHY!? Why is that your favorite book?' Whenever we share opinions, we should share the reasons for our opinions, because others want to know.

"When I said I didn't think my granola bar breakfast was very good, I gave you a *specific* reason why: Granola doesn't fill me up and I'm going to be hungry again in just a little while. If I said it wasn't very good because I didn't like it, well, you'd still wonder why. It's too general, too fuzzy a reason!

"So, let's sum this up: When we state our opinions, we have to *name* what the opinion is about specifically, like my granola bar breakfast, include how we *feel* about it, a granola bar is not a very good breakfast for me, and give *reasons.*

"Let's try stating some opinions together. Look at what you are wearing today. That will be our first topic. How do you feel about something you are wearing, maybe your shirt, pants, shoes, or socks? Why do you feel that way? Everyone think." (*Wait time*)

"Who wants to share their opinion? How are you feeling about something you are wearing today as well as reasons why you feel that way? Look here (*pointing to sentence frame*). You can use these words to start speaking if you need help."

I _____ (*like/don't like*) _____ because _____.

In my opinion, _____ *is/are* _____ *because* _____.

*I think*_____ *because* _____.

I believe _____ *because* _____.

Pete: I like the shirt I am wearing today because it has my favorite basketball team on it!

T: Okay, students, what did Pete say? (*Repeat together.*)

"Did he state his topic and how he felt about it? He sure did! He said he *likes* the *shirt he's wearing today!* And, what was his reason? He said he likes it *because* (that's a signal word that reasons are coming next!) his favorite basketball team is pictured on it!

"Perfect! He has the parts he needs for his opinion to make sense!"

Share some additional examples about this topic aloud, pointing out the topic, feeling, and reason(s) shared.

"Let's try another."*

Teacher and students complete other examples orally, using the sentence frame(s) as support as needed. Students think then pair-share with a neighbor. I circulate, listen in, and discuss examples so students get immediate feedback. I ask such questions as: Did the speaker state the topic? How he felt about it? Reasons why?

Remember, we are doing all this work *orally*. We are rehearsing and getting ready to write with confidence! Students can't be expected to write in a genre they don't understand, so all of this oral language work lays the foundation.

*Other possible topics you might use to stimulate discussion about opinions are

- A favorite ride, game, or food at an amusement park, carnival, or festival
- A favorite book
- A favorite character
- Opinions about our teacher or class
- A favorite movie or TV show
- A favorite game
- Opinions about favorite parts of the school day

Mix it up so students state opinions about *least* favorite rides, books, characters, class activities, and so on. It's important they get the idea opinions aren't always positive.

Be sure to model and reteach as much as necessary while providing plenty of immediate feedback.

Recap: Key Lesson Steps

1. Define opinion
2. Identify elements of opinions
3. Practice oral language

Wrap Up

K–2 students benefit from substantial oral language practice and rehearsal before they write. The oral language work done here lays the foundation for understanding the elements of opinion and confidently constructing one's own in written form.

Going forward, take time to discuss opinions throughout the day. During Companion Reading Lesson 1, you'll use shared writing to record the elements of an effective opinion on a chart. Refer back to the chart and sentence frames from this lesson to keep your opinion work on target.

Re-Identify Elements of the Text Type Using a Mentor Text

Getting Ready

The materials:

- Copy of *Stella Writes an Opinion* by Janiel Wagstaff or *Should We Have Pets?: A Persuasive Text* by Sylvia Lollis with Joyce Hogan and her second-grade class

- Document camera

- Sticky notes

- Chart paper

Context of the Lesson

This reading lesson uses a mentor text that focuses students' attention on the elements of an effective opinion, thus reinforces knowledge students began building in Booster Writing Lesson 1. Though the book *Stella Writes an Opinion* is a story, the author explicitly describes the parts of an opinion as the second-grade main character composes her own and, in so doing, changes the course of events at her school. Read the book once for enjoyment, then reread with the purpose of finding text evidence to answer a specific question: What are the elements of an effective opinion?

If you choose to use *Should We Have Pets?*, the elements of opinion are clearly present (student writers state their topic and opinion, provide reasons for their opinion, and include a closing), but they are not explicitly pointed out as they are in the *Stella* book. (Obviously, you could do the same with any other well-written opinion text. But, these two choices are appropriate for our younger students since they have a comfortable level of text complexity for the task at hand.)

The Lesson

"Let's enjoy this book *Stella Writes an Opinion* together. I'll share it on the document camera so you can follow as I read aloud. I'll stop at certain points so you can read with me, all voices together.

"This first read will be just for fun and to get a general idea of the whole story. I'm wondering based on the title, who is this Stella? Why does she write an opinion? What is her opinion about?"

Read the story aloud under the document camera, stopping at strategic points so students can chime in. After reading, have a brief discussion to answer the questions above. Refer back to the text, if necessary.

"Earlier today, we began learning the parts of effective opinions and practiced sharing our opinions about different topics. According to this text, what does an opinion writer

Core Connections

Grade 2
Reading Literature
  Standard 1
Ask and answer such questions as *who, what, where, when, why,* and *how* to demonstrate understanding of key details in a text. (Students will use text evidence to answer "what" questions: specifically, "what" elements writers include in their opinion pieces.)
Writing Standard 8
Gather information from provided sources to answer a question. (Noting and charting elements of opinion.)

Core Practices

- Read Aloud for Enjoyment
- Shared Reading Parts of the Text
- Revisit Text for Evidence
- Notation and Creation of an Anchor Chart
- Discussion

need to include first? Let's go back into the book and reread to answer this question."
(*State the topic and what you think about it.*)

As you reread a short section to find the answer, consistently model these three actions: point it out in the text, write the answer on a sticky note, and then post it in the book. "So, what is the topic of Stella's opinion? Let's find that, as well." (*I point it out in the illustration as well as in the words:* bringing back morning snack for second graders)

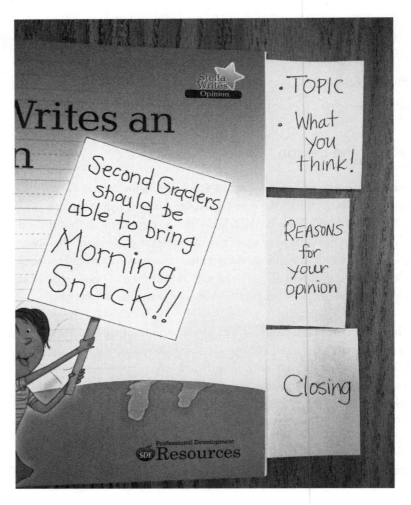

Source: Stella Writes an Opinion by Janiel Wagstaff (Peterborough, NH: SDE Professional Development Resources, 2015).

"According to the text, what does an opinion writer need to include next?" Again, reread the section, find the answer in the text (reasons for the opinion), point it out (or have a volunteer come forward to do so), and record it on a sticky note you post inside the book.

"What are the reasons Stella gives for her opinion? Let's find those in the text, too. (She gets hungry and can't concentrate on her assignments; she gets grumpy [low blood sugar]).

"Now, let's reread to find what an opinion writer needs to include last." Reread that section, find the answer in the text (closing), point it out (or have a volunteer come forward to do so), and record it on a sticky note you post inside the book.

But, wait. Ms. Merkley says that isn't enough. I've only stated my topic and what I think about it. You can't just say what you want, or what bugs you, or what you'd like to change. To write a good opinion, you have to have reasons to support it.

Reasons!

Well, most of us kids are pretty good at coming up with reasons.

Like when we try to get our moms to let us stay up 10 more minutes at night, we can come up with about a million reasons for that. For example:

1 Reading just one more book will make us so much smarter.

2 If we stay up later, we'll be more tired and fall asleep so much faster.

3 Ten more minutes in our whole entire lifetimes doesn't really add up to much.

Stuff like that.

Source: Stella Writes an Opinion by Janiel Wagstaff (Peterborough, NH: SDE Professional Development Resources, 2015).

So, I have my topic. I stated my opinion and my reasons for that opinion. Pretty good stuff!

Ms. Merkley says there's one more thing. Writers need to bring things to an end, like they do with stories, so we need to have a closing for our opinions. You know, like if you were giving a speech, you'd say something wise or funny that sums up your best ideas so people will remember them. This way, everyone knows you're done and can give you a standing ovation.

Source: Stella Writes an Opinion by Janiel Wagstaff (Peterborough, NH: SDE Professional Development Resources, 2015).

"We haven't discussed closings or conclusions for opinions yet; we'll get to that when we start writing our own. But, this book gives us an example of what an opinion is, what needs to be included in an effective opinion, and what an opinion writer does.

"Let's take a minute to create a chart listing the elements of an effective opinion that we've noted on our sticky notes. We can use our chart as a reference as we share and write our own opinions."

We use shared writing to record on chart paper: "What will make a good title for our chart? *(Something like "Effective Opinions.")* So, again, what does an opinion writer need to include first? Let's look at our sticky note." Continue this process, creating a list of the elements for opinion.

Effective Opinions ...

State your topic

Tell what you think about it

Give a reason for your opinion

Include a closing

Beginning Anchor Chart for Opinion Writing

Extend: If students easily grasp the elements of opinion, you might push their thinking deeper, reexamining sections of the text as necessary:

- What did Stella do to come up with possible topics for her opinion? How did she choose one? Are these strategies you could use?
- What do you think of Stella's reasons? Do they support her opinion? How do you know?
- What did Stella do to create a closing or conclusion she liked? Again, are these strategies you could use?

Examining questions like these could ultimately impact the quality of students' opinion writing.

Recap: Key Lesson Steps

1. Re-identify elements of opinion
2. Create a reference chart of these elements

Wrap Up

"Let's revisit something we discussed earlier: Why are opinions important? Why do they matter? Turn and talk with your neighbor about how Stella's opinion had an effect on her school. (*Listen in and share responses.*) See how important opinions can be? They can help us get our needs met or change something we don't like. They serve real purposes! Thanks for working with me to carefully reread and pick out the opinion elements from Stella's story. We can use the chart we've made to evaluate our writing; asking ourselves, 'Do we have the elements we need to have a convincing opinion?' That way we can work to make our opinions the best they can be. Like Stella said, 'Who knows what we opinion writers might change?'" (p. 29).

Oral Language Extensions

- "On your way out the door, think about your opinion: Did you like the book? Why or why not? Share your opinion with a neighbor at lunch!"

- "Notice the opinions you have throughout the day and into the evening. Tell your family what you learned about opinions. Share some of your opinions with them! Do they agree or disagree with you?"

Notes

2.

Booster
Reading
Lesson

Deeply Understanding
a Text to Stimulate Opinion Writing

Core Connections

Grade 2

**Reading Literature
 Standard 1**

Demonstrate understanding
of key details in a text.

**Reading Literature
 Standard 3**

Describe how characters in a
story respond to major events
and challenges.

**Reading Literature
 Standard 5**

Describe the overall
structure of a story,
including describing how
the beginning introduces
the story and the ending
concludes the action.

**Reading Literature
 Standard 7**

Use information gained
from illustrations and words
in a print or digital text to
demonstrate understanding of
its characters, setting, or plot.

Writing Standard 8

Gather information from
provided sources to answer
a question. *(Narrative story
mapping)*

**Speaking and Listening
 Standard 2**

Recount or describe key ideas
or details from a text read
aloud.

Getting Ready

The materials:

- Copy of *Prudence Wants a Pet* by Cathleen Daly or other title from the mentor text list on page 145
- Narrative Story Map (see example on the companion website)

Context of the Lesson

Prudence Wants a Pet is a great book to use to stimulate more thinking about, and ultimately the writing of opinions, but if you have another favorite picture book that involves a protagonist who voices a strong point of view, the basic moves of this lesson are easily adapted. As this story opens, Prudence wants a pet, but both her mom and dad say no and supply a reason for their thinking (Voila! Opinions!) The path Prudence takes to solve her problem is creative and hilariously attention grabbing. This lesson engages students in an interactive read aloud, story mapping, and retelling so they develop sufficient understanding of the plot and characters. These understandings are critical for composing reasoned opinions.

The Lesson

We preview the book cover and title and decide if we're about to read a narrative or informative book. Students decide *Prudence Wants a Pet* is a narrative. I then display the narrative story map and we quickly review what elements we expect to encounter. (If students have had lots of practice with this before, I have them turn and talk. Otherwise, I explain, while pointing to the map, "We'll likely find out the characters and setting right away, and then the main character will have some kind of problem or goal. Next, there will be attempts to solve the problem or reach the goal and finally there will be a solution or resolution at the end.")

"As we read, we'll be stopping to discuss the book, and we'll quickly note the narrative elements displayed here on our story map. I want you to be thinking about your opinion about the book, do you like it or not? Why or why not? This is a new book. Our library doesn't have a copy. (*I point to and explain the task.*) Our ultimate goal is to write our opinions and share them with the librarian so she can decide if she'd like to purchase of copy of the book for our school library."

I read the first few pages of the book and we stop to confirm the story elements so far (referring to the text and the illustrations). A volunteer comes forward and records our findings about the characters, setting, and problem on the story map. We then pair share so students consider how they think the problem might be solved. (*I listen in as they share and comment about what I heard.*)

I read to the next key juncture in the text and ask, "What do you think about Prudence's problem solving so far? Turn and talk. (*Again, I listen in and comment*). Yes, Prudence is creative isn't she? I heard Sharon say she can't believe the things Prudence tries to use as pets. Tell us more about that Sharon. (*After Sharon shares*) Who can piggyback off of what Sharon said? Let's add to our story map. What is the first thing Prudence does to solve the pet problem? We'll go back in the book and look again to make sure we're recording things correctly on our map. Then what? Then?" (*The class reexamines pages they've read and a volunteer records short notes on the Story Map.*)

"Now, using the story map, retell what has happened so far in our book. (*After sharing*) Mapping and retelling the story help us firm up our understandings of the book and can help us shape our opinions. Who's liking the book so far? Why?" (*Students share briefly about their opinions at this point.*)

I read on then ask, "Do you think the family is going to solve the problem? Why or why not? Turn and think together. (*Again, I listen in and share highlights.*) I heard Zach say the parents are starting to feel sorry for Prudence; they are essentially changing their opinions, aren't they? Zach thinks they'll get her a pet at the end. What in the text makes you think this, Zach? Come up and point it out in the book." (*After Zach shares, I reconfirm the words and pictures he used to make his inference and prediction.*)

At the story's end, "So, we were right. Prudence does get a pet! What do you think about this ending? Was it surprising? (*As students share, a volunteer comes forward and makes a note about the solution on the story map.*) Now turn to your partner one last time and retell the story together, referring to the map as needed."

Core Practices

- Interactive Read Aloud With Questions, Answers, and Discussion
- Revisit and Reread Text
- Story Map
- Retell the Story
- Pair-Share

Task

Write an opinion about the book *Prudence Wants a Pet*. Explain whether or not you liked it, and why you think that. Would you recommend it to other readers? Should our librarian buy a copy of this book for our school library?

Recap: Key Lesson Steps

1. Conduct an interactive read aloud
2. Complete story map
3. Retell story to partners

Wrap Up

"As we've been reading and examining *Prudence Wants a Pet*, I hope you've been thinking about your opinion of the book. Next, we'll look back and talk about our opinions at different points. We'll jot some notes to help us remember what we are thinking. Then, we'll discuss our opinions with each other."

Companion Website Resource

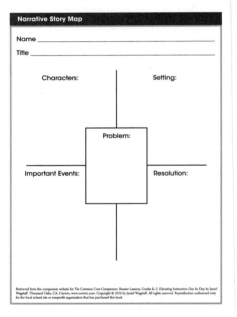

 Available for download at www.corwin
.com/thecommoncorecompanion

Notes

Revisiting the Text to Quick Jot Opinion Notes, Followed by Collaborative Conversation

2
Companion Writing Lesson

Getting Ready

The materials:

- Copy of *Prudence Wants a Pet* by Cathleen Daly
- Document camera
- Student think pads, writing notebooks, or scratch paper

Context of the Lesson

After reading and discussion, it's pretty easy for students to develop a quick opinion about a book. The purpose of this lesson is to get them to think more deeply about their emerging opinions. We reexamine sections of the text, discuss our opinions at each point, and take some quick notes (what I call *quick jotting*) to help us identify text evidence to support reasoning. Students then use their notes to engage in a collaborative conversation about the reasons for their opinions, thus further pushing one another's thinking.

The Lesson

"Let's take a few minutes to revisit sections of *Prudence Wants a Pet*. At each point, we'll discuss our opinions and note text evidence for those opinions in the illustrations and the words. This will help us more clearly identify and state our reasons for our opinions."

Revisit four or five selected sections from the text under the document camera. At each point, model jotting the page number, making an arrow up or arrow down to indicate your opinion, then jotting a few words of text evidence to support your opinion at that point in the book. Have students do the same in their notebooks.

For example, on page 14, I gave the book a thumbs-up, noting that I think Prudence is being creative and persistent in her problem solving since she wrote a sign for her lost pet (shown in the illustration) and she tries to use a shoe for a pet. On page 112 are my model jot and an example of a second grader's. (Note: I modeled jotting under the document camera while thinking aloud and referring to the text, then took my jot away so students wouldn't just copy my reasoning and evidence.)

Next, I ask students to reread their notes to prepare for a collaborative conversation about our opinions and reasons. They are encouraged to use their notes (and thus, text evidence) to help them explain their thinking, but they are not limited to what they've jotted on paper. I also encourage them to elaborate on their reasons and build off of or piggyback on one another's comments. We revisit sections of the text once again, for the purpose of adding details to our thinking. Students are also encouraged to add to their notes if something useful comes up while we're talking. This helps them understand

Core Connections

Grade 2
Reading Literature Standard 1

Ask and answer such questions as *who, what, where, when, why,* and *how* to demonstrate understanding of key details in a text. (Students will use text evidence to answer "what" questions: specifically, what details from the text support the reasons for your opinions?)

Reading Literature Standard 7

Use information gained from illustrations and words in a print or digital text to demonstrate understanding of its characters, setting, or plot.

Writing Standard 8

Gather information from provided sources to answer a question. (Students note their opinions, reasons, and evidence.)

Speaking and Listening Standard 1

Students participate in collaborative conversations with diverse partners about grade 2 topics and texts with peers and adults in small and larger groups while: following agreed-upon rules, building on others' talk, and linking their comments to the remarks of others, and asking for clarification as needed.

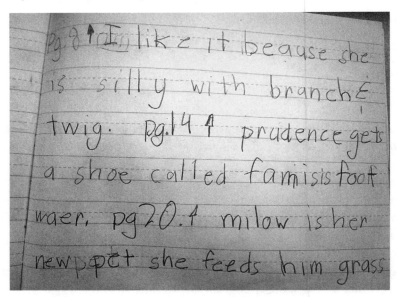

pg. 10 ↑ Pru. proactive
        wrote sign lost pet

pg. 14 ↑ Pru is creative
         persistent
         Shoe

pg. 20 ↑ Milo >funny
         Tire

My model: Quick jotting text evidence to support my opinion at different points in the text.

pg.8 ↑ I like it because she is silly with branché twig. pg.14 ↑ prudence gets a shoe called famisis foot waer. pg 20. ↑ milow is her new pet she feeds him grass

A student sample: Jotting text evidence to support her opinion at different points in the text. Notes are used for collaborative conversation and writing.

the notes are fluid—they can be added to, changed, used, or not used. Before we begin our conversation, we review the agreed-upon Collaborative Conversation norms.

T: Who'd like to begin? Tell us a bit about your opinion of *Prudence Wants a Pet* and why you feel that way. Use your notes to help explain your thinking.

S: I think the book is funny because Prudence uses things no one else would for a pet. I mean, who makes a branch into a pet?

T: Who has more to say about that?

S: I think it's funny, too, because she treats the branch like a living thing. She exercises it!

T: Yep, I agree. What else does she do with that silly branch? Let's look back in the book and see.

S: See, she tries to give it a water dish like a dog or cat!

T: There's an additional detail we saw in the illustration. You might add to your jots, if you have something about Prudence using the branch for a pet. So, it sounds as if you *like* the book because Prudence treats nonliving things like living pets. Is that right?

S: Yeah, even a tire.

S: She even names it! Mr. Round!

T: Thanks for the detail about the tire. You might add to your jots if that detail fits. Many of us agree she's funny. What else would you say about Prudence?

S: She keeps trying.

T: So, Prudence keeps trying. Who can say more about that?

S: Well, she tries thing after thing, a tire, a shoe, her brother. She doesn't give up. Then she gets those sea monster things.

S: Those things are a joke!

S: What do you mean?

S: Didn't you see in the picture how they were just lying there in the fish bowl like nothing?

T: Let's look at that page together. *(Revisits book with the class)*

S: Oh, yeah, like pulp!

T: Prudence keeps trying. Does that influence your opinion of the book? Does it make you like it or not like it?

S: I like it. She is a good example of someone who doesn't give up.

T: Hmmm, again, you might add something quickly to your jot if you have more ideas based on our conversation. Let's go back to Alberto's comment. What did you say again, Alberto?

S: I said she gets mad and gives up.

T: Why is that important?

S: Well, she wasn't like this big hero or something. She did give up and lock herself in the closet kinda like having a tantrum trying to get her way.

T: Does that action influence your opinion of the book?

We continue our conversation for about 10 minutes. Then, once again, I invite students to add to their notes if applicable.

Recap: Key Lesson Steps

1. Revisit sections of the text

2. Jot notes about opinions, reasons, and evidence

3. Have conversations about opinions, drawing from and adding to notes

---

Wrap Up

"We've taken time to revisit the book and jot notes to help us think through our opinions more deeply. The notes helped us share more thoughtful comments during our conversation. I hope you see how the notes are helpful and how they are never really done—you can add to them based on the thinking of others. As we write, I bet you'll even find you don't even use all of your notes. But the acts of taking notes and having a conversation help us better tease out our thinking. This will help us give the librarian clear reasons for our opinions. The more we tell her, the more she'll understand where we are coming from. You can use quick jotting or take notes yourself anytime you want to keep track of our build your thinking. We'll do this frequently as we prepare to write different kinds of texts."

Notes

Charting Character Development and Character Traits

3

Booster Reading Lesson

Getting Ready

The materials:

- Copy of *Prudence Wants a Pet* by Cathleen Daly
- Document camera
- Chart paper

Context of the Lesson

In this lesson, we examine and chart Prudence's responses to events throughout the story. We identify character traits she exhibits and provide evidence for our thinking. These activities deepen students' understanding of how a character's actions and personality can affect our opinions about texts. As we finish, we reexamine our opinions. Have they changed?

The Lesson

"Today, we're revisiting the book *Prudence Wants a Pet* one more time to watch how Prudence reacts to events in the story. What happens at the beginning, and what does Pru do? How does she react? What happens in the middle of the story and what does Pru do? How does she react? And so on. We'll reexamine illustrations and read some of the text then add to our Character Response graph to help us track our thinking. As we do this, we'll identify some of Pru's character traits or define her personality a bit more and jot those ideas on another chart. All of this work may help us better explain our opinions or may even change our opinions about the book. I'll think aloud for a bit to demonstrate.

"As the story begins (*showing the book under the document camera*), we see Prudence wants a pet but her mom and dad say no (*pointing to the text and rereading*). So, what does Pru do? She doesn't sit and whine or sulk. She takes matters into her own hands and decides to make her own pet. She grabs a branch and starts treating it like a pet (*again, pointing to illustrations and rereading just a bit*). What do her actions tell me about Pru? Well, I think she is a creative problem solver and a go-getter. I mean, she didn't just whine or wait for her parents to solve the problem for her. Instead, she tries to come up with something to solve the problem on her own.

"So, I'm going to list *go-getter* and *problem solver* on our Character Traits chart.* And, I'll make a mark here in the neutral response section of our Character Response graph to show I feel Pru didn't respond negatively or positively to the event of her parents saying no to a pet. She simply proceeded to go about solving the problem herself."

Core Connections

Grade 2

Reading Literature Standard 3

Describe how characters in a story respond to major events and challenges.

Reading Literature Standard 7

Use information gained from illustrations and words in a print or digital text to demonstrate understanding of its characters, setting, or plot.

Writing Standard 8

Gather information from provided sources to answer a question. *(Graph character responses, chart character traits.)*

Speaking and Listening Standard 1

Students participate in collaborative conversations with diverse partners about grade 2 topics and texts.

Core Practices

- Revisit Sections of Text
- Modeling
- Gradual Release of Responsibility
- Shared Writing to Create a Chart
- Pair-Share
- Evaluation and Discussion

Character Traits
Prudence

persistent

go-getter

problem-solver

silly/funny

creative

imaginative

positive

*Note: If this is the first time you've worked on character traits with students, start by having them think of characters they know well (like Froggy from the *Froggy* series by Jonathan London, Arthur from the *Arthur* series by Marc Brown, or George and Harold from the *Captain Underpants* series by Dav Pilkey). Discuss how these characters commonly behave and brainstorm a list of possible character traits together. Students need a lot of experience doing this so they become accustomed to analyzing characters' actions, thoughts, and words as a way of analyzing character development needed to work toward Reading Literature Standard 3.

I continue to model and think aloud, reexamining a few key illustrations and rereading a few key sentences about the next two major events in the story. I add to our Character Traits chart (if applicable) and mark our Character Response graph for each event, explaining my reasoning.

As we revisit the last three major events, I invite students to share their thoughts about Pru's reactions. We briefly discuss their comments then add to the Character Traits chart and mark our graph.

Discuss students' thoughts about Prudence now that they've examined her behavior closely across events in the story and identified some of her character traits. Have their opinions changed? Why or why not? Invite students to add to their quick jot notes, if they choose.

"Let's finish up our work today by voting. Think of your overall opinion of the book *Prudence Wants a Pet* now. Is it positive or negative? Do you like it or not? If you like the book, go to the right side of the room, if you don't like the book go to the left side." Once students are in their locations, have them talk to their neighbor about the main reasons for their opinions. Then, call on a few volunteers from both sides to share with the class. Last, ask, "Okay, think one more time, has your opinion changed now that we've listened to the reasoning of others? If it has, walk over to the other side." If any students change their opinion, have them share their reasoning.

> ## *Recap: Key Lesson Steps*
>
> 1. Revisit key sections of the text looking for a character's [Prudence's] response to events
> 2. Revisit sections of the text to identify a character's [Prudence's] character traits
> 3. Graph responses to events
> 4. Chart character traits
> 5. Model and gradually release responsibility to students, if appropriate

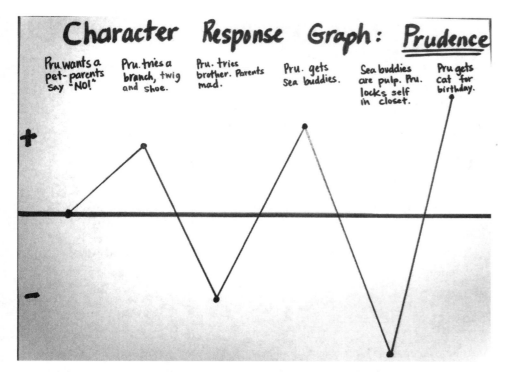

Character Response Graph: Prudence

Pru wants a pet-parents say "No!"

Pru tries a branch, twig and shoe.

Pru tries brother. Parents mad.

Pru. gets sea buddies.

Sea buddies are pulp. Pru. locks self in closet.

Pru gets cat for birthday.

Compare Character Response graphs from book to book. Do students see any patterns? Can they draw any conclusions about narratives from their observations?

Wrap Up

I end the lesson by explicitly telling students the skills they've worked on today, and how this sets them up nicely to turn to the next learning endeavor (planning). "We've done a lot of deep analysis today that adds to our understanding of the book. I think we are ready to plan our opinion pieces. We know what our opinions are and we have reasons to support them. Let's start that planning now."

Notes

Organizing Our Opinions With Thinking Boxes

Core Connections

Grade 2

Writing Standard 1

Students write opinion pieces in which they introduce the topic or book they are writing about, state an opinion, supply reasons that support the opinion, use linking words (e.g., *because, and, also*) to connect opinion and reasons, and provide a concluding statement or section.

Writing Standard 5

With guidance and support from adults and peers, focus on a topic and strengthen writing as needed by revising and editing.

Reading Standard 1

Ask and answer such questions as *who, what, where, when, why,* and *how* to demonstrate understanding of key details in a text. (Students will use text evidence to detail their opinions about the text.)

Core Practices

- Modeling
- Jot in Thinking Boxes
- Pair-Share
- Analysis Under the Document Camera
- Give Immediate Feedback

Getting Ready

The materials:

- Copy of *Prudence Wants a Pet* by Cathleen Daly
- Document camera
- Quick jot notes
- Charts we've created across the lessons
- Think pads, student notebooks, or scratch paper (students fold the paper into fourths and number the boxes)

Context of the Lesson

As students prepare to write their opinions, we scaffold the process using informal writing in Thinking Boxes (Wagstaff, 2011). I model, students share as we complete each box, and they receive constant feedback. (My students are accustomed to Thinking Boxes since we frequently use them to process what we are reading or learning and to organize our thinking for writing. If this strategy is new to your students, you'll have to slow the process down and provide even more thorough modeling and feedback.) We use the anchor chart we created in Companion Reading Lesson 1 (Effective Opinions) or a simple rubric to check our progress in our boxes as we go. This way, students can make immediate revisions. They also share from their boxes, to bounce ideas off each other, and rehearse their thinking aloud.

The Lesson

"We know from all the study we've done that in order to write an effective opinion, we need to first name our topic and state our opinion (*pointing to our anchor chart or the rubric*). Let's do that in Box 1. Take just two or three minutes to jot the title of the book and a few words about your opinion."

Students jot, I circulate and comment, partners share, one or two volunteers' examples are shown on the document camera, and feedback is given, checking for the book title and a few words that will lead to a clear opinion statement.

Next, I prompt students to think about the reasons for their opinions (as we've listed on our anchor chart and we see in the rubric), referring back to their quick jot notes and our charts. They list one reason in Box 2 and one in Box 3. They can talk about it before jotting and share with a partner to firm up thinking. This takes about 5 minutes. Again, I circulate, comment, and provide feedback for a few samples on the document camera, making sure students have two distinct reasons for their opinions.*

*Note: I invite students to add another reason to Box 4, if they'd like. If they choose to do this, the work that follows is simply pushed to the next box.

"Now, we need to tell more or elaborate about each reason (*pointing to rubric*). In each box, list some examples: What about the reason you listed made you like or dislike the book? Why is that reason important? Be as specific as you can and refer to your notes and our charts so you have details and evidence from the book to support your thinking and make it clear for your reader.

"Watch me for just a minute. (*I think aloud while jotting under the document camera*) Let's say this is my Box 2. I jotted 'Prudence is funny.' That's certainly true and a good reason for liking the book. But, *how is she funny? Why does this make me like the book?* I see here (*pointing to the story map and my quick jot notes*) Prudence picks a branch for a pet, a shoe, a tire, and even her little brother! Those are very silly. I mean, who picks those kinds of things for pets? (*I make a quick list in Box 2: picks pet: branch, shoe, tire, bro.*) See, those are specific things Prudence did that show she's quite a funny character! And, that's one of the reasons I like the book. I like funny characters. Remember, we discussed this quite a bit and even added *funny* to our Character Traits chart?"

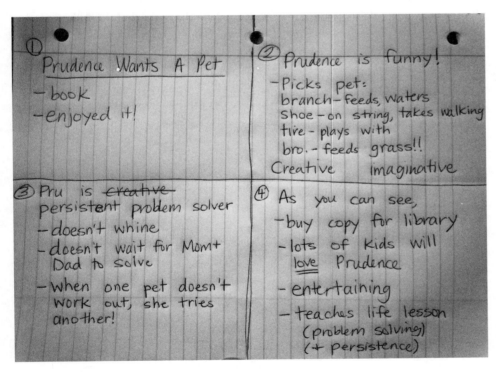

My Thinking Boxes for *Prudence Wants a Pet* (Box 4 is completed during Companion Writing Lesson 4). See other examples of Thinking Boxes in Sequences 1 (page 34) and 4 (pages 188–189).

Students are asked to tell more or elaborate in their own Boxes 2 and 3.

Students jot, I circulate and provide guidance, partners share, one or two volunteers' examples are shown on the document camera, and feedback is given: Have we explained thoroughly enough so our readers will understand why this reason makes us like or dislike the book? We also highlight examples of evidence that come directly from the text.

Recap: Key Lesson Steps

1. Organize opinion and reasons by jotting notes in Thinking Boxes

2. Model as necessary

3. Have students share and receive feedback

Wrap Up

Recap the work completed by saying something like, "We have a great start organizing our thinking for our written opinions. We've named our topic, given our opinion, cited reasons, and told more or elaborated on these reasons. Elaborating can be a little tricky. We need to explain our reasons clearly by using examples and details from the text. If we don't explain our reasons enough, listeners or readers are still left wondering, 'Why does he or she feel that way?'"

Companion Website Resource

Rubric for Opinion Writing	3—Got it!	2—Could be better	1—Not there
State your topic (Name the thing you have an opinion about)			
State your opinion (like, don't like . . .)			
Give reasons One Two			
Tell more about your reasons One Two			
Conclude			

 Available for download at www.corwin .com/thecommoncorecompanion

Our simple rubric for opinion writing based on where writers are right now in learning the text type.

Studying Mentor Texts: Concluding Opinions

4
**Booster
Reading
Lesson**

Getting Ready

The materials:

- Copy of *Stella Writes an Opinion* by Janiel Wagstaff
- Other mentor opinion texts that contain strong conclusions
- Document camera
- Chart paper

Context of the Lesson

Students often struggle with conclusions. In this lesson, we focus on studying the conclusions in mentor texts to help us craft our own. We revisit *Stella Writes an Opinion* and other mentor texts, noting the elements of effective conclusions.

The Lesson

"Yesterday, we jotted our opinion statements, reasons, and elaborations in our Thinking Boxes. Today, we'll study how opinion writers conclude their pieces so we can work on our own. Let's start by revisiting *Stella Writes an Opinion*. We'll reread specifically to identify what Stella does to craft her closing or conclusion. Then, we'll study the conclusions in a few other opinions to look for common elements."

Reread and discuss Stella's multiple attempts at her conclusion. Discuss how Stella uses words to signal her readers she's coming to the end of her piece. Have students read these together, repeating the signal words and phrases. Record these on a chart (*To sum up, As you can see, To conclude,*). "Like Stella, we can use these words to signal our readers we're ending our pieces. What else does she include in her conclusion(s)?"

Read her attempts again, noticing how she repeats her opinion then briefly revisits her reasons. On her last attempt, she also adds a wise thought at the end.

Compare Stella's conclusion to others. What other signal phrases might be used? Do authors always restate their opinion and revisit their reasons? Do they include anything else? It's great to pull the language for the elements of effective conclusions from the kids themselves when possible.

Core Connections

Grade 2
Reading Literature
  Standard 1
Ask and answer such questions as *who, what, where, when, why,* and *how* to demonstrate understanding of key details in a text. (Students will use text evidence to answer a 'what' question: specifically, what elements do writers include to compose effective conclusions in opinion texts?)
Writing Standard 8
Gather information from provided sources to answer a question. (Record signal phrases and conclusion elements.)

Core Practices

- Revisit Sections of Mentor Text
- Shared Reading Sections of New Mentor Text
- Record Conclusion Signal Phrases and Elements of Conclusions on a Chart

---

Recap: Key Lesson Steps

1. Study conclusions in mentor texts to identify elements
2. Chart elements

Wrap Up

Guide students to further see the purpose of the lesson: "You can see how useful studying mentor texts is as a strategy. When you're not sure how to do something in your own writing, you can find models, study them, and imitate what you see. Once you have the basics down, you can branch out and be more creative. Now that we have a better idea of what a conclusion for an opinion is and how one is written, let's get back to our Thinking Boxes, work on our own conclusions, then start drafting our pieces."

Rick Harrington Photography

Notes

Completing Thinking Boxes and Drafting Opinions

Getting Ready

The materials:

- Copy of *Prudence Wants a Pet* by Cathleen Daly
- Thinking Boxes in progress
- Document camera
- Quick jot notes
- Charts we've created across the lessons, including the new Conclusions chart

Context of the Lesson

Now that we've studied mentor texts with an eye for conclusions, we're ready to complete Box 4 of our Thinking Boxes. The same process is followed: I model (referring to charts), students jot, share, receive feedback, and refine their thinking when applicable. Once all four boxes are complete, a volunteer comes forward and we hold a public conference as a final check. Then, students talk out or orally rehearse their entire opinions. By this point, students have done the hard thinking and are very comfortably prepared to draft.

The Lesson

"We stopped working on our Thinking Boxes so we could study conclusions in some mentor texts. Now, using our Conclusions chart, let's think how we might close our opinion pieces about the book *Prudence Wants a Pet*. First, decide what signal phrase you think you'll use and jot it in the box. (*I model under the document camera and students jot in their boxes.*) We know we need to restate our opinion and reasons here at the end, so jot a few words about that. (*Again, I model and students jot.*) Last, and this is the hardest part, can you add a few wise words, ask a thoughtful question, or include a call to action?* Remember our purpose, if you have a positive opinion about the book, we'll share with the librarian to perhaps persuade her to buy a copy of the book for the school library. I think I'll try something with that (*jotting*) 'buy copy for library, lots of kid will love Prudence, entertaining, teaches life lesson . . .'"

*Note: If your students are having difficulty concluding their pieces, the additional piece of adding wise words, a thoughtful question, or call to action may be too much. If that is the case, leave this out until they are ready.

Core Connections

Grade 2

Writing Standard 1

Students write opinion pieces in which they introduce the topic or book they are writing about, state an opinion, supply reasons that support the opinion, use linking words (e.g., *because, and, also*) to connect opinion and reasons, and provide a concluding statement or section.

Writing Standard 5

With guidance and support from adults and peers, focus on a topic and strengthen writing as needed by revising and editing.

Speaking and Listening Standard 6

Produce complete sentences when appropriate to task and situation.

Core Practices

- Modeling
- Jot in Thinking Boxes
- Pair-Share
- Evaluate Progress Using a Rubric
- Give Immediate Feedback
- Talk-It-Out
- Draft and Revise Text

My Thinking Boxes

Students jot, I circulate and comment, partners share, and I lend feedback to the class on what I overheard, picking particularly good examples.

"Now, we're ready for a final check of our Thinking Boxes. Have we done the thinking required to write an effective opinion? Have we included all the elements we need?" A student volunteer comes forward with his Thinking Boxes so we can demonstrate checking our progress under the document camera. We use our anchor chart and rubric as a guide.

I discuss what element of opinion writing should be in each box, one box at a time. I demonstrate checking the volunteer's example (we often have a short "public conference" where feedback is given and the student reflects and perhaps revises), then all students reflect on the work they've completed in that particular box. The process continues for all four Thinking Boxes. This is a very useful formative self-assessment. Students have the opportunity to reflect on their thinking before drafting and address any lingering questions or problems.

You can use the opinion rubric shown on page 120 (it can be accessed on the companion website at www.corwin.com/thecommoncorecompanion.)

Talk-It-Out: So far, our Thinking Boxes have been used to organize and develop our thinking about our opinions. Now, they become a tool students use to rehearse orally before drafting. Make sure to model this process if it is new to your students (see A Snapshot of the Talk-It-Out Strategy on page 30).

"If you find you need more time to develop your thinking or you're missing something from our chart or rubric, go ahead and continue to work in your Thinking Boxes. If you think you're ready, get with a partner and take turns talking out your opinion using your boxes as a guide so you practice turning your notes into full sentences you can write in your drafts. I'll come around, listen, and help."

Next, with a quick bit of modeling, I prepare students to move into drafting. I am deliberate about referring to my Thinking Boxes to keep the writing organized. I also demonstrate constant rereading as a strategy for ongoing revision.

"Watch me for a minute (*thinking aloud while writing under the document camera*): Hmmm, (*pointing to my Thinking Boxes*) I need a statement where I give the book title and clearly state my opinion. Let me think what I said as I talked it out (*writing*), '*Prudence Wants a Pet* is an enjoyable book you'll want to read again and again.' (*I reread my writing*: Yep, I have it [*pointing to rubric*], like it, I'll keep going.) Box 2, oh yes, Prudence is funny. She picks crazy things for pets. I said something like (*writing*), 'First of all, Prudence is so funny. You may find tears rolling down your cheeks as you watch her try to make a branch, shoe, a tire, and even her little brother into pets.' (*I reread my writing.*) Now I need to elaborate using the details I have in my Thinking Box. I want to tell more about these crazy pets and what she does with them. I want the reader to see why I picked 'Prudence is funny' as a reason for liking the book.' (*Writing*) 'Prudence is so silly, she puts the shoe on a string and takes it for walks. She even feeds her little brother grass!' (*I reread my writing*) Wait, I keep using the same words: Prudence is *so*. Let me change my word choice." (*I cross out* so *and ask students,* "What could I say instead?" *and then make a revision.*)

We debrief about the modeling: "What do you think? I have a pretty good start. Did you see me use my Thinking Boxes, talk it out again, and reread my writing as I went along? Off you go, writers. Let's see what you'll do next!"

Students draft, I circulate, partners share, one or two volunteer examples are given feedback under the document camera, and we celebrate our efforts!

Recap: Key Lesson Steps

1. Finish Thinking Boxes

2. Review each box using anchor chart and rubric

3. Have students orally rehearse their opinions with partners by talking it out

4. Draft

Wrap Up

Remind students of the effectiveness of the process you've followed by saying something like, "As you draft, I hope you see that all the thinking and jotting you've done across the week is extremely helpful. You've organized that thinking in your Thinking Boxes. All the hard work is done. When we talk it out, we're ready to write. I hope you'll use these strategies in future writing." Students should get the time they need to draft, share with partners, and get feedback.

Exploring Multiple Forms and Purposes for Opinion Writing

Getting Ready

The materials:

- Mentor texts: Short opinion pieces (or excerpts from books, articles, etc.)
- Document camera

Context of the Lesson

Though students know the purpose for the *Prudence Wants a Pet* opinion piece is to share their opinions with the librarian and possibly influence her to purchase a copy of the book for the school library, it's important they get a broader sense of why people write opinions and the multiple forms those opinions might take. I read aloud and we engage in shared reading to examine several opinion pieces. We reread sections to look for clues as to the author's purpose for each piece. We also note the form the opinion writings take.

One of the best sources for opinion texts to review is those written by your own students. Keep copies over the years that show varied form, topic, purpose, and audience. Also, if you are able to really turn your students on to opinion so they're writing their own at home, on a blog, or other, you can study these pieces to review the objective of this lesson again at a later time.

The Lesson

"Let's look closely at some other examples of opinion texts to find out why authors write them. We know the purpose of our current opinion writing, but are there other reasons people write opinions? What form do those opinions take?"

Use a combination of reading aloud and shared reading (under the document camera) to examine varied opinion texts. I post these questions to focus the reading:

Why do you think the author wrote this opinion? What is his or her purpose? What forms can opinions take? (As we reread sections to answer these questions, volunteers come forward and point to the words (text evidence) that provide clues to the author's purpose.)

Texts you might use

- Letter from Luke to Jorge (see page 128)

    Purpose: to *persuade* Jorge to come to Luke's party; Form: letter

Core Connections

Grade 2
Reading Literature
  Standard 1

Ask and answer such questions as *who, what, where, when, why,* and *how* to demonstrate understanding of key details in a text. (Students will use text evidence to answer: What forms do opinions take? Why do authors write opinions?)

Core Practices

- Read Aloud
- Shared Reading
- Cite Text Evidence
- Discussion

- The letter from Red Crayon in the book *The Day the Crayons Quit* by Drew Daywalt

  Purpose: to *persuade* Duncan to give him a rest; Form: letter

- The first few letters from Alex in the book *I Wanna Iguana* by Karen Kaufman Orloff

  Purpose: to *persuade* mom to allow him to have the iguana; Form: letter

- https://childtasticbooks.wordpress.com/category/early-readersshort-chapter-books
  Scroll down to the review of the book by Holly. She is only ten years old.

  Purpose: to *share* her opinion with other readers and possibly *interest them* in the book. (The reviews by Sam are by Holly's mom.) Form: blog post

- https://childtasticbooks.wordpress.com/2014/10/29/review-dog-on-stilts
  Scroll down to another book review by Holly.

  Same purpose, same form as above

- http://www.startribune.com/opinion/commentaries/147833575.html
  Pick appropriate excerpts from this editorial that appeared in the *Minneapolis Star Tribune*. It was written by two sixth graders arguing to get more time to eat their lunches.

  Purpose: to *persuade* a change in policy; Form: op-ed article (Explain to students that these are opinion essays that appear in newspapers.)

- Social media posts on Facebook and Twitter: Most second graders have a pretty good understanding of Facebook and some classrooms have Twitter accounts. Screenshot a few appropriate Facebook posts to share. Open a Twitter account and share your class's opinions with others. Read appropriate tweets. Again, look at purpose and form.

- It would be great to bring in op-ed articles from your local paper if you can find some with appropriate content. Keep in mind, you might just read a short excerpt from the articles so students get an idea what they are about and why they were written.

Recap: Key Lesson Steps

1. Study mentor texts
2. Identify purposes for opinions
3. Identify forms of opinions

Wrap Up

Push students to think about how they might expand their opinion work: "We've learned opinion writing can take multiple forms, though its purpose is to persuade or influence others to do something or think something. Think of the many opinions you have that you might write about. Are there things you'd like to change here at the school, at your home, or in our community? Do you like to review books, movies, or games? You can add ideas for opinion writing as they come to you to your writers' notebooks or topics lists. Share your ideas because you may come up with something others might like to write about. Where might you share your opinion writing? If you decide to take on the challenge of writing and sharing additional opinions, make sure you let us know so we can read and discuss them here in class."

Dear Jorge,

Your mom told me you have a basketball game at the same time as my party. She said you get to decide if you play the game or come to my house. I hope you will come to my party. I think you will really like it. First of all, you have a basketball game every week for a while. Missing one game won't be a big deal. But, I only get to have this party once a year! If you miss it, there won't be another one for a whole year.

Another reason I think you should come to my party is that I came up with a special game to play that I know you will love! It is a ninja game! We will wear ninja headbands and run around the yard playing hide-and-seek. It's going to be a blast. I know you like ninjas and that's why I want to have the game at my party.

I hope you'll think hard about these reasons and decide to come to my party! You are a good friend!

Love,
Luke

Notes

Finish Writing and Celebrate!

The Lesson

At this point, students just need time to continue the process and finish their drafts. Model to get students reoriented, if necessary. Model rereading, making any revisions, talking out the rest of your piece from your Thinking Boxes, and then, continuing to draft. Circulate and provide feedback. Encourage children to share as they go, get feedback from peers, reread and revise, and check their final work with the anchor chart and rubric. When finished, deliver opinions to the librarian.

Recap: Key Lesson Steps

1. Finish drafting

2. Evaluate with rubric

3. Share with librarian

Wrap Up

Celebrate your students' efforts! "You've written your first opinion about a text and delivered it to the librarian! It will be interesting to hear what she thinks. (*You might encourage the librarian to write back to students or come and talk with them about how their writing influenced her thinking.*) You've worked very hard examining *Prudence Wants a Pet* and detailing your opinion. Are you excited to write other opinions? What might you write about?"

We get the most out of our experiences when we debrief. Debriefing helps students process the steps taken and strategies used to reach their end goals. This kind of talk solidifies their understandings of the process so they can take that knowledge and apply it in the future.

To debrief, I ask questions like:

- What strategies did we use to compose effective opinions?
- What steps did we take?
- What does this mean for our future writing?

Core Connections

Grade 2
Writing Standard 1
Students write opinion pieces in which they introduce the topic or book they are writing about, state an opinion, supply reasons that support the opinion, use linking words (e.g., *because, and, also*) to connect opinion and reasons, and provide a concluding statement or section.

Writing Standard 5
With guidance and support from adults and peers, focus on a topic and strengthen writing as needed by revising and editing.

Speaking and Listening Standard 6
Produce complete sentences when appropriate to task and situation.

Core Practices

- Modeling
- Draft Using Thinking Boxes
- Ongoing Peer-Sharing, Feedback, Revision
- Evaluate Finished Writing Using Rubric
- Share With Audience
- Celebrate and Debrief

A Snapshot of Moving From Opinions About Texts to Opinions About Topics

The standard for opinion writing is clear across the grade levels: students should be writing opinions about texts *and* topics. During this sequence, we've focused on an overall opinion about a book: Did we like it or not? Would we recommend it to other readers? Opinions about texts don't always have to be about overall reactions. Instead, students could write opinions about who their favorite character was and why, whether or not they liked how the problem was solved and why, or what the theme or lesson in the book was and why, for example. But what about opinions about topics?

Students have already learned the basics of opinion writing. They know why people write opinions, what elements must be present in effective opinions, and why those elements are important. All of this translates to opinion writing about topics. Be sure to point out what students already know that will help them write opinions about topics using your co-created charts. If you used one or both of the mentor texts listed in Companion Reading Lesson 1 (*Stella Writes an Opinion* and *Should We Have Pets?*), explain to students they've already studied opinions about topics! Further, *Prudence Wants a Pet* is also an opinion about a topic!

One way to dive into opinions about topics is to listen in to students' casual conversations at the coat rack or in the lunch line to see what topics are hot. These are great impetus for discussion. It's very useful to point out where the topic came from, "See, boys and girls, as we learned before, we all have opinions every day. Just today people from our class were talking about whether or not they thought it was fair to have different playground equipment on carts for upper grades versus lower grades. Let's talk more about this."

Point out how topics usually have more than one side. "When we look at a topic, there is often one side or point of view and another side or different point of view. Like in *Prudence*, she wanted a pet; her parents didn't. They had opposite points of view. When we try to decide our opinions on a topic, we have to examine both sides to really understand the issue. We have to look at why, or the reasons, some people feel one way about the topic and other people feel the other way. Then we can decide our own opinion.

"Let's take the topic that was being discussed today and look at both sides. Do you think it's fair that the upper grades have their own cart with different playground equipment than the lower grades have? What's good about this arrangement? What's bad about this arrangement?"

Create a T-chart with the headings Pros (good) and Cons (bad) at the top. List the topic above the T-chart. List students' reasons on both sides. If they can only come up with one side, you might bring in an upper grade student (or, if you're looking at some other topic, a person who can defend the other side) to talk about his point of view.

"Now that we have information about both sides of the issue, you have to examine it, think about it, and form an opinion. Everyone take a moment to do that. (*Think time*) Now briefly share what you're thinking with a partner." (*Give students a few minutes to talk*.)

"Before we hold a more formal discussion, jot down what your opinion is, and why you think what you do. Can you also jot a few notes to tell more about the reasons for your opinion? Then, we'll have a conversation."

Any time you need to vote on something for your class, you can hold a conversation about opinions. Again, if there are two sides to an issue, create a T-chart; if there are more perspectives, simply add columns. As students explain their reasoning, add notes to the chart so everyone can see the reasoning behind different perspectives.

Additionally, you can study short texts about topics. The resources listed in Companion Reading Lessons 1 and 5, and the mentor texts shared on pages 145 are useful. Help students identify the topic, opinion, and reasons supplied in written sources. Again, these could be T-charted. You might organize for opinion writing just as we did in this sequence, using Thinking Boxes.

The best writing is purposeful writing. If the students' opinions about topics can be sent out to an audience, do it! Students will feel empowered, especially if they get a response!

Notes

Kindergarten Adaptation

Core Connections

Kindergarten Writing Standard 1

Use a combination of drawing, dictating, and writing to compose opinion pieces in which they tell a reader the topic or the name of the book they are writing about and state an opinion or preference about the topic or book.

As we adapt opinion writing for kindergarten and first grade, we are reminded of the need to practice through conversation. Have lots of discussion about opinions. Model the academic vocabulary of the standard.* Some of these conversations may lead to writing, but many will not. Immerse your students in opinion thinking about topics and texts. This will greatly scaffold their abilities to write in the genre.

*Note: Use words like *opinion, texts, topics, reasons, reasoning, support* and *evidence.*

In kindergarten, we develop writing skills and knowledge by composing lots of *shared* pieces. After reading *Prudence Wants a Pet,* I ask students to tell their neighbor if they liked the book or not while I listen in. "I heard most of us like the book! I do, too! When we write an opinion about a book, we want to name the book or state its title then say whether we liked it or not. So, let's do that together.

"Let's practice out loud first. Who can help me? 'We liked _____ (the book *Prudence Wants a Pet*).'" Repeat the opinion statement a few times aloud. Then proceed to write it together on a large piece of chart paper using interactive writing (or sharing the pen).

Here's a quick snapshot of interactive opinion writing in kindergarten (also see A Snapshot of the Varied Writing Modes on page 76):

"So, our opinion is: 'We like the book *Prudence Wants a Pet.*' Let's write it by sharing the pen together. We, how do we spell *we*?"

Class: "W-*e*"

"Yes! That's a word on our Word Wall. Jamie, come up and write it for us please. Where do writers start on the page? Oh yes, here at the top left. (*Jamie writes* We) Now, *like*, /lllllllllll/, /llllllllll/. What letter do we need for that sound?"

Class: "*l*!"

"Yes, -*l*- just like in Leo's name. Leo, come up and write the -*l*-. I'll take the pen and write the rest of this word. (*Sounding out as I write*): /iiiiii/ i, /kkkkk/ k, and I remember the word *like* has an *e* at the end. Let's reread."

Class: "We like . . ."

"We need to name what we're writing our opinion about so our readers know. What are we writing about?" (A simple chart listing the elements of kindergarten opinion writing is really helpful. I point out where we are on the chart as we write.)

Class: "A book, *Prudence Wants a Pet!*"

"So, let's continue, 'We like the book . . .' Who can spell *the*? It's right there on our Word Wall."

The students and I continue to share the pen to write the opinion. We may even state a simple reason (kindergartners are very capable of this even though it is not required by the standard!). For example, "We like the book *Prudence Wants a Pet* because it is so funny!"

> **When we write opinions we:**
>
> - <u>Name</u> the topic or book
> - Say if we like it or don't like it

To extend the lesson, I encourage students to talk about what makes the book funny and go back into the text and illustrations to point those things out (though we may not write down any of these details). Additionally, after finishing the shared piece, I might ask students to now draw and write about their own opinion of the book or their favorite part. Naturally, they're given a chance to share their masterpieces!

Here a kindergartner is exceeding the standard by stating a reason for her opinion. After reading *The Paper Bag Princess* by Robert Munsch, students were asked to name their favorite character. Obviously, though it's not in the standard, we spend a lot of time talking about why we think the way we do. This way, you're bound to see reasons appear in students' writing.

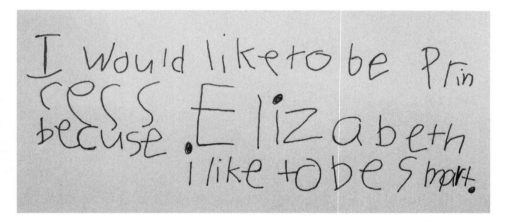

"I would like to be Princess Elizabeth because I like to be smart."

Core Connections

Grade 1
Writing Standard 1
Write opinion pieces in which they introduce the topic or name the book they are writing about, state an opinion, supply a reason for the opinion, and provide some sense of closure.

In first grade, we do a great deal of shared composing and we use interactive writing, too. Students learn what they need to include to write an effective opinion through these experiences. As we write together on chart paper, we stop to name and label the parts with sticky notes (for example, I write on the notes: name the book or topic, state opinion, reason, closing). The charts make useful references to come back to over time. And, as in kindergarten, I list the elements of the standard on a separate chart.

As first graders compose their own opinions independently, I break the standard down and begin by having them simply write an opinion sentence, naming the book or topic, and stating an opinion (just as they did in kindergarten). For example, "I really liked the book *Prudence Wants a Pet*." They might add a sketch to illustrate why they like the book. During sharing, I encourage them to talk about their reasoning by emphasizing *because*. . . . Once students are successful (and this shouldn't take long if they've been immersed in opinion talking and writing in kindergarten), I build in the other elements of the standard.

I scaffold the requirement for closure with sentence frames. Of course, students have the option of using these or coming up with their own conclusion. "I hope _____ (you'll enjoy this book, too)." "You should _____ (get a pet)!" We keep a running list of these frames that we add to over time. (When students struggle, I may help them pick a sentence frame to use.)

Young writers are proud to share their opinions with the class!

What's ahead:

What Do I See?
A Student Sample of Opinion Writing

Here's a second-grade student's opinion about *Prudence Wants a Pet*. Within the class pile, hers ranks in the middle.

Student strengths: Charlize shows many strengths. She meets the grade-level standard in the following areas: naming the book, stating her opinion, and providing a concluding section. She states one reason and provides elaboration ("Pru has a good imagination—she used a branch, umbrella, tire.") Though she writes more, obviously about what she likes, she doesn't use language that connects her statements to reasoning about her opinion.

> I like Prudence Wants A pet It is a very good book Pru. has a very good imaginathion. She used a branchy Unbrella, tire. She had some Sea monsters it looked like a Plup. But on Pru. birthday she got a Cat She named it branch and lived hapliy ever after. It was a very good book to me I want to read it again!

Follow-up lesson: After asking Charlize if she'd be willing to work on her writing in front of the class, I'd hold a public conference pushing her to reword how she begins her fifth sentence so the reader clearly knows it's another reason she likes the book. For example, we might try something like, "Another reason the book is good is because Pru got a cat for her birthday." Her sample would be excellent to use as the class learns about the purpose of linking words.

What Do I See?
A Student Sample of Thinking Boxes

This second grader used Thinking Boxes to develop his opinion about the book *Stellaluna* by Janell Cannon. He was the only person in the class who argued he did not like the book. His reasons were clever! I'd use this sample, not only to teach about how Thinking Boxes help us organize our opinion thinking and get ready to write, but also to reinforce the idea that having a dissenting opinion is absolutely welcomed, especially if you can explain your reasoning! An opinion is supposed to be what YOU think, not what your teacher thinks or your class thinks or your friend thinks—but what YOU think!

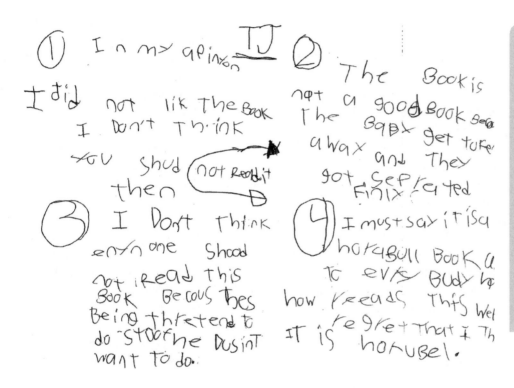

T.J. shows many strengths, especially in the points he picks to support his dissenting opinion. He certainly needs to elaborate more on each reason, name the book, and work on his sentence structures, but he has a great base to talk it out and clear things up via the questions his feedback partner asks. He may also need a conference with the teacher; but, I'd wait to see if I need to intervene after he drafts. (P.S. I love his strong voice. My apologies to Janell Cannon whose work I adore!)

In Thinking Box 1 T.J. wrote, "In my opinion I did not like the book. I don't think you should read it." (He's missing the title of the book, as per the standard.)

Box 2: "The book is not a good book because the baby gets torn away and they get separated." Here, T.J. referring to the bat baby being separated from her mother when they are attacked by an owl.

Box 3: "I don't think anyone should read this book because he's being threatened to do stuff he doesn't want to do." T.J. is referring to the fact that Stellaluna lands in a bird's nest and is forced, by the mother bird, to follow the rules of the house and eat bugs.

Box 4: "I must say it is a horrible book. Everybody who reads this will regret that. I think it is horrible."

Authentic Assessment:
Ideas for Evaluating Students' Learning

One of the most powerful ways we can assess students' development and help them grow is through student self-assessment. When students can identify elements in their writing that they're proud of or that have hit the mark, they are empowered much more than when we teachers point them out for them. After all, we want students to be reflective, independent learners. One way to focus their attention on rereading and self-assessing their writing is through the use of checklists.

Consider this second-grade example. Students wrote opinions about which would make better pets: cats or dogs. We brainstormed on a T-chart, discussed, chose a side, and I modeled writing parts of the piece, emphasizing elaborating on reasons (since students needed most work in this area). There was a paragraph frame available to support those who needed it, and I stopped students several times as they wrote to look at peer models on the document camera. I circulated and conferenced. The whole process took only two writing periods, the first mostly for brainstorming, T-charting, and talking, the second for informal writing, self-assessing using a checklist, and sharing.

Mya finished her piece then used a checklist to self-assess (see her work on the next page). She reread her opinion, checking to be sure she had included all of the necessary elements (including elaborating on her reasons). As you can see, she felt confident her opinion was complete.

Checklists are easy to adapt. Include the parts of your grade-level standard that you have thoroughly covered in instruction and that most students are demonstrating in their writing. In Mya's class, the students were ready to self-assess for all of the parts of the grade-level standard. But, if we hadn't covered elaborating on our reasons, for example, ("I can tell more about my reasons"), I would have left that part off of the checklist.

When students find something on the checklist is missing, they can find a partner who has also already self-assessed, but who has checked all the boxes, and ask for help.

Checklists are simple enough; they can be used with kindergartners and first graders. Using checklists helps writers solidify their understanding of the elements of a genre while also helping them feel confident that they can check their own work!

In my opinion dogs are a better pet then cats for two reasons first reason is some dogs don't shed as much as cats do becasve when Ih hug it I don't get hair on me. second reason tha play in the water I like it becouse tha can swim whith me th I am glad I have a dog thats wah I am glad I have a dog.

"In my opinion, dogs are better pets than cats for two reasons. My first reason is some dogs don't shed as much as cats do because when I hug it, I don't get hair on me. Second reason, they play in the water. I like it because they can swim with me. That's why I'm glad I have a dog."

Opinion Writing

I can state the topic or book ☑

I can state my opinion ☑

I can give reasons for my opinion ☑

   I can *tell more* about my reasons ☑

I can use linking words (because, and, also) ☑

I can provide a conclusion ☑

Peer Power:
Using Student Work as Mentor Texts

Peer models can be priceless. Sometimes, we model an aspect of writing numerous times, find and study examples in mentor texts, provide sentence frames or other scaffolds, and students still struggle. If we can find a peer model that even approximates the strategy, craft move, or element we're working toward, we can often boost students' understanding or willingness to risk attempting the same.

Since we don't want opinions to be reduced to simple lists of reasons, we encourage children to elaborate on their thinking. This can be difficult with youngsters, though. That's why Leni's example, on page 141, is a useful peer model. Here's what I might say as I share Leni's sample:

"Leni sets up a very clear structure for her writing. It's easy for me as the reader to follow. I see her opinion statement and that she is going to share two reasons for her opinion. She even labels them with the signal words *first* and *second*.

"I see her first reason has to do with living in a huge neighborhood where there may be 'bad guys.' So, she must be thinking that a dog is a better pet than a cat because it can be protective. She tells more or elaborates to help me understand her reason. She says, 'my dog can bite the bad guys or bark to warn my dad.' I'm glad she didn't just write, 'First, dogs are better pets than cats because they are better protectors.' I would have been wondering, 'Why are they better protectors? What does Leni mean?'

"Her second reason is very clear. She says, 'Second, dogs are more active than lazy cats.' She doesn't stop there. She goes on to explain using examples: 'dogs play fetch, tug-of-war, and they play in the water.' These examples are a form of elaboration or telling more about her second reason for liking dogs better than cats. I understand what she means by 'dogs are more active' because she included these examples.

"Often, writers just list the reasons for their opinions. They'll say something like, 'Dogs are better pets because they are protective and they are playful.' But listing reasons leaves the reader with lots of questions: How are dogs protective? When are they protective? Why would you need a dog's protection? And, how are dogs playful? What do they like to play? What do you like to play with your dog? Good writers know they need to explain their thinking, and with opinion writing, we have to explain our reasons. Thank you, Leni, for taking the time to elaborate!"

When we celebrate something specific, we often find other writers come forward to point out examples of attempts to do the same in their writing. I love this! Whenever possible, I use peer models to focus and refocus on teaching points.

In my opinion dogs are better than cats for two reasons.

First dogs are better than cats because I live in a huge neighenhood and there may be lots of bad guys my dog can bite the bad guys or bark to worn my dad. Second, dogs are more active than lazy cats because dogs are funner than cat because dogs play fech, tugawar and they play in the water. In conclusion dog are way better than cats so you should get a dog today.

If/Then Chart

If students are having difficulty writing opinions,	• Scaffold with conversation. Topics students are talking about make good fodder for discussion. Remind students to use the language of the standard. "My opinion is . . ." "I think this because . . ." Give them words to use (see Opinion Words chart at **www.corwin.com/thecommoncorecompanion**). • Have them use their Thinking Boxes to practice talking out their opinion without actually writing it. Do this frequently and you'll build their abilities to engage in opinion thinking that supports their opinion writing. • Simplify. For example, in first grade, have students simply name the topic or text and state their opinion or preferences rather than tackling all the aspects of the standard. Model, model, model whatever your focus is. Once they're doing well on your objective (in conversation and in writing), add to it. In this case, ask them to start stating a reason in their writing. Given where the second graders were in this lesson cycle, I simplified by not emphasizing the use of linking words as the standard requires (this was left off the rubric and not emphasized in instruction—yet). • Be sure to celebrate what they *are* doing well. Be specific. Show samples on the document camera for the sole purpose of celebration.
If students are having trouble elaborating on their reasons,	• Examine non-examples under the document camera (compose these yourself or use old anonymous samples from previous years). "Here's an opinion written by another second grader: 'I like the book because it has funny parts. You should read it.' What do you think? What questions would you ask the author?" This helps students see the need to elaborate, otherwise we're just left wondering! • Build sentences. Extract a students' reason from his piece, then talk with him to help him elaborate (in front of the class as a public demonstration, if he agrees). If the opinion is about a text, go back to the text to find details. Write the example on the document camera *before and after* so students clearly see the difference. For example, if he wrote "I like (title of book) because it was clever," ask, "Why was it clever? What specifically in the text are you referring to? Who was clever? When? How did this affect other characters, the plot, for instance?"

If/Then Chart

If students are having trouble writing distinctly different reasons for their opinions,	• Share non-examples. For example, "This student from last year said the book was funny for his first reason then said the book was entertaining because it had humorous parts for his second reason. Are those two different reasons?" • Acknowledge that it can be hard to determine whether one's reasons are distinctly different from one another. It takes a lot of thinking and may take some feedback and input from others to develop distinctly different reasons for our opinions. • Really, really, really celebrate when students share distinctly different reasons for their opinions whether in conversation, in notes, or in written opinions. Point strong examples out so everyone can build their understanding.
If students are having trouble writing conclusions,	• Create a chart with sentence frames. Build it over time with student input. Create the frames using the language from strong student examples and other mentor texts.
If, after much study, students still aren't including all the elements of opinion for the grade-level standard,	• Show models with the elements color coded and labeled (e.g., the opinion statement is green [title or topic and feeling], the first reason is yellow, the elaboration is orange, the second reason is red, etc.) • As students plan or prewrite, they color code the elements then color code them again in their drafts.
If motivation to write opinions is waning,	• Give students more choice. For instance, keep a running list of possible topics and allow students to pick from these or develop their own. • Find ways to share students' opinions outside your classroom to make their work more meaningful. • Keep informal opinion conversations going, but focus on other writing genres for a time. After intensively studying opinion writing, it should be revisited when it logically fits into the curriculum. Additionally, opinion writing can always be among the types of writing students choose to explore during open writing times.

(Continued)

If students' lack of spelling skills is interfering with their ability to write,	• Build and use a Word Wall. Do this over time with your students. Make sure to include high-frequency words as well as words with useful chunks to support spelling connections. Reference the Wall continually during modeled, shared, guided, and interactive writing (see Integrating Foundational and Language Standards on page 251). • Do Challenge Words lessons (see Integrating Foundational and Language Standards on page 251). These can even be done in small group so you can give students words to attempt that are right on their level. Spend more time doing the steps of the routine *together* to provide heavier support. Bonus: This work will increase students' decoding skills as well!
If students are stuck on content during the composing process and their partner sharing hasn't moved them forward,	• Have them meet with a group of *three* other students. (Obviously, they might conference with the teacher, but at times, a peer group is even more effective.) The student reads her piece and talks about where she is stuck while the group contributes ideas to move her forward. (I've had phenomenal success with this; again, sometimes kids surprise us!)
If students are excelling,	• Encourage them to "write more" or exceed the standard. For example, they could include more reasons for their opinions or extend their conclusions. • Ask them to serve as helpers to others, making use of a simple rubric, at times. • Naturally, these students should also have plenty of opportunities to go ahead with more choice writing.
If you have English language learners,	• Bring in related realia to support understanding when writing opinions about topics. • Meet in a small group to support them as they talk about their opinions. • Use sentence frames to scaffold their speaking and writing. • Compose shared pieces together using sentence frames.

Mentor Texts

The Day the Crayons Quit by Drew Daywalt: Duncan's crayons write letters arguing they need a rest. Each crayon gives reasons and elaborates for an entire page!

I Don't Want to Be a Frog by Dev Petty: Little frog simply does not want to be a frog and he has all kinds of reasons why. Instead, he wants to be different animals like a pig or a cat. Big frog counters his arguments. But, it's a surprise character at the end who helps little frog see the trouble with his reasoning. This book is an instant smash hit and a shining example of an opinion mentor text!

I Wanna Iguana by Karen Kaufman Orloff: This mentor text follows Alex as he writes letters to his mom arguing for a pet iguana. His mom writes back with her reasons why he shouldn't get one. Students love the humor! This is a great book for talking about opinions in general and supporting opinions with reasons, in particular.

I Wanna New Room by Karen Kaufman Orloff: This book is a follow-up wherein we hear Alex argue for a room separate from his little brother. He writes to mom and dad about his reasons. They write back with theirs. Great mentor text like its predecessor.

Prudence Wants a Pet by Cathleen Daly: When Prudence says she wants a pet, her dad says no and states his reason. Her mom says no and states her reason. Later in the book, her dad gives another reason. So, even if you don't read the book and have students write their opinions about it, you might consider it a mentor text.

Should There Be Zoos: A Persuasive Text by Tony Stead and Judy Ballester's Fourth-Grade Class: This book is chunked into sections: students' writing that argues *for* zoos, students' writing that argues *against* zoos, and even a section on steps students took to write their opinions. Since it is chunked in this manner and addresses a topic of high interest, it is suitable to use (even if in bits and pieces) for K–2. The student samples show aspects of the opinion writing standards. Students give clear, elaborated reasons for their opinions and include interesting introductions and lots of voice.

Should We Have Pets: A Persuasive Text by Sylvia Lollis and Joyce Hogan and her Second-Grade Class: This is the perfect mentor text for our K–2 students. Again, like its predecessor, the students compose pro and con opinions about a relevant and engaging topic. They provide explicit reasons for their thinking. Best of all, these authors are second graders! Read this book and your students will want to write their opinions on the topic, too!

Stella Writes an Opinion by Janiel Wagstaff: Ms. Merkley asks her second-grade class to write opinions. Stella chooses to write about why they should be able to bring a morning snack to school. Ms. M. guides the class to include all the elements of an effective opinion and, though she struggles, Stella very successfully fulfills the requirements and changes policy at her school in the process!

Here are other books wherein children share opinions and supply reasons for them:

Can I Keep Him? by Steven Kellogg

Earrings! by Judith Voirst

Hey, Little Ant by Phillip and Hannah Hoose

I Want a Dog by Dayal Kaur Khalsa

My Brother Dan's Delicious by Steven Layne

Red Is Best by Kathy Stinson

Summer Stinks by Marty Kelley

Super-Completely and Totally the Messiest! by Judith Voirst

Here are a few picture books I deliberately choose for opinion writing because they are so engaging. I list ideas for opinion writing for each title.

The Circus Ship by Chris Van Dusen: The horrible nature of the circus manager, the kind villagers, and clever problem solving have all the kids riveted to their seats. In one two-page spread, the animals are hidden within the village (this is part of how the problem is solved) and the kids can't get enough of searching for them. They'll enjoy writing opinions about the characters, how the problem was solved or whether the resolution was fair to all the characters involved.

I Must Have BoBo! by Eileen Rosenthal: This story details the epic battle between a young boy, Willy, and his crazy cat, Earl, as they fight over possession of Willy's beloved sock monkey. It's hilarious! Students can write their opinions of Willy or Earl's actions or how they would solve the problem (the book ends without a solution).

National Geographic Readers: Cats vs. Dogs by Elizabeth Carney: This book is the perfect fact-finding treasure trove that can be used to add to students' background knowledge leading up to writing opinions on the topic of which make better pets: cats or dogs?

One by Kathryn Otoshi: This wonderful book addresses bullying. Students can write opinions about the characters' actions or how the problem was solved. This book can help you launch important collaborative conversations!

The Paper Bag Princess by Robert Munsch: Because the characters in this book are so glaringly different, it's great to have students pick a favorite character and tell why he or she is the favorite. Or, since the ending is so shocking, students take great pleasure in telling their opinions about how Prince Ronald treats Princess Elizabeth after she saves his live. I love to use Robert Munsch books in general because of their humor.

Z Is for Moose by Kelly Bingham: You probably already know this one! Have your students write their opinions about Moose's behavior. Outrageous!

Extending the Work

One general point about extending the work that is important to keep in mind is that any text that is part of the study can be displayed on a chalkboard tray or in a bin for students to pick up and reread individually, in pairs, or check out for home reading. The more students read and engage with the texts the better. Additionally, you and your students can do book talks on titles that go along with the study but are not part of the lessons.

Beyond the ten lessons in the sequence, I would spend two to three more weeks heavily focused on opinion writing until I feel I've guided students through enough experiences that they really have the text type down. After this in-depth study, I want them to be able to share opinions aloud on an ongoing basis and pick up writing opinions at any time, as if they've never stopped. The anchor charts we make along the way will help us refresh our memories about what elements are needed for effective opinions, but students should be so immersed in this type of speaking and writing throughout the year that the use of the charts falls off. Like anything, with practice and feedback, processes become easier, and opinion writing is no exception.

Keep in mind, any text might lead to opinion writing, and topics for opinions are everywhere. Have students write plenty of *quick opinions* that they share informally as they get the hang of it. Spend extended time developing *only some* of these. It's more important students produce a good volume of writing then it is to have several pieces published. Give them plenty of opportunities to informally self-assess since they benefit greatly from this, rather than feeling they must revise, edit, and publish much of what they write.

Companion Website Resource

Available for download at www.corwin
.com/thecommoncorecompanion

LESSONS	**READING** Speaking and Listening	**WRITING** Speaking and Listening
6	**Lesson 6:** *Narrative Reading to Form an Opinion* • Shared reading under document camera: *Click, Clack, Moo: Cows That Type* by Doreen Cronin (or other engaging narrative).	**Lesson 6:** *Share Opinions Orally* • Complete Narrative Story Map. • Reexamine anchor chart: Effective Opinions. • Share opinions about the text as a whole orally.

7	**Lesson 7:** *Revisit Text*
	
	 • Revisit *Click, Clack, Moo*, rereading key sections.
		Lesson 7: *Quick Write Opinions*
		
		 • Model and students . . .
		
		   ○ Jot notes about opinions, reasons, and evidence as sections of text and illustrations are reviewed.
		
		   ○ Quick Write: Opinion about the book as a whole.
		
		   ○ Peer or self-assess using rubric or checklist.
		
		   ○ Share examples under document camera: "What do we see that the writer has done well?"

8	**Lesson 8:** *Conversation About a Relevant Topic*
	
	 • Discuss class-related topic: an example, "Should we always line up boy, girl, boy, girl?"
		Lesson 8: *Form an Opinion About the Topic and Share*
		
		 • Create T-chart example: Yes/ No
		
		 • Model and students . . .
		
		   ○ Jot notes about your opinion (in Thinking Boxes or other).
		
		   ○ Practice sharing opinions aloud from notes.
		
		   ○ Take notes home, share opinion with family member.
		
		   ○ Does family member agree or disagree?

9	**Lesson 9:** *View Media to Prepare for New Topic*
	
	 • Share family members' opinions from the day before.
	
	 • Discuss: What is your favorite toy and why?
	
	 • View related media to spark conversation: https://www.youtube.com/user/EvanTubeHD
	
	 (Evan reviews tons of toys on his YouTube channel.)
		Lesson 9: *Plan Opinions*
		
		 • Model and students . . .
		
		   ○ Complete Thinking Boxes about favorite toy topic.
		
		   ○ Refer to Effective Opinions anchor chart.

LESSONS	READING Speaking and Listening	WRITING Speaking and Listening

10		**Lesson 10:** *Write and Share Opinions*
		
		• Model and students . . .
		   ○ Check each Thinking Box using rubric.
		   ○ Talk it out using Thinking Boxes.
		   ○ Draft using Thinking Boxes (could be in a letter format).
		   ○ Share and get feedback.
		   ○ Highlight some samples on document camera.
		   ○ If appropriate, take writing home to share with family audience.

11	**Lesson 11:** *Prepare for Opinion Discussion and Writing on a New Topic* • "What destination would make your favorite field trip and why?" or "Which of these choices would you prefer for a field trip and why (list choices)?" • Stimulate discussion and note-taking by viewing photos of field trip destinations (I use Google Images to find photos and we closely examine them to generate thinking and talk).	**Lesson 11:** *T-Chart and Jot Notes* • Have class brainstorm and do T-chart of pros of different field trips (number of columns based on number of field trip destinations). • Have students decide own favorite. • Model and students . . . ○ Jot notes about favorite.
12	**Lesson 12:** *Collaborative Conversation* • Have a collaborative conversation about favorite field trip using notes. • Add to notes based on discussion. • Has your opinion changed?	**Lesson 12:** *Quick Write and Share Opinions* • Model beginning a quick write based on collaborative conversation and notes. • Have students quick write based on collaborative conversation and notes. • Have students self-assess and share.
13	**Lesson 13:** *What's Your Favorite Children's Book?* • Read interview protocol and understand how to interview family member or friend about their favorite children's book (download a copy at **www.corwin.com/thecommoncorecompanion**).	**Lesson 13:** *What's Your Favorite Children's Book?* • Have students interview family member or friend about his or her favorite children's book. (Might pair up with another class of older students to do the interviews at school rather than home) • Have students take notes.

LESSONS	**READING** Speaking and Listening	**WRITING** Speaking and Listening
14	**Lesson 14:** *Reread, Share, and Converse* • Reread notes to prepare for sharing. • Share interview with a peer. • Circulate, listen, and look for patterns: Were certain books named several times? • Have collaborative conversation: Share highlights from interviews. What did we learn from doing these interviews?	**Lesson 14:** *Independent Task* • "Write an opinion in which you explain which part of the school day is your favorite. Be sure to name your topic, share your opinion, and reasons for your opinion and include a closing. You might use Thinking Boxes to organize your thinking before you write." • Even though this is an independent task, remind students to refer to helpful charts and to use the rubric or checklist to assess their work. (If you don't feel your students are ready for this independent task, do a few more quick opinions about other texts or topics to prepare them. Be sure to give as much feedback as possible on the document camera and have students check and assess their opinions using the anchor chart, rubric, or checklist.)
15		**Lesson 15:** *Complete Independent Task*
16	**Lesson 16:** *Debrief* • What did we learn about opinions? • What is important when it comes to writing opinions? • What strategies do you think are most helpful? • Why would you continue to write opinions? • What other topics might you write about? Who might you share your opinions with?	**Lesson 16:** *Ongoing Opinion Writing Topic Search* • Keep eyes, ears, and minds open for opinion topics (teacher and students). • Make notes about possibilities for opinion writing on a class running topics list or on students' individual topics lists or in writing notebooks.

Integrating Comparing and Contrasting With Publishing Using Digital Tools

In this lesson sequence, students compare and contrast two texts and three short video clips on the same topic. The text sources are a narrative book and an informational article. With the narrative, students first closely study its illustrations to glean information and then confirm these facts by reading the article and other sources. To culminate the experience, the teacher and students work together to compose a shared informative text on the topic and turn it into a lively digital publication using Photo Story 3.

Though this sequence is designed for first grade, it contains several instructional staples easily included in kindergarten and second-grade compare-and-contrast experiences and topic investigations (see grade level adaptations on pages 182–185).

Conner demonstrates talking out information about bats from a graphic organizer. The class offers feedback about the quality of his attempt. Does he sound ready to write? YES!

This sequence could be used as an introduction to comparing and contrasting, or could occur after students have had experience with this skill. Many teachers like to introduce compare/contrast with narrative texts rather than informational, finding students can grasp it more readily. Here, we are looking closely at sources not just for the sake of comparing and contrasting per se, but for the purpose of *confirming* facts as a step toward incorporating them into informative writing about hermit crabs.

The culminating writing project is done in the shared-writing mode. When working with first graders, it would be best to engage in this sequence after students have completed a shorter informative writing experience involving both shared and independent modes.

The ideas in the sequence are universal and can be used with whatever topics and sources best fit your needs. I encourage you to start with a narrative, as we do here, because students are so easily engaged with a fun story. The story work gives them a compelling purpose to compare the information they've gleaned with other sources.

Core Connections

Focus Reading
Informational Standard
9 integrated with
Writing Standard 6
Reading Informational
Standards 1, 2, 4, 5, and 7
Writing Standards 1, 2, 5,
6, 7, and 8
Speaking and Listening
Standards 1, 2, 5, and 6

Task

Compare and contrast information about hermit crabs from a story, article, and video clips. Use the information to write an informative piece and turn it into a digital Photo Story.

What Teachers Guide Across the Week

LESSONS	READING Speaking and Listening	WRITING Speaking and Listening
1	**Lesson 1:** *Reading Narrative Text* • Review the task. • Define compare and contrast. • Identify purposes for reading. • Read *Is This a House for Hermit Crab?* for enjoyment. • Retell story. • Read story second time for possible factual information. • Closely examine illustrations for possible factual information.	**Lesson 1:** *Jot Sticky Note Details* • Have students jot information from *Is This a House for Hermit Crab?* on sticky notes.
2	**Lesson 2:** *Reading Informational Text* • Identify purposes for reading. • Utilize text features to predict and confirm. • Read "Hermit Crab Information" article once for general understanding. • Read article again for factual information and to underline key details. • Retell key details to a partner. • Clarify word meanings using context clues.	**Lesson 2:** *Jot Sticky Note Details Then Compare and Contrast* • Have students jot facts from the informational article on sticky notes. • Have students compare and contrast notes: Which contain information confirmed in both the narrative book and informational article? Which contain information that is different? • Add sticky notes to the Same/Different chart.
3	**Lesson 3:** *View Short Video Clips to Build Knowledge* • View three short video clips. • Use first viewing to identify main topic. • Re-view while asking questions and making comments. • Partner-share key details or facts seen in each clip.	**Lesson 3:** *Jot Sticky Note Details Then Compare and Contrast* • Have students jot facts they see depicted in the videos on sticky notes. • Have students compare and contrast notes: Which contain information that is the same across all three sources? Which contain information that is different? • Sort sticky notes on the Same/Different chart. • Have students quick write a reflection.
4	**Lesson 4:** *Which Ideas Are Most Important? Sort and Categorize* • Revisit article and text features. • Re-sort sticky notes into categories of information. • Brainstorm headings for shared writing.	**Lesson 4:** *Organizing Ideas With Thinking Boxes* • Revisit headings students decided upon. • Determine order of main ideas for shared writing (revisit article as mentor). • Reread sticky notes. • Jot, sketch, and label about each of these in Thinking Boxes (hermit crabs' bodies, habitat, and food). • Talk-it-out to prepare to write.
5	**Lesson 5:** *Mentor Text: Picture Glossaries* • Reread article, noting use of context clues for difficult words. • Study mentor text's picture glossary. • Have students create their own picture glossaries using the words *pincer, scavenger,* and *nocturnal.* • Label and post a student's picture glossary for future reference.	**Lesson 5:** *Compose Shared Text, Celebrate With Photo Story* • Cooperatively compose a shared informative text across two or three days. • Utilize Thinking Boxes. • Incorporate headings and questions. • Type finished copy for students. • Create Photo Story with students. • Post to class Web page. • Debrief about process.

What Students Do Across the Week

Young children become fascinated with hermit crabs as they study their features and learn where they live and what they eat, reading across three sources: a narrative book, an informational article, and three YouTube videos. Each source brings something novel to the experience and opportunities for comparing and contrasting.

Students take the work of finding facts that are the same and different very seriously, jotting furiously on as many sticky notes as possible. (You may want to limit the number of sticky notes you give students!) They love the opportunity to post their notes on the Same/Different chart. This seems to lend an air of importance to their work and results in enthusiastic discussion about where notes belong and why.

> **Literacy Moves**
>
> - Use varied sources
> - Jot notes
> - Chart to compare and contrast
> - Incorporate text features in shared writing
> - Discussion
> - Publish with digital tools

Students actively engage with each source. The narrative book provides some factual information in the text, and the realistic illustrations beg close examination and generate a lot of questions about what may be true of real hermit crabs—and what may not be. Now they have an authentic purpose to investigate another source to see if they can verify information as factual. Students study and utilize text features in the informative article, underlining key information they will revisit later in the week. Watching and rewatching the video clips is an absolute favorite mode of study for students; there is lively conversation as they watch a hermit crab change shells, eat, and walk across a rocky beach.

After sorting and categorizing their sticky notes, students sketch, label, and jot in Thinking Boxes. Since they'll work together as a class to compose a shared text at the end of the week, they need to agree on the focus of the writing and hone in on the information related to those foci. They decide what headings will be used and work in Thinking Boxes to summarize important details. Sources are revisited during this process.

All aspects of the recursive writing process are utilized as students work together with me to negotiate their informative piece about hermit crabs. We work from their Thinking Boxes, talking out their main ideas and details. Over the course of a few writing sessions, we cooperatively decide on all aspects of our composition. Students are so proud of their accomplishment!

The final fun comes when we work together to create a Photo Story. Students work with me to pick pictures from Google Images or other search engine to accompany their writing. They pick music and decide on formatting issues. The final product is posted on the class Web page for all to enjoy bringing more real purpose to students' efforts!

Finally, we take time to reflect on the process. What aspects of this learning sequence will affect students' thinking and writing as they move forward?

Reading Narrative Text

Getting Ready

The materials:

- Copy of the task (page 151) to display
- Kid-friendly definition of compare and contrast
- Copy of *Is This a House for Hermit Crab?* by Megan McDonald
- Document camera

Context of the Lesson

We launch into this sequence by understanding and building excitement for our ultimate goal (the task) and clearly defining what it means to compare and contrast. Then, we read a narrative book, once for enjoyment and again to glean information about real hermit crabs from the text and illustrations.

The Lesson

"Today we launch an exciting study! We will be reading and viewing sources of information on hermit crabs so we can write about them and create a wonderful digital story to share on our class Web page. Let's look at the task (*read together*). There are some words here you may not understand. It says we will 'compare and contrast information.' What does that mean? Let's look at a simple definition.

"When we <u>compare</u>, we look for things that are the same or similar between two or more things.

"When we <u>contrast</u>, we look for things that are different.

"Let's think about times when we've compared and contrasted in the past. We've made groups of items that have qualities that are the same. Do you remember when we grouped shapes by the same colors and then regrouped by the number of sides they had? We put shapes that had three sides together and those that had four sides were sorted together, for example. That was comparing. We compare stories, noting how authors of narratives often follow the same plan. The stories include the same elements: settings, characters, problems, and solutions. Who can think of some other examples of comparing? (*Share examples.*)

"When we contrast, we look for differences. If we think about the stories we've compared again, yes, they have the same elements (settings, characters, etc.), but we've looked at how the settings are different from story to story or the characters are different. That's contrasting. I've seen many of you contrast at lunchtime. You talk about how what you have in your sack lunch is different than what your neighbor has. I've even

Core Connections

Grade 1

Reading Informational Standard 1

Ask and answer questions about key details in a text. (*What real hermit crab facts can we learn from this book and its illustrations?*)

Reading Narrative Standard 2

Retell stories, including key details.

Reading Informational Standard 7

Use the illustrations and details in a text to describe its key ideas.

Speaking and Listening Standard 2

Ask and answer questions about key details in a text read aloud.

Core Practices

- Explicitly Define a Key Term or Skill
- Read First for Enjoyment and Gist
- Retell the Story
- Revisit Text Again for Specific Purposes (finding factual information, studying illustrations)
- Modeling Use of Text Evidence

seen some of you trade items based on those differences! Who can think of some other examples of contrasting? (*Share examples.*)

"This week, and into next, we'll be comparing and contrasting information from sources on hermit crabs. We'll see what each source has that is the same and different from the other sources we study. We'll closely examine this book (*I hold up the book*), an informational article (*I hold up the article*), and watch some short video clips. We'll jot down facts that are the same and different, then sort them on a chart. Along the way, we'll learn a lot of interesting information about hermit crabs! We'll use this information in our writing!

"Today, we'll read *Is This a House for Hermit Crab?* It is a narrative story. We'll read it the first time to just enjoy it and get the gist of the story."

I read the book under the document camera. Students retell the story to a partner.

"We'll read again, this time for a specific purpose. Some of what we read and saw in the illustrations seemed like real information, other parts were definitely not real— they couldn't be true of real hermit crabs. When something couldn't happen in real life, we call it *fantasy*. For example, a real hermit crab would not try to make a rock, a tin can, or a plastic pail its home. Its instincts would have it look for another shell, not one of those things. So, we know this is fantasy. I mean, how many hermit crabs have you heard of walking around with rocks or pails on their backs? But there are other things we can notice in the words and illustrations that could be true for real hermit crabs. We'll focus on those. Watch me as I think aloud and you'll see what I mean."

We read the book a second time. I invite students to read with me. I think aloud about what could be real information both from the text and from what I see in the illustrations. For example, on the first page I model: "I see it says 'Hermit Crab was forever growing too big for the house on his back.' The words *forever growing too big* let me know he's growing all the time. I know living things grow. So I'm sure that's true. The words *too big for the house on his back* point me to his shell. I'm thinking a real fact could be that as hermit crabs grow, they outgrow their shells." On the third page I continue, "The illustrations look very real (*as I talk about the details in the pictures, I point to them*). I see the hermit crab lives in a shell. It has long antenna. It has six legs showing, one with a really big claw. I'll need to check with other sources, but I bet this really is what a hermit crab looks like. I also see it walking along the sand near the shore. I bet this is a clue to where real hermit crabs live." I continue thinking aloud about what could possibly be factual information and, if the students seem eager and ready, invite volunteers to come up and point out information in the text and illustrations and share their thoughts and questions. I sum up, "See how important it is to closely study illustrations when you're reading? Often there are many additional clues to help you understand what you're reading if you take the time to look closely, ponder, and ask questions."

> ## Recap: Key Lesson Steps
>
> 1. Study the task
>
> 2. Define compare and contrast
>
> 3. Read narrative story for enjoyment
>
> 4. Retell the story
>
> 5. Model using the text and illustrations to find possible real information about hermit crabs
>
> 6. If ready, invite students to do the same and provide feedback

Wrap Up

"Next, we'll read the story again, this time stopping to jot notes on sticky notes about hermit crabs facts we are learning."

Isaac relishes the opportunity to read his writing to the class.

Jot Sticky Note Details

Getting Ready

The materials:

- Copy of *Is This a House for Hermit Crab?* by Megan McDonald
- Sticky notes for students
- Same/Different chart
- Document camera

Context of the Lesson

After reading and closely examining the text and illustrations in *Is This a House for Hermit Crab?* twice, we're ready to jot the probable facts we've gleaned about hermit crabs on sticky notes. We won't be able to compare and contrast yet, since this is our first source of information.

The Lesson

I hand out sticky notes to students and tell them to wait to write on them until instructed.

"It's time to jot some notes so we can compare and contrast what we're learning from this book with other sources once we study them. First, we need to either write the word *book* or the letter *b* in small handwriting at the top left of a sticky note (*I model then ask students to do the same*). This way, we know which source the information came from.

"Now, I'll page through the book again and model jotting some notes about what facts we thought we found. First, I see the text on the first page and see the words *forever growing too big for his house*. This reminds me that we think as hermit crabs grow, they change shells. The whole book is about this! So, I'll jot a few words to remind me of this. (*Working under the document camera, I jot 'change shells as grows' on a sticky note. I invite students to do the same.*) On the next few pages, we studied the illustrations closely and determined a lot of information about hermit crabs' bodies. I'll jot what I think we learned on another sticky note. I need to label it *book* first, then I'll jot . . ." (*6 legs, big claw, 2 antenna*). As I continue, if students are ready, I invite them to contribute their thoughts and model jotting notes under the document camera while I guide and provide feedback. We jot four or five facts from the book.

I show children the Same/Different chart we'll be using to compare and contrast. "You can see, as we study and jot notes, we'll put things that are the same in two sources up here at the top where it is labeled *Same*, and those that are different down here at the bottom where it is labeled *Different*. Since we only have information from the book today, we'll

Core Connections

Grade 1

Reading Informational Standard 1
Ask and answer questions about key details in a text (and we jot notes).

Reading Informational Standard 7
Use the illustrations and details in a text to describe its key ideas (and we jot notes).

Writing Standard 7
Participate in shared research and writing projects.

Writing Standard 8
With guidance and support from adults, . . . gather information from provided sources to answer a question (note-taking).

Speaking and Listening Standard 2
Ask and answer questions about key details in a text read aloud.

Core Practices

- Revisit Text
- Modeling
- Guided Practice
- Jot Notes
- Discussion

just pile up our notes and put them in the column labeled *Book*. Tomorrow, after we read, study, and jot notes on our informational article, we can start to compare and contrast." I have the children pile up their sticky notes and place them in the Book column.

Recap: Key Lesson Steps

1. Revisit source

2. Model jotting notes on possible facts from text and illustrations

3. Have students jot notes based on teacher model

4. If ready, invite students to model finding facts and jotting notes and provide feedback

Wrap Up

"What do you think of our first hermit crab source?" The students and I discuss their thoughts about the book. "Tomorrow, we'll read an informational article. I bet it will help us confirm whether or not what we have on our notes are true facts. In the meantime, I wonder what you might be able to find out about hermit crabs on your own?"

Companion Website Resource

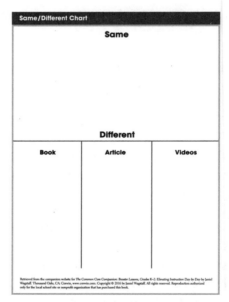

 Available for download at www.corwin .com/thecommoncorecompanion

Reading Informational Text

Getting Ready

The materials:

- Copy of "Hermit Crab Information" article for each student (see page 162)
- Document camera

Context of the Lesson

We're ready to dig into our second source: an informational article. We use the headings to predict what we will read in each section and confirm or disconfirm as we read the first time. After reading for general understanding, we discuss our reactions. Then, we reread, stopping to underline key details in each section and share these with a partner.

The Lesson

I hand out copies of the article, "Hermit Crab Information" (see page 162). "What do you notice right away that's different about this source than yesterday's?" We discuss how this is an article, not a book. It has a title and headings, which we've encountered in other informational reading, but no photographs or diagrams. It appears to be giving us real information. (*Point out to students that they have just compared and contrasted!*)

"I heard someone say since the title is 'Hermit Crab Information,' this article should be about true facts about hermit crabs. I expect the same thing since the word *information* is right there in the title. I see the first heading is *Description*. A description tells what something is like. So, I expect to read what hermit crabs are like in this section. Let's read and see." We read the first section together. "It did tell us what hermit crabs are like. It's about hermit crab bodies. I see those words in the first sentence. Let's read the next heading together: *Habitat*. A habitat is where something lives, so I'm sure we'll find out where hermit crabs live in this next section." We read the section together then agree we just read about where hermit crabs live. "Read the next heading and talk to your neighbor about what you think we'll find out in the next section." After sharing, we read and confirm the section is about what hermit crabs eat. "Now this last heading is *Behavior*. Again, tell your neighbor what you think we'll find out." After partner-talk, we read and point out that we've learned a few things about what hermit crabs do.

"Now that we've read it once, what do you think about this article? How does it help us as we work on learning about real hermit crabs? Turn to your neighbor and talk." I listen in then recap some of what I heard. "I heard some readers say they learned some new information in the article. Other people said they heard some of the things we

Core Connections

Grade 1

Reading Informational Standard 1

Ask and answer questions about key details in a text.

Reading Informational Standard 4

Ask and answer questions to help determine or clarify the meaning of words and phrases in a text.

Reading Informational Standard 5

Know and use various text features to locate key facts or information in a text.

Reading Informational Standard 7

Use the illustrations and details in a text to describe its key ideas.

Speaking and Listening Standard 2

Ask and answer questions about key details in a text read aloud.

Core Practices

- Read First for General Understanding
- Utilize Text Features
- Modeling and Guided Practice
- Revisit the Text for Specific Purpose (to underline key details)
- Retell Key Ideas
- Clarify Word Meanings
- Discussion
- Partner-Talk

read about yesterday. Those are useful observations. We'll reread the article again more slowly, this time underlining the key details or facts under the headings. The headings really are helpful in this article, aren't they? They point us right to the main or big ideas we're learning about hermit crabs."

As we reread a second time, I begin by thinking aloud about the key details under the first heading and why I'm underlining certain words. Students follow my model, underlining as I go. "This first section is describing hermit crab bodies. (*Rereading under the document camera*) 'Hermit crabs have soft bodies, which they hide in shells they find on the sea floor.' I see the words *soft bodies* and I'm going to underline them because this is important. I thought their bodies looked hard from the illustrations in the book yesterday; this says they are soft. (*Rereading*) 'which they hide in shells they find on the sea floor.' Again, we saw this in the book yesterday. We know they 'hide in shells,' (*underlining*) we saw that in the illustrations, and it seemed they must have to *find* the shells (*underlining* find *and* sea floor) because that's what the whole book *Is This a House for Hermit Crab?* was about!" I continue this process throughout the first section: reading a detail, underlining key words while I think aloud about their importance, and comparing what we are reading in the article to my memory of what we read the day before. Of particular note is how hermit crabs actually have ten legs, not just the six we could see in the book's illustrations; they are a reddish-brown color; and they have *two* pincers (*we note the context clue "claws"*) on their front legs, not just one big claw.

"Now that we've underlined key facts in this first section, turn to your neighbor and retell what we've learned about hermit crabs' bodies. You may look back at your underlines to help you." I circulate and listen in to check for understanding.

Since we've done plenty of other informative reading and have had experience highlighting and underlining, I turn more of the work over to students on the next three sections. "Let's read the next section under the heading *Habitat*. (*We read together.*) Who can tell me the key words or details there? Why are these key?" After discussion, a volunteer comes forward to underline *land* and *ocean*. "Okay, turn to your neighbor and retell what you've learned about where hermit crabs live."

We complete the other two sections, one at a time, with students coming forward to think aloud and underline key words under the document camera while I provide guidance. We discuss the context clues for the words *scavenger* and *nocturnal*. At the end of each section, I continue to have the students retell what they've learned, using their underlines, if needed.

Wrap Up

Review learning and forecast next steps by saying something like, "What do you think about the details we noted yesterday from the book? Were they true facts? What have we learned that is new? (*After discussion*) Next, we'll jot brief notes on sticky notes using our underlining as a guide. Then we'll go back to our sticky notes from yesterday and carefully compare and contrast them to today's, placing them in the right spots on our chart."

Notes

Description

Hermit crabs have soft bodies, which they hide in shells they find on the sea floor. They move from shell to shell as they grow. Six of their ten legs poke out from the shell, which they use to walk along the sea floor or along the sand. They are a reddish-brown color. They have two pincers, or front claws, on the first pair of walking legs.

Habitat

Hermit crabs can live on land or in the ocean.

Food

Hermit crabs are scavengers; they feed on food they find. They eat turtle eggs, dead fish, fruit that has fallen from trees, and just about anything along the bottom of the ocean.

Behavior

Hermit crabs are nocturnal animals, hiding during the day to avoid predators.

When threatened, they pull into their shells and cover the door with their large claw.

Jot Sticky Note Details
Then Compare and Contrast

Getting Ready

The materials:

- Students' copies of "Hermit Crab Information" article with their underlining
- Students' sticky notes from previous lesson
- New sticky notes for each student
- Same/Different chart
- Compare/contrast definition
- Document camera

Context of the Lesson

Once again, we've read a source twice and are ready to jot facts on sticky notes. The underlining we did in the article will help students have a high degree of success with this task. Once we have our new sticky notes written, we'll reread the notes we generated while reading the narrative *Is This a House for Hermit Crab?* and compare and contrast them, adding them to our Same/Different chart.

The Lesson

I hand out sticky notes to students and tell them to wait to write on them until instructed.

"It's time to jot some notes on what we've learned about real hermit crabs, just like we did yesterday. First, we need to either write the word *article* or the letter *a* in small handwriting at the top left of a sticky note (*I model then ask students to do the same*). This way, we know these notes came from the article. We'll need to know the source when we compare and contrast our facts.

"The underlining we did will help us go straight to the important facts and details. Jotting notes should be pretty simple, but we have to keep our wording short. That's why we focus on key words when we underline. Let's see (*looking at the article under the document camera*), the first words I underlined are *soft bodies*. I'll jot that on my first sticky note (*jotting under the document camera*). Next, I underlined (*pointing*) *hide in shells*, *find*, and *sea floor*. Those are perfect words for my next note because they all relate to the same thing: how hermit crabs live in shells and that they find them, not grow them. It also reminds me where they find them. Those are important facts." I continue this process throughout the first section: pointing to and rereading my underlined facts and thinking aloud as I add them (or choose not to) to my sticky notes.

Core Practices

- Revisit Text
- Modeling
- Guided Practice
- Jot Notes
- Compare and Contrasting on a Visual (chart)
- Discussion

Time Crunched?

Getting the notes from the article may be enough work for the day. You can always wait until the following day to compare and contrast on the chart.

Next, I turn more of the work over to students, again because I am confident they understand the task, have enough prior experience to be successful, and because their underlining will guide them. "Who would like to come up to the document camera with their article and sticky notes and help us jot notes for the next section under the heading *Habitat*?" I stand by as the volunteer talks and works, providing guidance as needed. We continue in this fashion through the whole article.

"We have quite a few notes from the article! It was rich with information! Now, we're ready to compare and contrast the information we have. (*I pass back the notes from yesterday.*) Remember what it means to compare and contrast? Let's read the definition again (*we read the definition together*). Before we start comparing and contrasting, let's reread all of the notes we've taken. Get with a partner and share. (*After sharing*) Now be sure the notes are sorted on your desk: which came from the book and which came from the article? Remember, we wrote *book* or the letter *b* and *article* or the letter *a* on each note to help us. (*After sorting time*) Let's start by comparing: looking for facts or details that are the same. Many of you have been talking excitedly about this already. It's great to learn something new then have it confirmed from another source, isn't it? Okay, who found a similarity or something that is the same?"

Students take turns telling the class about similarities, holding up their notes. Once we all agree on an example, that volunteer comes up and places his or her notes under *Same* on our chart. The rest of the students then look to see if they have similar notes on that particular fact or detail and, if they do, they come up to place them on the chart.

As we finish comparing notes that are the same, "We have many facts or details that are the same in the book and article. Now, we'll *contrast* our findings. Let's look at what we learned from each source that is different." We follow the exact process as before to find what is different. Volunteers explain their thinking then come up to post their notes. The rest of the students post notes about that fact or detail afterwards.

Recap: Key Lesson Steps

1. Revisit source
2. Model jotting notes on facts
3. Have students jot notes based on model
4. Invite volunteers to model note-taking for class
5. Review definition of compare and contrast
6. Reread all notes and sort into two sources
7. Invite volunteers to share notes that are the same across the two sources
8. Ask students to post notes to the *Same* section of the chart
9. Invite volunteers to share notes that are different
10. Ask students to post notes to the *Different* section of the chart

Wrap Up

"Wow. We have a lot of information already! We learned some details or facts in both sources and some we found in just one. I love how excited you are about comparing and contrasting! Tomorrow we'll examine one more source: some video clips of real hermit crabs in action! We'll jot some notes and add these to our chart, as well. At that point, we'll know a great deal about hermit crabs!"

Some similarities:

"they can live in the ocean or live on the land."   **"cover the door with a claw."**

Some differences: "Porcupine eats hermit crabs." Yep, that is one hermit crab predator. But it's called a pricklepine fish. ☺

3

Booster Reading Lesson

View Short Video Clips to Build Knowledge

Getting Ready

The materials:

- Video clips

Core Connections

Grade 1

Reading Informational Standard 1

Ask and answer questions about key details in a text. *(We do this with video.)*

Reading Informational Standard 2

Identify the main topic and retell key details of a text. *(We do this with video.)*

Reading Informational Standard 7

Use the illustrations and details in a text to describe its key ideas. *(We do this with video.)*

Speaking and Listening Standard 2

Ask and answer questions about key details in a text read aloud. *(We do this with video.)*

Context of the Lesson

Students get so excited to see real nature in action! Today is a favorite day since we view three short video clips of hermit crabs. Again, we're looking for hermit crab facts, so we view and re-view for that purpose. After we watch once, we decide on the main topic of each clip. Once we watch again, I ask students to retell the key details they saw to a partner. There's a whole lot of talk going on throughout!

I used the following short video clips since they relate to main ideas we've already encountered. If these clips are no longer available, it's quite easy to find others that will fill the bill.

Hermit crab changing shells (play from :50 onward)

http://www.youtube.com/watch?v=0jZe_VGLRYI

Hermit crab eating

https://www.youtube.com/watch?v=CMKbJJ04rXg

Hermit crab using front six legs to walk along rocky beach

http://www.youtube.com/watch?v=qVBH-nwdyjQ

The Lesson

"Today, we have the opportunity to see real hermit crabs in action. We'll watch three short video clips. As we watch this first time, I want you to think, 'What is the main topic of this clip? What is the videographer trying to show us?' We'll talk about that after viewing once, and then we'll have the chance to watch again."

We watch each clip in the order I've listed them above. Students are fascinated! After our first viewing, we discuss the main topic of each clip. Since each is focused on one particular subject, this is pretty simple for students to do.

"As we watch this second time, please make a comment or ask a question that comes to mind. We'll stop the video, examine what we see closely, and discuss." Most often, students wonder what the crab is eating in the second clip. Students usually deduce

Core Practices

- View Video Clips First for General Understanding
- Identify Main Topic of Each Clip
- Discussion
- Re-View for Specific Purpose
- Retell Key Ideas
- Partner-Talk

that it's some type of fruit, since they read about that in the article—a pretty impressive text-to-media connection!

After each clip, I ask students to share the details they saw with a partner. In the first clip, we see the hermit crab change shells. It does this quickly. We can see its soft body as it comes out of the first shell. We replay this a few times so students get a good look. In the second video clip, we pay a lot of attention to how the hermit crab eats. We notice its mouth must be under its head since it is putting the food there after it tears it away with its large pincer. In the third clip, we notice how the crab is using its six front legs to walk and how it goes into its shell to hide.

Recap: Key Lesson Steps

1. View video clips first time for main topic
2. Re-view each clip and have students ask questions and comment
3. Have students share key details from the clips with a partner

Wrap Up

"Who's ready to write down what we saw? We'll do that right now!"

FYI

Often, when using clips from the Internet, I turn the sound off. Sometimes, we'll watch first without me talking or questioning; I just listen to students' comments (they can't help but make them!). Other times, we watch while I narrate, so I'm sure students hear the most important information I'd like them to walk away with. This is especially useful for YouTube videos which may have great video but poor audio. For this lesson sequence, we watched in silence once, and then watched again as students asked questions and made comments.

Notes

_____

Integrating Comparing and Contrasting With Publishing Using Digital Tools 167

3

Companion Writing Lesson

Jot Sticky Note Details Then Compare and Contrast

Getting Ready

The materials:

- Three video clips
- New sticky notes for each student
- Same/Different chart
- Document camera
- Think pads or scratch paper for quick write

Context of the Lesson

With a third source in the mix, we have a lot of information. We jot a few notes about the details we viewed in the video clips and compare and contrast these to what we already know and have posted on our chart. We end the lesson with a reflective quick write.

The Lesson

I hand out sticky notes to students and tell them to wait to write on them until instructed.

"Now, we'll jot notes on what we just viewed in each video clip. Again, we have to be picky about the words we write to remind us of important details and facts. First, we need to either write the word *video* or the letter *v* in small handwriting at the top left of a sticky note (*I model and then ask students to do the same*).

"Okay, let's think about the main topic in the first clip. What is it?" A student shares that this clip was about a hermit crab changing shells. "Yes. What details did we see? Tell your neighbor again." As students share, we jot a few words on sticky notes like: *changes shells as it grows, changes shells quickly, soft body*. As with the other lessons, I model first, then turn the reins over to students as I stand by and guide as needed. We repeat this process for the other two clips.

"Now, let's reread our notes to ourselves and sort them on our desks. Which notes have details that are the same as another source, either the book or the article or both? Which notes have details that are different from the other sources? (*After giving students time to sort*) Okay, who has a detail that is the same?" A volunteer shares her note and her thinking, and like before, we discuss what she has to say and she posts her note on the chart under *Same*. Then students with notes containing similar information do the same. After we've worked through the notes that are the same, we work through those that have differences and place them on our chart.

Note: Some of the notes may have to be moved. For example, we first had the notes about soft bodies as different under the article heading. But, we saw the soft body again in the first video clip and noted it. Now, this detail must be moved to the *Same* category since it was found in two sources.

"Wow, look at all we've learned. And, as we study our chart, we see that by comparing and contrasting, we were able to confirm many facts, even those we thought we found out from a narrative picture book! At the same time, we learned several new facts from the various sources." We discuss students' reactions to the chart.

"As we finish up today, I'd like you to do a quick reflection. Think about the three different sources we used to learn about hermit crabs: the book, the article, and the video clips. Which do you think was the best source for learning information? I'm curious about your opinions here. Which source do you think was best and why?" I allow students about 7 minutes to write, and then they share their thinking in small groups. I circulate and listen in and we discuss as a whole class.

Core Connections

(Continued) conversations with diverse partners . . . with peers and adults in small and larger groups (*discussion following quick write*).
Speaking and Listening Standard 2
Ask and answer questions about key details in a text read aloud.

Recap: Key Lesson Steps

1. Revisit media sources

2. Jot notes for each source

3. Sort notes on our Compare/Contrast chart

4. Conduct a quick write reflection

Core Practices

- Revisit Sources
- Modeling
- Guided Practice
- Jot Notes
- Compare and Contrast on a Visual (chart)
- Quick Write
- Sharing and Discussion

Wrap Up

"Do you remember how we discussed using what we learn to write about hermit crabs and then make a digital Photo Story? That's what we'll be working on next! We have to make some decisions: out of all these facts and details, which are the most important to include in our writing? That will be a big job. Think about it tonight: which facts do you think will be most important to include? What was most important or interesting to you as we learned about hermit crabs? We'll start organizing tomorrow!"

We discussed his opinion and how using a variety of sources is important to us as learners. This is a big "aha" I want my first graders to take with them for future learning!

Time Crunched?

Poring over notes from three sources and a chart can take longer than you anticipate. So be open to adjusting this lesson so that the quick write occurs at a later juncture; you'll just need to refresh students' memories more before they write.

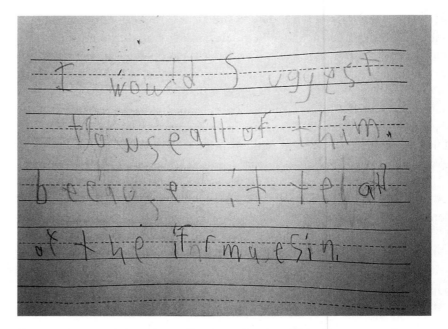

One first grader's quick write reflection about which source was best and why: "I would suggest to use all of them because it tells all of the information." (Ha! I agree!)

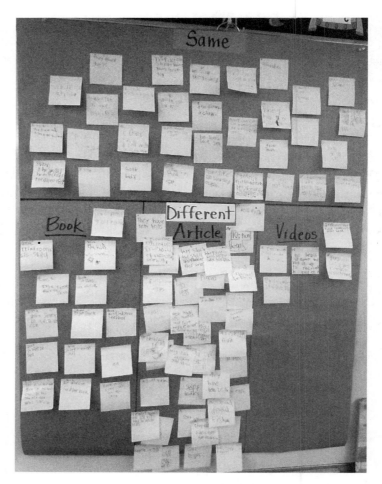

Here is our chart. You can see, we got in a great deal of compare and contrast practice!

Which Ideas Are Most Important? Sort and Categorize

4

Booster Reading Lesson

Getting Ready

The materials:

- Student copies of the article "Hermit Crab Information"
- Compare/Contrast chart

Context of the Lesson

In this lesson, we reread the notes we compared and contrasted on our chart to determine the most important ideas we learned about hermit crabs. We decide to use the article as a mentor text, borrowing some of its structure for the informative writing we'll complete.

The Lesson

"As we look at our Compare/Contrast chart, we see we have a lot of facts or details about hermit crabs. We have to decide which facts are most important and how we will organize the information we share in our writing. Let's start by looking back at our informational article. Since we are writing an informational text, we can use the article as a model to help us organize our information." We reread the article one more time.

"Now that we've reread, talk to your neighbor about the text features you see. Remember, we used them to help us when we first read the article." I circulate and listen. "I heard some people share how the article starts with a title then has headings and sections of information. I also heard how the headings tell what information will follow. If we use the article as a guide, we could think about organizing the information we gathered under headings. So, let's start by rereading the notes on our chart and sorting them into categories that could go under headings."

We reread some of the notes and quickly realize we have three main categories: information about hermit crab bodies, information about where hermit crabs live, and information about what hermit crabs eat. Though we have other notes, three categories of information are plenty for first graders to focus on. We group the sticky notes together.

"Look back at the article and reread the headings. Talk with your neighbor. What headings might we use for our categories of information? What should we call each of these groups?" (*After share time*)

"Let's hear your ideas. I'll write them down and we'll vote."

I write students' ideas for headings on the board and we vote. We decide on *Body*, *Habitat*, and *Food*.

Core Connections

Grade 1

Reading Informational Standard 1

Ask and answer questions about key details in a text.

Reading Informational Standard 2

Identify the main topic and retell key details of a text.

Reading Informational Standard 5

Know and use various text features to locate key facts or information in a text.

Core Practices

- Reread Text
- Re-Identify Text Features
- Reread Sticky Notes
- Categorize Notes
- Determine Importance
- Partner-Talk

1. Reread the article

2. Identify text features

3. Resort sticky notes to identify most important information and information categories

4. Brainstorm and vote for headings to use in shared writing

"Now that we have the headings we'll use, let's clarify the information we know so we're ready to write. We'll do that by working in Thinking Boxes."

Wrap Up

Save the wrap up for after Companion Writing Lesson 4, which you can present on the same day as this reading lesson.

Companion Website Resource

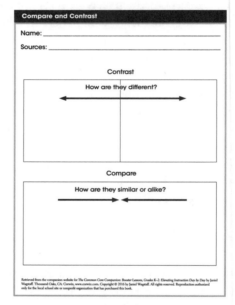

Available for download at www.corwin .com/thecommoncorecompanion

Organizing Ideas With Thinking Boxes

Getting Ready

The materials:

- Copy of the article "Hermit Crab Information"
- Sticky notes sorted into categories
- Document camera
- Think pads or white paper

Context of the Lesson

Students clarify the main ideas and details we'll include in our shared writing by jotting and sketching in Thinking Boxes. The information recorded in the boxes will help us talk out the details we'll write.

The Lesson

"Writers often organize their thinking before they begin to compose a piece. Today, we'll do that in Thinking Boxes. We'll use the headings you voted on (*Body*, *Habitat*, and *Food*); one for each box. We'll jot, sketch, and label about what we've learned for each main idea. What should we begin with? Talk with your neighbor." As students look back at the article again, they decide to follow the progression of main ideas in that mentor text.

"So, our *first* main idea will be hermit crabs' bodies. Let's fold our paper into four boxes and label Box 1. (*I model on the document camera as students work.*) We'll reread our sticky notes for that category of information. Then, you jot, sketch, and label to remember what you think is most important to include in our writing under that heading. I'll model up here, but you don't need to copy what I do. Do your own thinking in the box. We'll share some examples." We reread our notes for the main idea of 'hermit crabs' bodies, jot and sketch in Box 1, and student volunteers share their thinking under the document camera. The class and I provide feedback.

We continue this process for Box 2, *Habitat*, and Box 3, *Food* (see a student sample on pages 188–189).

"Now, I'd like you to get with a partner and talk out the information in your boxes. Before you do, I'll model. Listen how I talk in full sentences so it doesn't sound like I'm just reading notes or labels. I also need to talk out what I'm showing in my sketches. This should also be done in full sentences that make sense. As I talk it out, it should sound close to how it will sound when we write it." (*I model a non-example and example. We discuss my examples. Students partner up and talk it out.*)

Core Connections

Grade 1

Reading Informative Standard 1

Ask and answer questions about key details in a text.

Reading Informative Standard 7

Use the illustrations and details in a text to describe its key ideas.

Writing Standard 7

Participate in shared research and writing projects.

Writing Standard 8

With guidance and support from adults, . . . gather information from provided sources to answer a question (*Thinking Boxes*).

Speaking and Listening Standard 6

Produce complete sentences when appropriate to task and situation (*talking it out*).

Core Practices

- Utilize Article as Mentor Text
- Revisit Notes
- Modeling
- Guided Practice
- Jot Notes
- Sketch and Label to Clarify Information
- Talk-It-Out
- Sharing and Discussion
- Immediate Feedback

Thinking Box 1: Bodies

"Moving into bigger shell

hermit crab

small shell

bigger shell"

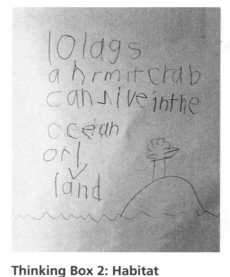

Thinking Box 2: Habitat

"10 legs / a hermit crab / can live in the / ocean / or / land"

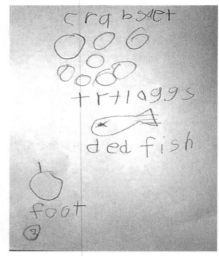

Thinking Box 3: Food

"crabs eat / turtle eggs / dead fish / fruit"

Recap: Key Lesson Steps

1. Revisit article as mentor for organization
2. Reread sticky notes for each category of information (the main ideas)
3. Jot, sketch, and label in Thinking Boxes
4. Share and provide feedback
5. Model talking it out using Thinking Boxes
6. Have students talk it out with a partner to prepare to write

---

Wrap Up

"We've done a lot of great work today. Writers should keep their writing focused. We've stuck to our main ideas, picked out the most important details, and jotted about them to help us move forward. Talking it out always helps us prepare, as well. Do you feel ready to write? What has helped you prepare? (*We have a brief discussion.*) Tomorrow, we'll have our Thinking Boxes standing by to help us as we write our informational piece."

Compose Shared Text, Celebrate With Photo Story

5

Booster
Writing
Lesson

Getting Ready

The materials:

- Student's Thinking Boxes
- Chart paper
- Photo Story 3 downloaded to computer (or iPad)

Context of the Lesson

Notice, I've flipped the order of lessons here at the end of the sequence. Once we compose our shared *writing*, we complete the final *reading* lesson, studying a mentor text to help us understand picture glossaries. Since we're not including a picture glossary in this text, I wanted to wait to study it so students would stay focused on the task at hand. All the reading and writing work we've done culminates in the creation of our shared informative text about hermit crabs. *It takes two or three sessions to cooperatively compose.* I then type the final version, so everyone receives a copy, and work with students to create the Photo Story we post on our class Web page.

The Lesson

"Okay, writers, we've already made a lot of decisions about this piece of informative writing. We know our three main ideas and our headings. We know the details we'll record under each and we've rehearsed by talking it out. Now, let's create our masterpiece!

"Writers sometimes start with the title or they skip it and move on. Does anyone have an idea for a title right now? (*I record students' ideas and we pick one.*) We've decided on a very straightforward title that basically just states the topic: Hermit Crabs. (*I write* Hermit Crabs *at the top of the chart paper.*) Talk to your neighbor, what should we write to get readers into our piece? How shall we introduce it? (*After partner-talk, I have a few volunteers share what they came up with. We pick one based on student response, or I just pick one, since we don't want to get bogged down voting on everything and we can always come back and change it later*). So, we've decided we'll introduce our piece with the statement, 'We learned about hermit crabs.'" (*I record this on the chart.*)

"Our first heading is Body (*I record this in bold on the chart.*) How might we introduce this section to our readers? We could start with a question, like we've seen in other informational writing. Talk to your neighbor about a question that may work here (*pointing to the chart*)." (Looking at the photo of our shared writing on page 176, you can see we started with, "Did you know hermit crabs live in a shell?" But, once we wrote on and came back and reread, we made revisions to that sentence. This is what

Core Connections

Grade 1
Writing Standard 2
Write informative texts in which they name a topic, supply some facts about the topic, and provide some sense of closure.

Writing Standard 5
With guidance and support from adults, focus on a topic, respond to questions and suggestions from peers, and add details to strengthen writing as needed.

Writing Standard 6
With guidance and support from adults, use a variety of digital tools to produce and publish writing, including in collaboration with peers.

Writing Standard 7
Participate in shared research and writing projects.

Speaking and Listening Standard 1
Participate in collaborative conversations (*debriefing at end of sequence*).

occurs when we constantly reread as we compose. It's an active, thinking process. Revision and editing are not just tacked on at the end.)

"Let's reread. (*We reread our title, introduction, heading, and first sentence.*) What should we say next to give more detail about how hermit crabs live in shells? Look back at your Thinking Boxes and talk to your partner." (*After partner-talk, I have a few volunteers share and I write on the chart. We write the first section, rereading and making changes as we go.*)

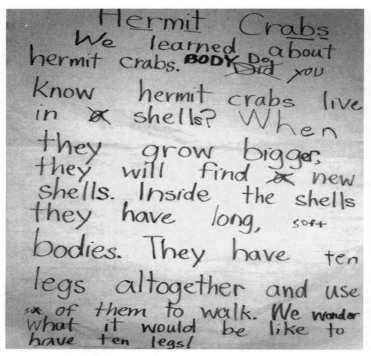

Depending on students' stamina, you may want to compose one section under one heading each day. It's a useful strategy to write and then leave the text for a bit before coming back to it so you have fresh eyes as readers. This often leads to more revision and a better final piece.

We continue to work through each section in the same way. I record the heading we decided on. We stick with the structure we've started, asking a question to introduce each new section. Using our Thinking Boxes, we talk about the details with partners. I call on volunteers and we pick an idea, I record it, and we move on, again knowing changes can be made.

On our final rereading of this piece, we decided to go back in and add some voice. We didn't want our writing to read like a list of facts. We decided to add questions at the bottom of each section to once again involve the reader a bit and add some humor. We also added a conclusion to the piece.

Once our informative text was complete, I typed it so everyone could have a copy. We reread it and sent it home for the students to share.

To begin our Photo Story, we worked as a class as I projected the project on the screen. We picked the cover image and music together. Then, over the course of the next several days, I called back small groups of children to help me pick images from Google Images to go along with our text. This is such a simple program to use (it leads you through the process step by step) and it produces such a polished, professional looking product. We posted our Photo Story to our class Web page.

Time Crunched?

Do you need more than three days to do the shared writing? Take the time it needs! Students in Grades K–2 present a vast range of developmental stages of reading and writing, so take your cues from your own class.

Recap: Key Lesson Steps

1. Cooperatively compose shared writing on chart paper

2. Elicit ideas from student volunteers, pick one, and record

3. Reread as you write, make ongoing changes

4. Cooperatively create a Photo Story

5. Post on class Web page

Wrap Up

We debrief about what we've learned after we've completed all aspects of the project. We talk about why comparing and contrasting was important and why utilizing several sources was helpful. We revisit the idea of carefully examining illustrations for information. We recap how using the article as an organizational mentor helped move our writing forward and what we learned by, once again, using Thinking Boxes to prepare for writing. I ask if students have learned anything new about writing from our shared writing experience. Lastly, I ask students to reflect on what they feel is the most important learning they'll take with them for their future work.

Notes

5

Companion
Reading
Lesson

Mentor Text: Picture Glossaries

Getting Ready

The materials:

- Copy of mentor text *National Geographic Kids: Pandas* by Anne Schreiber or other informational text with picture glossary
- Copies of article "Hermit Crab Information"
- Think pad or scratch paper
- Document camera

Context of the Lesson

As we read the informational article "Hermit Crab Information," we came across three words in particular which were difficult. Though we were able to use the context clues to figure them out, I want students to have an understanding of picture glossaries as a useful informational text feature. In this lesson, we study the picture glossary of an informational book, and then play with the idea of what one might look like given the domain specific vocabulary in the hermit crab article.

The Lesson

"Looking back at the informational article we read, we found there were three words in particular which were difficult. It's important to know how to work out the meaning of such words, because many informational texts have words that are like these; they are specific to the topic and you may not know them.

"Let's reread and find the first one. (*We reread under the first heading* Description, *until we get to the word* pincers.) Finish reading the section. Talk to your neighbor about how we figured out this word. (*I listen in.*) I heard some friends say we read on to help us. We did, we saw that the text said "front claws," and that helped a lot. I also heard a friend say we saw the huge front claws in the story *Is This a House for Hermit Crab?* and we talked about them then. So, we had some understanding of what the pincers look like before reading the article, though we didn't know the word. And as we read on in the article, there was more information there to help us figure out the word meaning. Let's read on until we come to the next word we had to work to figure out."

We reread and discuss the context clues for the words *scavengers* and *nocturnal*.

"So, for these three difficult words, there were clues in the words around them that helped us figure out what they meant. This is not always the case, however. Sometimes authors don't include as many clues to word meanings. But, there may be another feature in the text, particularly in informational books, that can be helpful.

Core Connections

Grade 1

Reading Informational Standard 4

Ask and answer questions to help determine or clarify the meaning of words and phrases in a text.

Reading Informational Standard 5

Know and use various text features to locate key facts or information in a text.

Core Practices

- Study Mentor Text
- Identify Purpose of Text Feature
- Guided Practice
- Utilize Context Clues
- Partner-Talk

"Here is a book on pandas (*I show it under the document camera.*) We see a Table of Contents which shows us the main ideas about pandas that are included in the book. Here, at the end of the list, I see Picture Glossary on page 32. (*I turn there.*) Oh yes, we've seen picture glossaries before. Talk to your neighbor about what picture glossaries are and how they are helpful."

Students share their thoughts and we discuss. "Let's study the example of the picture glossary in this book. What does each entry have? Talk to your neighbor."

We note how each entry has the vocabulary word, a short definition, and a picture.

"Would a picture glossary have been helpful for the hermit crab information? If so, what might it look like? Talk to your neighbor." Students agree a picture glossary would be a useful tool and it could include the three words we worked on—*pincer, scavenger,* and *nocturnal*—but might also include the word *predators*, since other readers may not know what that means.

"Let's play around with our own picture glossary to help use remember what they are, what they have, and why they are important. Take out your think pad. Take a minute to sketch the words as best you can, label them with the vocabulary word, and give a really short definition. If you're having trouble, you can work with a partner or come up front for help." I write the words on the board for students. Then, I invite those who are having trouble to come up to the front rug so I can guide them. I show them my quick sketches and we tease out simple definitions.

Students share their quick picture glossaries with each other. "Is there a volunteer who'd allow us to make a copy of her picture glossary so we can post it to remember this text feature?" If there are many volunteers, I pull a random name. We label the picture glossary and its elements with bright sticky notes.

Recap: Key Lesson Steps

1. Reread the article, noting tough vocabulary and context clues

2. Study mentor text's picture glossary

3. Have students create picture glossaries to go with the vocabulary we worked on

4. Share

5. Keep one example for future reference

Wrap Up

"I hope you've learned a little more about picture glossaries today and how they can be beneficial to informational readers. Be sure to use them in your independent reading when you see they are available. (*I make a point of following up, reading aloud other informational texts with picture glossaries, and including such texts in guided reading.*) And, as you write other informative texts, consider including one to help your readers. You'll have this reference from today (the student sample we labeled) to help you if needed."

A Snapshot of Comparing and Contrasting With Narrative Text

A simple way to get young students started comparing and contrasting narrative texts is to first have them master narrative text structure. One effective tool is to maintain a simple story map labeled *setting, characters, problem, solution*. My students and I refer to it whenever we are identifying story elements in our read alouds or shared reads, for example. We start this routine very early in the year, beginning with modeling and then moving to guided practice. After plenty of practice and inclusion of these elements in our conversations about stories, I do some formative checks. Can students easily talk about these elements with peers, using the proper vocabulary? Can students independently sketch narrative text structure on paper, so I know they have a concrete mental picture? Can they fill out a simple Narrative Text Map?

Once students know the basics, they can compare and contrast these elements quite easily. What are the settings of the two texts? How are they alike and different? Who are the characters in the two texts? How are they alike and different? What is the problem in both texts? Are there similarities and differences? How is the problem solved? Similarities, differences? Using sticky notes and a Same/Different chart, as we did in this lesson sequence, will engage students in interacting with two or more texts.

Conversations about story elements can go deeper than surface level comparisons. Students *start* by making observations like "The characters in both books are animals," "One story takes place in a city and the other takes place in the country," and "The problem in both stories is bullying." They're using the foundational knowledge we've set in place and from there, we can work toward more higher-level thinking:

- What characteristics or personality traits do the characters have? How do you know? (Pay attention to what the characters say, do, think, and how they respond to other characters and events in the story.) Now, what do we notice about how the characters are alike and different?

- How do the characters change throughout the course of the story? Are there similarities or differences there?

- How do the characters' personalities affect the way the problems are solved? Are there similarities and differences there?

- How are the themes in the stories the same and different?

For example, in the stories *Stand Tall, Molly Lou Melon* by Patty Lovell and *Hooway for Wodney Wat* by Helen Lester, both characters have disadvantages. Students could start by comparing these (Molly, the shortest girl in first grade, has buck teeth and a horrible voice, and is a klutz. Wodney has a speech impediment and is very shy and quiet from being constantly teased.) But, then, looking deeper, how does Molly handle her differences compared to Wodney? We have to look at what each character says and does to determine this. Molly is confident and outgoing, while Wodney is meek and worn down. He tries to hide inside his jacket. Both are challenged by a bully, and though they handle the adversity in different ways, both are triumphant in the end. (Compare and contrast: How did each character win out over the bully? Do you think their different personality traits affected how this happened in each story? Why?) Finally, it would be challenging to explore this: "Which character changed the most by the end of the story? How do you know?" Students have to synthesize everything they've seen the two characters say and do throughout each book and compare and contrast that information to answer. Likewise, students have to put together all of the events in the two books to analyze their themes. "What life lesson might the authors be trying to teach? How do you know? Are the lessons the same or different?" Now, there's some higher-level thinking!

FYI

How might we make comparing and contrasting narratives purposeful for our learners? I'm always thinking about *why* we do what we do. What authentic purpose does comparing and contrasting serve? With narratives, you might think about having students compare and contrast two stories, then decide which is better so they can recommend it to others. Here's an ongoing activity: Display two books you've read on a shelf for students to compare and contrast. Once it's decided which is better and why (sticky-note sharing, collaborative conversation), students write a recommendation for the class newspaper or website or to post in the library. Even better, students read the summaries of books, compare and contrast, and decide which they'd most like to read as the next class novel or book club pick and why.

Notes

Core Connections
_____

Kindergarten
Reading Informational
   Standard 9
With prompting and support, identify basic similarities and differences between two texts on the same topic (e.g., in illustrations, descriptions, or procedures).

In adapting this sequence for kindergarten, first I limit the number of sources we compare and contrast to just two. We study a modified version of the "Hermit Crab Information" article (see page 183) along with an emergent, informational text: *Pet Hermit Crab* by Robin Nelson (though any early level text on hermit crabs will do). (The videos are a great source, but they primarily contain confirming information, not new information. You might show the videos after comparing and contrasting the two texts, since students enjoy this medium so much.)

When reading the article, we use Thinking Boxes to interact with the text. We read and reread one section at a time, then record our learning in each box. In Box 1, students sketch and jot about hermit crab bodies while I model; then we share. In Box 2, we focus on where hermit crabs live, and in box 3, we jot about what hermit crabs eat. Student responses are more emergent than those of the first graders, but the acts of pausing the reading, rereading a section at a time, discussing, then jotting, sketching, and labeling, plus sharing, all serve to deepen students' understanding.

We also use Thinking Boxes as we work our way through the book. We stop to discuss, jot, sketch, label, and share: Box 1 hermit crabs can be pets in aquariums; Box 2 hermit crabs eat almost anything; Box 3 hermit crabs need water and to keep their bodies wet; Box 4 hermit crabs live and protect themselves in shells.

Rather than sticky notes, we keep a list of similarities and differences on a Venn diagram labeled *article* and *book*. We use interactive writing (sharing the pen) to record on the diagram. I then have students talk out the Venn diagram with a neighbor, so they practice the language of comparing and contrasting (*I model this first and provide a list of helping words:* but, like, too, also, however). If students really struggle, I provide some sentence stems like

In the article we learned _____. But, in the book we learned
_____.

Both the book and article showed _____.

Depending on your students' interest in the topic, you might end the lesson sequence here by simply having a collaborative conversation about what they learned. If students are still highly interested, you could use shared writing to compose an informational text, again, using their Thinking Boxes as a guide, but keeping the text shorter. Of course, kindergartners love cooperatively producing photo stories, too!

What Are Hermit Crabs Like?

Hermit crabs have soft bodies. You wouldn't know that because they hide them inside shells! When they grow, they have to change shells. They find new shells on the sea floor.

They have ten legs, but only six poke out from their shells. The two front legs have claws. One is big and one is small. They use the big claw to tear food and to close the opening of their shells when they hide.

Where Do Hermit Crabs Live?

Hermit crabs can live on land or in the sea.

What Do Hermit Crabs Eat?

Hermit crabs eat food they find on the ground. They eat turtle eggs, dead fish, and fruit. They eat anything they find on the bottom of the sea.

Core Connections

Kindergarten
Reading Literature
  Standard 9

With prompting and support, compare and contrast the adventures and experiences of characters in familiar stories.

You'll notice the kindergarten standard for comparing and contrasting literature asks us to use "familiar stories." Many K teachers use different versions of simple fairy tales like "Goldilocks and the Three Bears" or "The Gingerbread Man." Various versions of the same story make comparing and contrasting an easier task, since the differences tend to jump out at students.

I definitely would not shy away from using other, non-familiar stories for comparing and contrasting, though (see mentor texts on page 196). Obviously, stories can become very familiar after reading and rereading several times! So, don't limit students' experiences based on the language in the standard.

Note: For more ideas on comparing and contrasting literature see A Snapshot of Comparing and Contrasting With Narrative Text on page 180.

Companion Website Resource

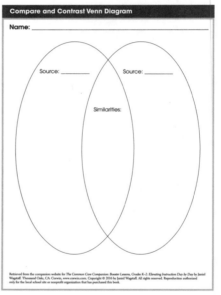

Available for download at www.corwin .com/thecommoncorecompanion

---

Notes

_____
_____
_____
_____
_____
_____

As long as my second graders have had plenty of informational writing experience leading into this lesson sequence, the biggest adaptation I make is to differentiate how we complete the informational writing at the end. The comparing and contrasting described in the sequence as is, hits the standard perfectly and even reaches beyond it (since we compared three sources).

I give students the choice. If they'd like to work on a shared piece with me, I invite them to the rug area to engage in shared writing, using the same procedure I use with the first graders. If they'd like instead, they can work on their own piece independently or with a partner. The guidelines include that they must still use the three categories of information we decided on when we categorized our sticky notes, though they may word these headings any way they wish, and they need some type of introduction and conclusion.

If students are even further along, I open the experience up to even more choice and responsibility by inviting them to work individually or with a partner to compare and contrast sources (two or three) on an entirely different topic. They are required to find the sources and run them by me, but then they can use a similar process to what we did during the sequence, comparing and contrasting using sticky notes, sorting their notes to categorize, deciding on headings, and drafting text.

Note: For ideas on comparing and contrasting literature see: A Snapshot of Comparing and Contrasting With Narrative Text on page 180 and Authentic Assessment on page 190.

> ## Core Connections
>
> **Grade 2**
> **Reading Informational**
> **   Standard 9**
> Compare and contrast the most important points presented by two texts on the same topic.

Notes

Katlyn and Harlan reread an informative text about hermit crabs. Even a little bit of daily rereading adds up! I'm also excited they want to reconnect with the information!

What's ahead:

What Do I See?
A Sample of Shared Writing

Our first grade shared writing was completed in sections over several days.

> **Hermit Crabs**
> We learned about hermit crabs. **BODY** Did you Know hermit crabs live in a shells? When they grow bigger, they will find a new shells. Inside the shells they have long, soft bodies. They have ten legs altogether and use six of them to walk. We wonder what it would be like to have ten legs!

> **Habitat** Do you know where hermit crabs live? They live in the ocean and walk on the sea floor. Would you like to live in the ocean? They also live on land.
> **FOOD** Do you know what hermit crabs eat? They eat turtle eggs, dead fish, fruit that falls from trees and almost anything! Yummy! Would you eat dead fish? No!

> It was sure fun learning about hermit crabs. Would you like to be a hermit crab?

The first characteristic of the writing that stands out is its structure. We worked together using headings to keep our facts and details focused and organized. The use of headings is a great organizational strategy first graders can grasp to help them write their own informational texts.

This shared-writing piece becomes a valuable model to keep and refer to for future writing. We can use it to remind us of valuable text features for informational writing (though certainly more of these could be added), how to use headings to organize a piece, and even the pattern of using questions to introduce and conclude the piece and varied sections. Once a piece like this is done, it's very effective to go back with students and vibrantly label (i.e., fluorescent-colored sticky notes) these elements for future reference.

Notice the revision and editing. Modeled, shared, and interactive writing are the most effective ways to teach these processes. Students need to see that we reread and reread and reread as we compose. This leads us to make changes as we go or find mistakes and fix them. We changed the verb from past to present, then kept that parallel throughout the piece. We changed *shell* to *shells* to go along with the plural subject *they* and took out the *a*. I don't use the technical grammatical terms with first graders, but I can point out how "They have shells" makes sense and "They have shell" does not. In terms of revision, though it's hard for you to see, we actually decided to add more voice when we were two-thirds through the piece. That's when we went back and added "We wonder" and the "Would you . . . " questions at the end of each section, which led us to the structure of our conclusion.

What Do I See?
A Student Sample of Thinking Boxes

These Thinking Boxes were completed by Caleb, a first grader, during this lesson sequence. Remember, though I modeled up front, students were encouraged to jot, sketch, and label what *they* thought the most important information in each category was. This was a useful way for students to prioritize their learning and rehearse for writing.

Caleb has a good handle on some critical details for the three main ideas. In Box 1 he uses lines to indicate what he is labeling (a common feature of diagrams), and an arrow to show how the hermit crab is moving to the bigger shell.

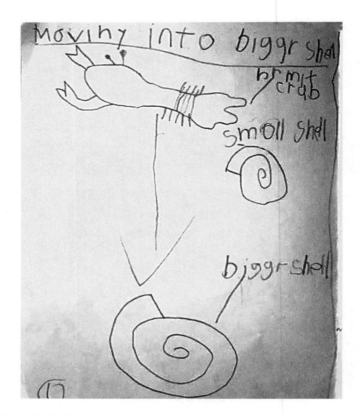

Thinking Box 1: Bodies

"Moving into bigger shell

hermit crab

small shell

bigger shell"

Thinking Box 2: Habitat

"10 legs / a hermit crab / can live in the / ocean / or / land"

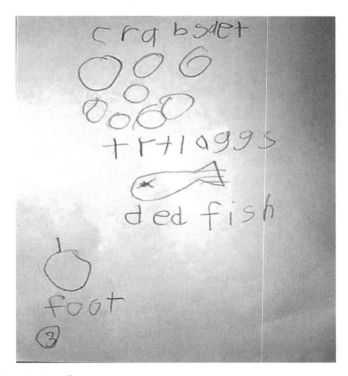

Thinking Box 3: Food

"crabs eat / turtle eggs / dead fish / fruit"

I needed to check with Caleb about where he included the information "10 legs." It doesn't fit in Box 2, where hermit crabs live (notice, this is the only box without a heading; maybe this is what threw him off—those headings are valuable tools!).

When students rehearse for writing by talking out their notes, they practice composing whole sentences aloud. As I listened to Caleb talk it out, I noticed he still needed guidance on this concept. When he moved from Box 1 to Box 2, he simply said, "Ten legs." I said, "Ten legs what? Or what has ten legs?" With this feedback, he was able to restate that fact in a complete sentence.

Authentic Assessment:
Ideas for Evaluating Students' Learning

Teachers often ask me how to assess Reading Informational Standard 9 (along with Reading Literature Standard 9), which expects students to be able to identify basic similarities in and differences between two texts on the same topic. I remind them that it can be sufficient for students to merely sort their notes into rows labeled *Same* and *Different*. After all, students don't have to *write* to meet the standard, they only need to compare and contrast the informative or literary elements included therein.

However, if you think your students are ready to compare and contrast in writing, and you want to use it as an assessment, consider having students independently fill in a Venn diagram following reading. Another way is to have students write a short summary paragraph in which they compare and contrast (I recommend you do this second grade and beyond). But remember, in order to do either of these as an assessment task, students have to have had plenty of prior practice with both.

Following is an example of a Venn diagram filled out by Luke, a first grader. The class read *Boy + Bot* by Ame Dyckman and *Those Shoes* by Maribeth Boelts. Since I wanted to use the Venn diagram as an assessment tool for standard 9, I didn't discuss or have students pair-share about similarities and differences. We did have a conversation about the possible themes, though. In looking at Luke's independent work, you can easily see he is skilled at comparing and contrasting. He notes the characters Boy and Bot and Jeremy and Antonio as being different, though similar in that they are all boys. He notes the problems are different (he wrote about two in each book) and that in one story there is a resolution but in the other, there really isn't. Last, he even noted a similarity

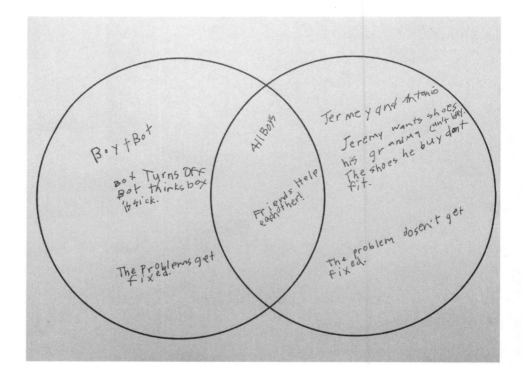

in the themes across the two texts: "Friends help each other!" I say he has a firm grasp on standard 9! (Again, these students had lots of prior experience with Venn diagrams, making this a fair assessment to give.)

Another type of authentic assessment is to judge students' abilities to compare and contrast in oral conversation. Keeping anecdotal records or observational data can be challenging. You need plenty of opportunities to observe every student and a form for keeping data.

Companion Website Resource

Observational Chart				
Student Name	Date	Topic/Text	Compare	Contrast

 Available for download at www.corwin .com/thecommoncorecompanion

Peer Power:
Using Student Work as Mentor Texts

Second grader Dax writes about reading the book *Dear Primo* by Duncan Tonatiun (see a sample of his work, retraced in pen for readability, on the facing page). In this book, two cousins, one living in America and one living in Mexico, write letters back and forth to each other about their lives. It has a simple-to-follow compare and contrast structure, so students are generally successful talking and writing about what's the same and what's different.

In using Dax's writing as a mentor, I would call attention to his very clear introduction. The reader knows we will be hearing about childhood customs in Mexico and the United States. Dax introduces the subject of each sentence then uses the words *but* and *and* to compare and contrast. He uses this sentence structure throughout the writing: "Notice, writers, how Dax sticks with this structure: 'Carlito rides a bike to school, **but** Charlie takes a subway. At recess, Carlito plays futbol, **but** Charlie plays basketball.' Since Dax uses this same pattern over and over, it's easy to understand the comparing and contrasting examples."

If you make a copy of the students' work before showing it under the document camera,* the student can stand by and highlight the points you are making. For example, Dax could highlight the introduction as we talk about it, and the *buts* as we address his sentence structure.

*Note: Often, if the writing is informal, the students will agree to highlight or make notations right on his original copy. Obviously, this decision depends on what will happen with the writing next.

In conferencing with Dax, I point out the "*and* monster," as I call it. Since it's not a good idea to start sentences with *and* in general (we all know how young writers often fall into the trap of starting every sentence with *and*), I show him how to cross it out and start the sentence with the next word instead. This requires rereading to make sure the change makes sense, but it often works. Since so many students need the same lesson, I create a short piece with the "*and* monster" problem. I project it and talk with the students about making revisions. Another way to handle this is to keep samples from year to year, remove the names, and use these to show how to correct writing problems during targeted lessons.

Another point for Dax to consider is to define the Mexican terms he refers to. Those who have not read *Dear Primo* may not know what *futbol*, *The Day of the Dead*, or *Las Posadas* are. He could add some details about these to really help readers understand the differences.

Lastly, with Dax's permission, the class could brainstorm how he might conclude his compare/contrast piece. Although it is always helpful to get input from other writers, he has the final say about what he'll do next.

In Dear primo we learned about the customs of kids in Mexico and the United States Carlito rides a bike to school but Charlie takes a subway undergound to get to school. And at recess Carlito plays futball but Charlie plays basket ball. On the weekend Carlito goes to the open air market but Charlie goes to the super-

market. But Carlito celebrates the day of the dead and posads And Charlie celebrates Thanksgiving and halloween. And Charlie gets a slice of pizza before going home. But when Carlitos gets home he makes quesadillas.

If/Then Chart

If students are struggling to compare and contrast,

- Compare and contrast with concrete objects such as colored pattern blocks, felt pieces, and fruit, for example. Make sure students understand the concepts of same and different.

- Compare and contrast pictures, starting with simple images first, then moving to the more complex.

- Simplify. Work on just *comparing* across two text or sources. Once students are proficient at finding similarities, start looking for differences.

- Constantly model. Infuse your daily think alouds with connection making. This is one way to compare experiences and texts and immerse students in this kind of thinking.

- Practice with oral language first. Provide students with a list of helpful compare/contrast words (but, like, too, also, both, however, whereas, only one) and sentence frames to scaffold their oral language (In the article we learned _____. But, in the book we learned _____. Both the book and article showed _____.)

- Limit the number of sources to compare and contrast.

- Start with sources that have a compare and contrast structure where similarities and differences jump out at students (see mentor texts on page 196).

- Compare and contrast the literal and concrete, not items that require thinking beyond the text like characters' motivations or themes. Move to this level when students are more skilled.

- Use the Venn diagram as a staple. It's easier to compare and contrast on a chart like this than on sticky notes. As students work in a Venn diagram, they can quickly see what information they have (for example, they may have several differences) and what information they need to go back in and look for.

- Stick with the same graphic organizer. Rather than giving students many different organizers to use for comparing and contrasting, stick with just the Venn diagram. Sticking with one is less confusing, builds in necessary repetition, and helps students create an image of the structure in long-term memory.

If/Then Chart

If motivation to compare and contrast is waning,	• Compare and contrast in a different genre. If you've been comparing and contrasting with informative sources for a while, switch to narrative. • Give students more choice. Once students have more skills, let them choose two books to compare and contrast, even if they stick to the basics like settings, characters, problems, and solutions. You might be surprised by what they can do! • Find ways to make comparing and contrasting text purposeful. Can students compare and contrast two books on the same topic and suggest one of the books for purchase to the librarian or principal based on what they find? Can they recommend a book to a neighboring class based on a compare and contrast of information ("We think you'll learn the most from this book because . . .") or based on how a problem was solved or the theme of a narrative? • Let students compare and contrast with sticky notes they place right inside books. Make sure they share their findings with peers!
If students are excelling,	• Allow them to compare and contrast sources of their own choosing. Have them show you the sources they've found before they launch into the work. How will they compare and contrast? What will they do with their findings?
If you have English language learners,	• Have these students work with a partner to jot sticky notes and to sort the notes into categories. • Encourage them to rely on your model more heavily as they create their own Thinking Boxes. • Meet in small groups to support them as they talk out their Thinking Boxes. Model turning one jot, sketch, or label into a sentence. Have students repeat your sentence. Continue one piece at a time. • Use sentence frames to scaffold their speaking and writing.

Mentor Texts

The following texts have a compare/contrast structure built right in!

Biggest, Strongest, Fastest by Steve Jenkins: As the title suggests, this book compares and contrasts animals that are the biggest, strongest, and fastest. Each animal is compared to something children can relate to. For example, the ant's amazing strength is compared to a man's. There are also direct comparisons. The blue whale, the largest animal that has ever lived, is followed by the Etruscan shrew, the smallest mammal, which can sleep in a teaspoon.

Other Steve Jenkins's titles are perfect for comparing and contrasting, including *Actual Size, Just a Second, What Would You Do With a Tail Like This?, What Do You Do When Something Wants to Eat You?, Sisters and Brothers, Eye to Eye*, and *The Beetle Book*.

Dear Primo by Duncan Tonatiun: Here you have the story of two cousins. One lives in America and one in Mexico. They write letters back and forth and in so doing, compare and contrast all aspects of their lives. I love the inclusion of the Spanish words.

National Geographic Readers: Cats vs. Dogs by Elizabeth Carney: Here again, within one book, you have a whole lotta comparing and contrasting going on! Since kids love dogs and cats, you'll have no trouble with engagement with this one! The table of contents is a great aid in pointing you to aspects of cat- and dog-ness you may want to analyze. I bet you'll learn something even you didn't know!

Same, Same, but Different by Jenny Sue Kostecki-Shaw: Like *Dear Primo*, two pen pals, one from America, one from India, find out how their lives are different and the same through their letters. There's a lot to compare and contrast in the beautiful collage illustrations.

Shark vs. Train by Chris Barton: Whereas the titles above present real information, this one is crazy fantasy. Hilarious scenarios ensue as Shark and Train challenge each other to various contests. Lots of opportunities to compare and contrast! My favorite comparison comes when neither Shark nor Train can score at videogames because, similarly, neither of them has thumbs!

Town Mouse, Country Mouse by Jan Brett: A different take on the traditional tale with Brett's amazing illustrations to entertain and delight.

Who Would Win? series by Jerry Pallotta: Pallotta pits one animal against another, and in so doing, sets up the perfect compare and contrast texts. Though there isn't a table of contents at the beginning, there is a checklist of topics to compare on the last page. This can serve as a way to focus students' attention on particular items you'd like to have them compare and contrast. Boys especially like this series!

The following are some of my favorite texts to use for comparing and contrasting:

KatKong and *Dogzilla* by Dav Pilkey: Compare and contrast characters, plot, and endings in these humorous tales of the mice citizens of Mousopolis versus the enormous cat and dog beasts.

Mousetronaut and *Mousetronaut Goes to Mars* by Mark Kelly: Compare the two creative tales of Meteor, the mouse who goes into space, twice!

Stellaluna by Janell Cannon: Compare and contrast birds and bats!

Where the Wild Things Are by Maurice Sendak and *The Salamander Room* by Anne Mazer: Compare and contrast the boys' character traits, their imaginations, the illustrations (how nature grows to fill their rooms), and story endings.

Books by Robert Munsch: Compare common elements across his many books: the mischievous main characters, zany secondary characters, the repetition of lines, and his use of onomatopoeia.

Series

Books in a series provide plenty of opportunities to compare and contrast. I suggest jumping on the series your students are most interested in. Here are some that have been student favorites in my classrooms over the years:

A to Z Mysteries by Ron Roy

Click, Clack, _____ by Doreen Cronin

Diary of a _____ by Doreen Cronin

Don't Let the Pigeon_____ by Mo Williams

I Know an Old Lady Who Swallowed a_____ by Lucille Colandro

If You Give a _____ a _____ by Laura Numeroff

The Black Lagoon series by Mike Thaler

Captain Underpants and the Ricky Ricotta series by Dav Pilkey

Flat Stanley series by Jeff Brown

Fly Guy series by Tedd Arnold

Magic Tree House series by Mary Pope Osborne

Extending the Work

Let's open up more choice and independence. Remember, the standard we're focused on is comparing and contrasting across texts. This means students can compare and contrast what they see in illustrations, pictures, and photographs, and still be working toward the standard. They can do the work orally and still be moving toward the standard. Obviously, getting them to write about similarities and differences pushes them even further.

The extensions below allow students to choose what they will compare and contrast and who they will work with. If this makes you nervous, I must tell you, I've done this with kindergarten students with astonishing success. They get very excited when they see all the sources and choices, and they relish working with others to find similarities and differences. Sharing their findings ups the motivation even further!

LESSONS	READING Speaking and Listening	WRITING Speaking and Listening
6	**Lesson 6:** *Peruse Sources* • Bring in a variety of sources on animals (make sure there are a least two sources on each animal): books, magazines, articles. Invite students to bring in sources, as well. • Have students peruse sources. • What jumps out as the same and different? • Discuss.	**Lesson 6:** *Pick a Topic, Compare and Contrast Visuals* • Have students pick a source and topic, find another source on a matching animal. • Have students choose to work alone, with a partner, or group of three. • Have students peruse the two sources together. • What is the same and different in the illustrations, photos, charts, or diagrams? • Jot notes on sticky notes, place them in the sources.
7	**Lesson 7:** *Share Findings and Read* • Talk about the similarities and differences in the illustrations, photos, charts, or diagrams with a peer or another twosome or threesome. • Dig into the text. Use the table of contents, headings, and topic sentences to guide what you choose to read.	**Lesson 7:** *Compare and Contrast Info in Text* • Note similarities and differences in the words and text. • Jot notes on sticky notes, place them in sources.
8	**Lesson 8:** *Share Findings* • Talk about the similarities and differences in the words and text with a peer or another twosome or threesome.	**Lesson 8:** *Summarize Findings* • Have students draw a diagram of their animal, labeling the information they've learned from comparing and contrasting their sources. • Have students write a short summary of your findings. • (This may take more than one session.)

LESSONS	**READING** Speaking and Listening	**WRITING** Speaking and Listening
9	**Lesson 9:** *Present* • Divide the class into four or five groups. Students share their diagram or summary with the group. • If you can, videotape snippets of the presentations and share them on your class Web page.	**Lesson 9:** *Collaborative Conversation* • Discuss this process. What was easy? What was hard? Would students repeat this process for any reason? What other audience may be interested in hearing students' findings?
10	**Lesson 10:** *Peruse Sources* • Bring in a variety of fairy tales and fractured fairy tales. Invite students to bring in sources, as well. • Have students peruse sources. • What jumps out as the same and different? • Discuss.	**Lesson 10:** *Pick a Tale and Compare and Contrast Illustrations* • Pick a fairy tale and a matching source (either a different version of the fairy tale or a fractured version of the fairy tale). • Have students choose to work alone, with a partner, or group of three. (Grouping will depend on how many sources you have. If all students need to work in small groups of three based on source availability, that is OK.) • Peruse the stories. • What is the same and different in the illustrations? • Jot notes on sticky notes, place them in the books.
11	**Lesson 11:** *Share Findings and Read* • Talk about the similarities and differences in the illustrations with a peer or another twosome or threesome. • Read the stories.	**Lesson 11:** *Compare and Contrast Text* • Note similarities and differences in the words and text. • Jot notes on sticky notes and place them in books.
12	**Lesson 12:** *Share Findings* • Talk about the similarities and differences in the words and text with a peer or another twosome or threesome.	**Lesson 12:** *Represent Learning or Invent Something New* • Have students draw an event or scene from one story. Label how the other story was different. • Have students write a short summary of how the stories were alike and different. • Write your own version of the story. You may include things that are the same and different from the versions you read! • (This may take more than one session.)
13	**Lesson 13:** *Present* • Divide the class into four or five groups. Have students share their drawings, summary, or story with the group. • If you can, videotape snippets of the presentations and share them on your class Web page.	**Lesson 13:** *Collaborative Conversation* • Again, debrief about the process and consider what other audience may be interested in hearing students' presentations?

Integrating Informative Writing With Use of Text Features

Andy talks out his notes on Caine to rehearse for writing.

In this lesson sequence, students learn to write to inform with purpose and structure. Their purpose is to read and then view media closely to become experts about an interesting topic so they can share their findings with the rest of the student body. They use the structure and features of a newspaper article as the format for their publications.

This sequence is designed for second grade, although imitating a structure is a useful strategy for helping kindergartners and first graders compose informative texts (see grade-level adaptations on pages 230–233).

This ambitious sequence could occur later in the year after students have done other informative and explanatory writing. Students already understand the purpose of informative texts and have engaged in shared projects, investigating and writing about topics as a class. They've read closely, taken notes, organized findings in graphic organizers, and shared short speeches with partners and small groups on assorted topics. They've also independently written short, informative pieces. Along the way, they've learned to recognize common text features that support informative writing, though using these features in their own writing hasn't been an instructional goal.

The sequence builds from this base, focusing on using learned processes (reading closely, taking notes, organizing thinking, talking it out, writing) and ups the ante by charging students with tackling text *and* media to gather information, using simple text features in their independent writing, and producing more formalized products (individual newspaper articles) that will be printed and publicly shared.

In kindergarten and first grade, an even wider base of experiences with informative texts would be wise before tackling a task like this one, though a class might publish a shared newspaper article. Teachers might differentiate, especially in first grade, by working with a small group of individuals that are ready, again after much prior experience, to take on such a task independently. Regardless of the final product, the processes described within the sequence can be adapted for K and first-grade informative work (see pages 230–233).

Core Connections

Focus Writing Standard 2 integrated with Reading Informational Standard 5
Reading Informational Standards 1, 2, 3, and 6
Writing Standards 5, and 8
Speaking and Listening Standards 1, 2, and 6

Task

You will write an informational article about Caine for classroom newspaper. How did Caine use his imagination? How did Caine and his friend Nirvan change the world? Copies of the newspaper articles will be available to our whole student body.

What Teachers Guide Across the Week

LESSONS	READING Speaking and Listening	WRITING Speaking and Listening
1	**Lesson 1:** *Reading With Purpose and an Eye for Evidence* • Review the task. • Identify purposes for reading. • Read informational article once for gist, secondly for strategic highlighting of evidence. • Model and think aloud, gradually releasing responsibility to students.	**Lesson 1:** *Two-Column Notes* • Have students create two-column notes: one column for each writing target or main idea. • Have students revisit the article, noting highlights. • Have students jot notes in appropriate columns. • Model and think aloud, gradually releasing responsibility to students.
2	**Lesson 2:** *Close Reading of Media: Caine's Arcade Video 1* • View Caine's Arcade Video 1 all the way through. • Discuss general understandings.	**Lesson 2:** *Revisit Media and Add to Two-Column Notes* • Rewatch video 1, stopping at strategic points. • Have students discuss and add notes to appropriate columns. • Model and think aloud, gradually releasing responsibility to students (if appropriate).
3	**Lesson 3:** *Close Reading of Media: Sections of Caine's Arcade Video 2* • View selected segments of Caine's Arcade Video 2. • Discuss general understandings.	**Lesson 3:** *Two-Column Notes Additions, Organizing Notes, Talking Out Caine's Story* • Rewatch selected segments of Video 2. • Have students discuss and add to notes. • Have students reread notes, numbering them in sequential order. • Have students talk out Caine's story with partners. • Model and think aloud, gradually releasing responsibility to students.
4	**Lesson 4:** *Study Mentor Texts: Newsela Newspaper Articles* • Identify text features of newspaper articles. • Label text features and discuss their purposes. • Model and think aloud, gradually releasing responsibility to students.	**Lesson 4:** *Compose Headlines, Headings, and Begin to Draft* • Have students brainstorm and pick headline. • Have students brainstorm and pick two headings. • Have students talk out Caine's story using two-column notes. • Model beginning to draft. • Have students begin to draft.
5	**Lesson 5:** *Exploring Deeper Meanings: Caine's Arcade Updates and Conversation* • Shared Reading: Updates from Caine's Arcade website • Collaborative conversation: What can we learn from Caine's story? Considering all the facts, what deeper meanings might we find? • (Students have think and jot time before conversation.)	**Lesson 5:** *Finish Draft, Peer Check, Teacher Conference, Publish!* • Model throughout the process. • Have students finish drafts. • Have students check with peer using Peer Checklist. • Confer with writers. • Publish on newspaper template. • Publicize (announcement) and make copies available to the study body.

What Students Do Across the Week

Students focus on learning about an interesting topic by closely reading an informative article and viewing primary source videos. They analyze a prompt to determine their writing targets and work to find and note details about these main ideas. Since they'll ultimately write newspaper articles and share them with the school, they study mentor articles to understand and use their main features. It's a grand celebration when they announce their publication to the school and distribute their articles!

Literacy Moves

- Identify writing targets from a prompt
- Read and write for informative purposes
- Read text and media closely and take notes on text evidence
- Use primary sources
- Draft with ongoing revision
- Engage in collaborative conversations
- Conference with partners and teacher
- Share, celebrate, publish, and publicize

Caine Monroy is a real boy who became famous for his creative use of cardboard. His story is perfect to study with students since it centers around engaging content (what kid wouldn't like their own cardboard arcade?) and leaves them thinking about deeper meanings like making a difference in the world or helping others, for example. Given this content, students happily invest in reading and rereading, viewing and re-viewing, note-taking, organizing notes, drafting, conferencing, revising, editing, and publishing! This is writing worth taking the extra time and effort to publish and share with an outside audience.

As always, we keep the writing focused. Since we work together to identify the two writing targets, we stay glued to finding details about these main ideas throughout the course of our work. This helps the students have more success as they organize content and write about it.

Additionally, we take the study of text features to another level by including them in our writing. Students have seen titles (in this case, headlines), headings, pictures, and captions, as well as other text features before. They've studied their purposes in informative texts. Now, they are charged with composing and utilizing their own. Though this is more challenging than you might think (especially coming up with appropriate headings), it is well worth the struggle since students get a much firmer grip on text features when they have to create and use them in their own writing.

When the newspaper articles are ready, students publicize their work by making an announcement to the school over the loudspeaker. This is a purposeful, if a bit scary, speaking opportunity: one that is naturally connected to the overall task—and to speaking and listening standards. Students are really excited the day their articles are received by the student body.

As is true for all of the lesson sequences, final reflection is critical. I want students to generalize their learning: Which of these processes will be most helpful for informative writing in the future? They're asked to make a quick list or write a short paragraph about the most important things they've learned. In K and first grade, we reflect orally, creating a short list together that we can come back to in the future.

As noted earlier, this is an ambitious project. Keep in mind the processes involved are more important than the final outcome. Students take away a great deal of meaningful learning from this sequence and the extended work that may follow!

Reading With Purpose
and an Eye for Evidence

Getting Ready

The materials:

- Copy of the task (page 200) to display
- Kid-friendly definition of what informative writers do
- Copy of article for each student: "Caine Monroy: A Boy With an Imagination"* (see page 209)
- Document camera
- Highlighters: two colors

*Note: As I wrote this article based on my own research of Caine Monroy, I purposefully did not include headings. In Companion Writing Lesson 4, students are charged with creating their own headings and I did not want them to simply copy them from the article.

Context of the Lesson

Students must understand the task so they have a clear purpose for reading. We study the task carefully to identify the purpose and the main writing targets (or the main ideas students will be writing about). Students need to understand that as informative writers they must be focused and accurate, especially since they will be publishing information. To that end, we review our definition of what informative writers do. We read the article once to get the gist of Caine's story then reread a second time to highlight strategically.

The Lesson

"I'm so excited about what we'll be doing next as readers, writers, listeners, speakers, and thinkers! We're going to be reading and viewing information about a very special boy then sharing what he did with our whole school! Let's look at our task carefully so we understand what we'll be doing. (*Point to the task and read it aloud to students.*)

"We'll be writing newspaper articles. Don't worry about how to write them specifically yet, we'll study some examples and figure that out before we draft. In the articles we write, we'll be focused on two things, can you find what they are? Tell your neighbor. (*After quick sharing*) Yes, we'll be writing about how Caine used his imagination and how Caine and his friend changed the world (*underlining sections of the task*). Who will our audience be? Share. (*After quick sharing*) Yep, our whole school will have the chance to read our articles! (*Allow time for* ews *and* ahs!)

"So, writers, we'll be studying information then sharing what we've learned as informative writers. Let's review our description of what informative writers do."

Informative Writers . . .

- **Become experts about their topic**

- **Stay focused**

- **Write clearly and accurately**

- **Share what they learn!**

 Available for download at www.corwin.com/the commoncorecompanion

"We've done this kind of writing before, but we haven't shared with such a wide audience. Discuss with your neighbor your thoughts about this project."

(*I listen in, share highlights, and discuss any questions or concerns.*) "Sounds like you are as excited as I am and you don't even know who Caine is yet! So, let's dive into an informative article and see what we can find out about him, how he used his imagination and changed the world. This first read will be to get the gist of who Caine is and what he did."

I display the article on the document camera and read it aloud, inviting students to read with me as they follow in their own copies. We make few stops during this reading: once about half way through for a pair-share and formative check, "Discuss what you've learned so far with your neighbor," and once again at the end.

Next, we have a quick conversation about whether or not this information is relevant and interesting enough to share with the student body (thus, reviewing purpose). The students are excited about what they've learned during our gist reading. (Essentially, at age nine, Caine built his own cardboard arcade using boxes and tape. A special customer came and was so impressed that he made a video of Caine's Arcade and put it on the Internet. The video became very popular, inspiring kids from all over the world to create fun games from old stuff. Now there is a Cardboard Challenge each year to encourage people to use their creativity just like Caine did.) If you study Caine with your class, I'm confident your students will be thrilled about the idea of becoming "Caine Experts" and sharing his motivating story.

For our second read, we review our writing targets (*again, I underline these questions in the task: how Caine used his imagination and how Caine and his friend changed the world*) and how we'll have to reread closely to find precise information about these main ideas. I begin by modeling and thinking aloud, reminding students how to sift through information in the article, and strategically highlight the most important details (*we've worked with information in this way many times before*).

"As an informative writer, I have to read and reread this article carefully, looking for important details about my targets. I'm thinking about our first focus: How did Caine use his imagination? I remember this is written about in the first few paragraphs of the text. So, let's go back, reread together, and I'll think aloud as we go. I'll also highlight the most important words. Let's use yellow for this target or main idea, so we can easily find information again when we take notes later.

"In this first paragraph, I'm learning that Caine made his own arcade. The first three sentences tell about that and even end with the exact words 'to make his very own arcade!' (*I highlight these words.*) As I read on, I see it says exactly what he used: boxes and tape from his dad's car parts store (*I highlight the words* boxes, car parts store, *and* tape). That is the focus of this paragraph and it's the gist of what Caine did.

"The second paragraph (*rereading quickly while tracking*), tells me about the first game he made, how he made it, and that he went on to make other games. So, what is important there in terms of 'how Caine used his imagination'? It would be interesting to share a bit about his first game and how he made it and I read that right here (*I highlight the words* first game, basketball hoop, box *and* taped the hoop). Plus, it's pretty important that he went on to make more games or he wouldn't have ended up with an arcade (*I highlight 'kept making new ones'*).

"Readers, are you noticing how I'm highlighting just a few words or phrases? Remember, we try to highlight strategically like this, not highlight whole chunks of text, so that when we go back, we can find information easily, and when we write, it's much easier to put details into our own words.

"Let's read this next paragraph together. What is the main idea here? What may be important for our first writing target?" We read together, discuss the main idea (Caine created other imaginative things for his arcade, but he didn't have any customers), and highlight.

"We're already to the middle of the first page of the article. Let's read this paragraph together, again figuring out the main idea of this section and if any of the information is important for our purposes."

After reading together, a student shares what he thinks is the main idea and why, pointing to text evidence under the document camera. Then we note, "Look! We have some important information about our second writing target (how Caine and his friend changed the world). If Nirvan Mullick hadn't come to the store, hadn't seen Caine's arcade and been so impressed, a video wouldn't have been made and all the other events that followed would not have happened!" Students independently highlight (this time, with green since this is the second main idea) and pair-share what they've noted. I highlight just the word *video*.

This process continues throughout the remainder of the article. We proceed paragraph by paragraph, noting the main idea of each paragraph and highlighting details relevant

Time Crunched?

Stop here and continue this work the following day during a second reading session. You might also need to chunk the work into two sessions if your students are losing stamina.

to our writing targets. I give students as much support as needed for success, but I gradually back away, allowing volunteers to come forward, share their thinking under the document camera, and receive feedback.

Recap: Key Lesson Steps

1. Study the task to determine purpose, audience, format, and writing targets
2. Review what informative writers do
3. Read article once to get the gist of the information
4. Reread to identify the main idea of each paragraph and highlight text evidence on writing targets
5. Model and gradually release responsibility to students, if appropriate

Wrap Up

"Thankfully, there are other sources of information about Caine that we can study to learn even more. It's important to study several sources and confirm facts if we're going to be Caine experts and write newspaper articles about him. Why might it help to examine a few different sources? *(Students share ideas.)* Today, we've done a good job of figuring out the main ideas of the article we read and highlighting details that go along with our two writing targets. Now, we'll use our highlights to take some notes to help us organize and remember our thinking."

Notes

Two-Column Notes

Getting Ready

The materials:

- Students' own copy of their highlighted article
- Document camera
- Think pads or scratch paper for notes
- Chart paper

Context of the Lesson

Students have already completed two readings of the informative article "Caine Monroy: A Boy With an Imagination." We've studied it closely together, identifying the main idea of each paragraph and highlighting key details that go along with our writing targets. Now, we need to better organize the information we've identified and take notes so we can remember our thinking and prepare for writing.

The Lesson

"We have a lot of information about how Caine used his imagination and how he changed the world just from this one article. We've been highlighting in two colors, our first writing target in yellow and our second in green, so we've already done some organizing. Let's create two-column notes that we can add to when we watch the videos on Caine's website. In the first column, we'll put key details that answer the question, 'How did Caine use his imagination?' and in the second column we'll put key details that answer the question, 'How did Caine and his friend Nirvan change the world?' We'll work on one target at a time."

I model and think aloud, jumping right to the highlights in the article. "As I look at my highlights, I have another chance to rethink, 'Is this important and really focused on how Caine changed the world?' If it is, I can make a quick note. Notice, it's helpful to strategically highlight like we did because our notes are pretty much done for us. If we highlight whole sentences, we still have to figure out what key word or words to jot in our notes." I continue through the first few examples, thinking aloud. Students then add to the first column in their notes.

"Now, let's work on the second column together. Our green highlights detail how Caine and his friend changed the world. Who would like to come forward, reread, and evaluate their first highlight and jot a note in column 2?" A volunteer comes forward, places his work under the document camera, and I guide the process as needed. When the volunteer is finished, students work on their own notes as I circulate and provide assistance. We continue in this manner until we have completed our second column of notes.

Core Connections

Grade 2

Reading Informational Standard 1

Ask and answer such questions as *who, what, where, when, why,* and *how* to demonstrate understanding of key details in a text. *(We reexamine our highlights in the article to verify these details are important to our targets.)*

Writing Standard 8

Gather information from provided sources to answer a question *(creating written notes in two columns: key details about our two writing targets).*

Speaking and Listening Standard 2

Recount or describe key ideas or details from a text read aloud. *(Students retell Caine's story using their notes.)*

Speaking and Listening Standard 6

Produce complete sentences when appropriate to task and situation *(talk it out in full sentences).*

Core Practices

- Revisit the Text
- Modeling
- Note-Taking
- Gradual Release
- Pair-Share
- Talk-It-Out
- Discussion

"We've completed our notes from the first article. Let's turn to a partner, as we often do, and talk out our notes, reviewing what we've learned about Caine so far." (If your students are not accustomed to 'talking-out' their understandings in whole sentences, you'll have to model and have them practice. Be sure to give them feedback on this process. See A Snapshot of the Talk-It-Out Strategy, on page 30.)

Recap: Key Lesson Steps

1. Reexamine highlights in the article
2. Create two-column notes on writing targets
3. Model and gradually release responsibility to students, if appropriate
4. Share with a partner, talking out what's been learned in whole sentences

Wrap Up

We debrief about the processes we've undergone so far as we've worked toward the task. We might even chart these in list form. (For example, study the task, determine writing targets, determine form and audience, and read information to get the gist. Reread information looking for key details that answer questions about the topic. Strategically highlight key details in different colors. Jot notes in columns, one column for each main idea or writing target.) We discuss: What has been important about each step? Would you use these processes in the future? When? Why?

Notes

Caine Monroy: A Boy With an Imagination

Caine Monroy spent his summer vacation putting his imagination to good use. Caine always loved going to arcades and playing games. So, the 9-year-old decided to make his very own arcade! He used boxes from his dad's car parts store, lots of tape, and creativity.

For his first game, Caine used a small plastic basketball hoop he won at an arcade. He cut the front off a box and taped the hoop to the back. Stand back and shoot! You're playing mini-basketball! Caine loved his game so he kept making new ones. He used the space in the front of his dad's store to set up the arcade.

Caine's imagination didn't stop there. He made a prize wall and had tickets for his games. He made and hung signs for "Caine's Arcade" and he patiently waited for customers. But, none came.

One day, a very special customer stopped by. His name was Nirvan Mullick. He needed something from the car parts store, but when he saw Caine's creation he had to stop and talk to him. He ended up buying a "Fun Pass." Nirvan was impressed with Caine's imagination and his arcade, so he asked Caine's dad if he could make a video to help bring more customers in to play.

Nirvan put the video on the Internet and the rest is history. Caine's Arcade became very popular. He had a lot of customers! So Nirvan and Caine decided to try to help other people use their imaginations.

Have you heard of the Annual Cardboard Challenge? Each October, schools, families, and other groups around the world challenge people to build things using cardboard and other stuff. Then, they share their creations. The Cardboard Challenge has become very popular in just a few years. Many kids from countries all around the world participate. Thanks to Caine Monroy, more people are now using their imaginations to invent something new. And, that's fun to do!

Close Reading of Media: Caine's Arcade Video 1

Getting Ready

The materials:

- Caine's Arcade Short Film (Video 1): http://cainesarcade.com

Core Connections

Grade 2
Reading Informational Standard 1

Ask and answer such questions as *who, what, where, when, why,* and *how* to demonstrate understanding of key details in a text. *(In this lesson, we watch Caine's Arcade Video 1 once for the gist. We watch again during Companion Writing Lesson 2 to closely study the video and identify additional key details related to our two target questions.)*

Context of the Lesson

Students will now get the chance to view Caine's digital story! The film is truly inspiring and just plain fun! It is under eleven minutes long, so I suggest watching it one time all the way through to build general understanding, then when you move on to Companion Writing Lesson 2, watch the video a second time, stopping to talk and take notes on the writing targets.

The Lesson

"As we learned in the article we read, Nirvan Mullick made a video of Caine's arcade, which was put on the Internet on the Caine's Arcade website. This will be another source of information that will help us become Caine experts! Are you ready to meet Caine and Nirvan? We'll watch the short film all the way through once to get a general idea of what it's about. Also, watch for more information about how Caine used his imagination and how he and Nirvan changed the world. After watching, we'll talk about it. Then, we'll watch again, stopping at points to take notes."

Core Practices

- Utilize Digital Primary Sources
- Discussion

Recap: Key Lesson Steps

1. Discuss purpose for watching film
2. Watch the film once for enjoyment and to get the gist

Wrap Up

Wrap Up will occur after Companion Writing Lesson 2.

Notes

Revisit Media and Add to Two-Column Notes

Getting Ready

The materials:

- Caine's Arcade Short Film (Video 1): http://cainesarcade.com
- Two-column notes students have been working on (see the companion website for a template)
- Document camera

Context of the Lesson

This lesson takes right off where Booster Reading Lesson 2 left off. After enjoying Caine's Arcade Short Film (Video 1) first for the gist, students need the opportunity to view the film again, stopping to take notes on writing targets. In this lesson, they primarily add to the first column of their notes.

The Lesson

"As we view Caine's video again, we'll stop to take notes on our two writing targets: how Caine used his imagination and how he changed the world. I know you are already thinking of many details from our first viewing. But, as we watch again, we'll pick up on more information, figure out what is important, and reconfirm what we already know from our first source, the article. Just as we read the article twice, viewing the video twice will help us get a deeper understanding of our topic and take more accurate notes. We'll stop the video in several spots and jot down our thinking."

As we come across important information, I stop the video and model, thinking aloud,* while adding to my two-column notes. I reread what I already have, then, as I add notes, I talk about why those details are important. Then, students add to their notes. If they're ready, I release responsibility to them. Next time I stop the video, I ask a volunteer to come forward and add to her notes while talking about what she's adding and why she's adding it. I provide feedback and continue this process until Video 1 is finished.

*Note: At times, I might stop the video to think aloud about how I am reconfirming information I already noted from the article. Since I've come across it again in this primary source, I can be confident it is accurate.

Details you might discuss and add in column one (in shorter, notated form; see student sample, page 236):

Caine created the arcade over summer vacation

His first game was mini-basketball

He added many other games

His arcade was so big, he took over his dad's whole auto parts store

He made his own T-shirt and office

He created a prize wall

He crawled in a box underneath the game and pushed tickets out when a game was won

He made "Fun Passes" $2 for 500 plays

Recap: Key Lesson Steps

1. Stop film while watching the second time

2. Note important details; discuss

3. Jot additions to two-column notes

4. Model and gradually release responsibility to students, if appropriate

---

Wrap Up

I wind things up by reinforcing the process and the reason for the work: "Look at all we did! This first video helped us add a lot of details to our first column of notes. We'll view a second video, which is also posted on the Caine's Arcade website. We'll dive into that film tomorrow, following the same process we did today, viewing it closely and taking notes. You'll find lots of information there that is especially useful for our second writing target."

Companion Website Resource

Two-Column Notes	
Name: _____	
Topic: _____	
Main Idea	Main Idea
Details	Details

 Available for download at www.corwin .com/thecommoncorecompanion

Close Reading of Media:
Sections of Caine's Arcade Video 2

Getting Ready

The materials:

- Caine's Arcade Short Film (Video 2): http://cainesarcade.com

Context of the Lesson

The second video focuses mainly on how Caine and Nirvan changed the world. Watch the selected segments listed below. As you move from segment to segment, discuss what students are noticing. This first viewing is to increase general understanding. Notes will be taken during the second viewing (Companion Writing Lesson 3).

The Lesson

"As you look at your two-column notes, I'm sure you notice you have many details for our first writing target, but not nearly as many for the second. There is one more video on the Caine's Arcade website that we'll watch now. You'll find many details about how Caine and Nirvan changed the world. We won't watch the whole video; instead, we'll only view segments. Just sit back and take them in. As we move from segment to segment, we'll discuss what we're noticing."

I suggest watching these segments since we work with younger students:

Start to 0:51

1:52–3:49

6:03–7:24

(There is a section about "The Imagination Foundation" in the middle that I skipped because I think it's a bit complex and I want to keep our focus narrow.)

Core Connections

Grade 2
Reading Informational
    Standard 1
Ask and answer such questions as *who, what, where, when, why,* and *how* to demonstrate understanding of key details in a text. *(In this lesson, we watch selected segments from Caine's Arcade Video 2 once for the gist. We watch again during Companion Writing Lesson 3 to closely study the segments and identify additional key details related to our two target questions.)*

Core Practices

- Utilize Digital Primary Sources
- Discussion

Recap: Key Lesson Steps

1. Discuss purpose for watching film
2. Watch the selected segments once for enjoyment and to get the gist

Wrap Up

Wrap Up will occur after Companion Writing Lesson 3.

3
Companion
Writing
Lesson

Two-Column Note Additions, Organizing Notes, Talking Out Caine's Story

Getting Ready

The materials:

- Caine's Arcade Short Film (Video 2): http://cainesarcade.com
- Two-column notes students have been working on (download a template at www.corwin.com/thecommoncorecompanion)
- Document camera

Context of the Lesson

After enjoying segments of Caine's Arcade Video 2 first for the gist, students need the opportunity to view them gain, stopping to take notes on writing targets. In this lesson, they primarily add to the second column of their notes.

The Lesson

This lesson takes right off where Booster Reading Lesson 3 left off.

"As we view the same segments of the video again, we'll stop to take notes on our two writing targets: how Caine used his imagination and how he changed the world. As we did yesterday, I'll model first then ask volunteers to come forward and lead us with their thinking as we add to our notes."

We rewatch each segment. I stop the video and model thinking aloud to add to my two-column notes. I reread what I already have, then, as I add notes, I talk about why those details are important. Then, students add to their notes. As we continue, I release responsibility to students. I pause the video, ask a volunteer to come forward and add to his notes, while talking about what he's adding and why he's adding it. I provide feedback and continue this process until we've reviewed all the segments in Video 2.

Details from these segments that you might discuss and add to column two (in shorter, notated form):

Video released—hugely popular right away

On the national news

Kids send in examples of their cardboard creations (list some)

Cardboard Challenge every October

www.cardboardchallenge.com

Involving countries all over the world

"We have a great deal of information jotted in both our columns now. Though we've gathered details in the two columns, they are not in sequential order. We better reread our notes and number them to indicate what happened first, second, third, and so on in each column. That way, when we retell Caine's story and write about it, it will make sense."

I model rereading my notes in column one. I think aloud, numbering the ideas in sequential order. Then, I model talking it out to make sure it makes sense. I ask students to listen to how I talk it out in whole sentences as if I was reporting what I've learned in an informal speech and remind them to do the same when it is their turn. Next, students number their notes in column one, then talk it out with a partner to make sure it makes sense. If it doesn't, they need to make changes to the numbering of their notes.

We repeat this process for column two. If students are ready, I have a volunteer come forward to think aloud and model numbering her notes in sequential order. I provide feedback. Students number their notes then talk it out with a partner.

Recap: Key Lesson Steps

1. Rewatch selected segments of Video 2
2. Note important details; discuss
3. Jot additions to two-column notes
4. Number notes in sequential order
5. Talk it out to a partner
6. Model and gradually release responsibility to students, if appropriate

Wrap Up

"Given all the study we've done over the past three days, how many of you are feeling like Caine's Arcade experts? Do you feel like you know a lot about our writing targets? Do you feel ready to start writing? Turn to your partner and tell them what you think about Caine and Nirvan. What kind of people are they? Why do you think this is important?

"Since we'll be writing newspaper articles, we'll need to study how those are written. We'll do that tomorrow. In the meantime, feel free to share what you've learned about Caine with your family at home. The more you retell the information, the better prepared you'll be to write about it! Also, be thinking about what all this information means to you. What is important about Caine's story? What qualities do Caine and Nirvan have as people? You might also share what sources you've used to learn about Caine and what we've done with the information so far."

Study Mentor Texts:
Newsela Newspaper Articles

Getting Ready

The materials:

- Two kid-friendly newspaper articles
- Document camera

Core Connections

Grade 2

**Reading Informational
   Standard 5**

Know and use various text
features to locate key facts
or information in a text
efficiently.

Context of the Lesson

In order to write newspaper articles, students must become familiar with common elements of their structure and the purposes of those elements. We examine two newspaper articles from Newsela.com, noting the text features, labeling them, and discussing the author's purpose for using them.

Core Practices

- Study Mentor Texts
- Identify and Label
  Text Features
- Modeling
- Gradual Release
- Determine Purposes
  of Text Features
- Discussion

The Lesson

"As with any new text type we write, we need to read and study examples to get a sense of what authors do in the genre. I have two newspaper articles for us to examine together. We need to examine how the articles are structured and what text features the authors' use so we can get an idea of how to craft our own articles."

We examine the articles together under the document camera. As we read, we discuss the features we see and how they go along with the text. I think aloud, "The first thing I notice is the title of the article. In newspaper articles, these are called *headlines* (*I label the headline*). Headlines serve to catch readers' attention and, in just a few words, give them a sense of what the article will be about.

"Let's look at this second article. Do you see a headline? Let's read it together." After talking again about the headline's purpose and what the article may be about, a volunteer comes forward and labels *headline* in the second article.

"Let's go back to our first example. I notice it has a picture or photograph like other informational text types (*I label the photograph*). We know from our experience as readers that pictures, diagrams, and photographs can hold a lot of information that help us understand what is in the text or even give us new information beyond the text. Let's talk about this example." We examine the photograph and talk about what it adds to our understanding of the article.

We examine the second article for the same feature, asking a volunteer to come forward and label the photograph. Again, we discuss how it aids our understanding.

"Going back to the first article, what other features do you notice?" I guide students to notice and label the headings. "Why might an author use these headings? What are you noticing they do?" Once a few students have shared their thinking (and hopefully connect to our prior experiences with headings!), I guide them to realize headings in newspaper articles serve the same purpose as headings in other informational reading. "They give the reader a heads up as to what is coming in the next section. Notice, they do this in just a few words, and they are often in bold print like they are here. What do you expect to read under each heading? Turn to a partner and talk." As students turn and talk, I circulate, listen in, and then bring them back together to discuss highlights. A volunteer labels the headings.

We examine the headings in the second article, and talk about their purpose and what we expect to read next. A volunteer labels the headings. (Notice the misspellings of *headline* and *headings*. If this was going to be used as an ongoing reference, we would fix those with white-out tape.)

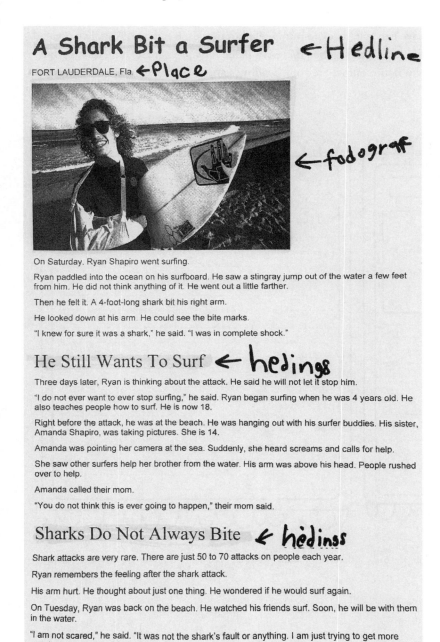

A Shark Bit a Surfer   ←Hedline

FORT LAUDERDALE, Fla. ←Place

←fodograf

On Saturday. Ryan Shapiro went surfing.

Ryan paddled into the ocean on his surfboard. He saw a stingray jump out of the water a few feet from him. He did not think anything of it. He went out a little farther.

Then he felt it. A 4-foot-long shark bit his right arm.

He looked down at his arm. He could see the bite marks.

"I knew for sure it was a shark," he said. "I was in complete shock."

He Still Wants To Surf   ← hedings

Three days later, Ryan is thinking about the attack. He said he will not let it stop him.

"I do not ever want to ever stop surfing," he said. Ryan began surfing when he was 4 years old. He also teaches people how to surf. He is now 18.

Right before the attack, he was at the beach. He was hanging out with his surfer buddies. His sister, Amanda Shapiro, was taking pictures. She is 14.

Amanda was pointing her camera at the sea. Suddenly, she heard screams and calls for help.

She saw other surfers help her brother from the water. His arm was above his head. People rushed over to help.

Amanda called their mom.

"You do not think this is ever going to happen," their mom said.

Sharks Do Not Always Bite   ← hedings

Shark attacks are very rare. There are just 50 to 70 attacks on people each year.

Ryan remembers the feeling after the shark attack.

His arm hurt. He thought about just one thing. He wondered if he would surf again.

On Tuesday, Ryan was back on the beach. He watched his friends surf. Soon, he will be with them in the water.

"I am not scared," he said. "It was not the shark's fault or anything. I am just trying to get more people to be aware of the water."

Recap: Key Lesson Steps

1. Examine newspaper articles

2. Identify, label, and discuss the purpose of the text features

3. Model and gradually release responsibility to students, if appropriate

Wrap Up

"We have a pretty good sense of what features to include in our newspaper articles. Let's quickly review the features we studied. (*I point to the labeled text features and ask students to name them, then turn to their neighbor and explain their purpose.*) As we write our own, we can refer back to our labeled examples, if needed. Also, I've created this template for you to use. Notice there is a place for you to create a picture, if you like. I'll help you figure out where your headlines and headings belong once we get that far."

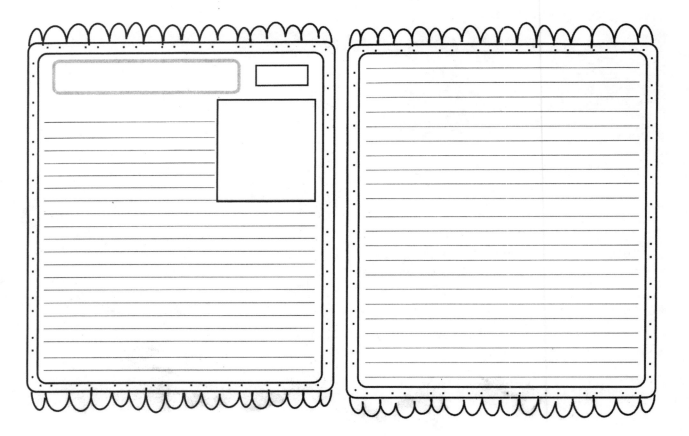

Source: Author-created template using the "Fun and Simple Borders" by Anita Goodwin. Used with permission. (https://www.teacherspayteachers.com/Store/Anita-Goodwin)

Available for download at www.corwin.com/thecommoncorecompanion

Compose Headlines, Headings, and Begin to Draft

Getting Ready

The materials:

- Think pad or scratch paper
- Two-column notes (download a template at www.corwin.com/thecommon corecompanion)
- Document camera

Context of the Lesson

In this lesson, students review the information in their two-column notes and brainstorm titles and headlines for their articles. I model beginning to draft my article, first talking it out from my notes then starting with my title and first headline. Students do the same. They'll need at least two writing sessions to complete their drafts.

The Lesson

"We're ready to get writing! Let's begin where we just left off, by brainstorming some possible titles for our newspaper articles." Students volunteer possible titles and I write them on paper under the document camera. We discuss whether the titles proposed capture the whole of what we will write. Students record the title they think they'll use on their own paper.

"We know the notes in our first column are about how Caine used his imagination. This will be the first section of our articles. Let's brainstorm headings that may work for this section." Students volunteer possible headlines and I record them. (If students are proposing headings that are too long, we go back to our mentor articles and study the headings, counting how many words they have.) We discuss their examples. Will these headings work for our purposes? Will they help the reader know what to expect in this section? Students record their first heading on paper.

"The notes in our second column detail how Caine and his friend changed the world. We'll need to come up with possible headings for this section." We follow the same process as above.

"Okay, we've recorded the headline and two headings. If you change your mind as you draft, you certainly can revise them, but now that we have them written we won't forget the work we've done so far. Now, as we get ready to draft, let's take a minute to talk out Caine's story one more time, using our notes. Remember, we numbered our notes in sequential order so our information will be organized. Practicing aloud makes the writing easier since you can talk out trouble spots. Everyone find a partner and begin." I circulate, listen in, and assist.

- Incorporate Text Features Into the Writing
- Brainstorm Examples
- Modeling
- Talk-It-Out Using Notes
- Draft
- Sharing
- Feedback

(*After a few minutes*) "Sounds like you are confidently reporting what Caine did! Let's start writing. I'll begin modeling for a few minutes then it will be your turn."

I model copying my title from my think pad, then recording my first heading underneath. Next, I show how to work from my sequentially numbered notes, thinking aloud and talking it out, to draft the beginning of my first section. I ask students one of my favorite questions after modeled writing: What did you see me do as a writer? We briefly discuss the strategies they saw me use and students begin their own drafts. I circulate, providing assistance and feedback.

As we close our writing workshop for the day, students are given time to share. Then, a volunteer or two (or a student whose sample shows something I'd like to use for a teaching point) comes forward to showcase his writing under the document camera. We talk about what is going well and where we are headed.

Recap: Key Lesson Steps

1. Brainstorm headlines and headings
2. Jot down selected headline and headings
3. Talk out Caine's story using two-column notes
4. Model beginning to draft
5. Have students begin to draft
6. Sharing and feedback

Wrap Up

"We're off to a great start drafting our newspaper articles. We'll continue to draft tomorrow. I'm impressed with how accurately you are reporting what you've learned. This is so critical in informative writing. We have to be accurate. That's why we worked so hard reviewing our sources and composing our notes. Think about where you are in your writing overnight and we'll get back to drafting tomorrow."

Notes

Exploring Deeper Meanings:
Caine's Arcade Updates and Conversation

Getting Ready

The materials:

- Caine updates list from website
- Document camera
- Think pads or scratch paper for jotting

Context of the Lesson

Informative writing shouldn't be just a spewing out of facts. Rather, we want students to synthesize what they've learned and think, "Is there a deeper meaning here? Is there a life lesson we can learn? What does this mean to me, to my classmates, to the world?" Given we work with K–2 students, we must scaffold this kind of higher-level thinking with modeling and engaging in collaborative conversations wherein we loan children language that may assist them. When we push for this kind of thinking and work to express it, we lift the level of possibilities for all students. One of my favorite quotes from Lucy Calkins speaks to this: "The conversations we have in the air become the conversations we have in our minds."

The Lesson

"This list of updates is directly from the Caine's Arcade website. We'll read it together to see what has happened since the second video was posted." We read the list using shared reading and discuss the points. (*I got the list from cainesarcade.com. If you scroll down, you'll come to the heading, "1 Year Later: Caine's Arcade Updates." Choose some points to read and discuss. You'll also find plenty of other humorous items and engaging articles you might want to explore at another time.*) In the future, you may want to check Caine's website yourself to see if there are more updates and to continue to learn about Caine.

"Now as writers and thinkers, let's reflect on all we've learned about Caine, Nirvan, and what they've accomplished. What characteristics do Caine and Nirvan possess that have led to their success? When you put all the facts and events together, do you think there is a deeper meaning here? Is there a life lesson we can learn? What does this story mean to you, to our class, to the world? Take a moment to think. You might jot down a few notes in your think pad. We'll follow up with a conversation." (*Give students think and jot time.*)

(*Quickly review conversation rules and norms.*) "Okay, would someone like to start us out? What are you thinking that goes beyond the facts or events?"

Core Connections

Grade 2
Reading Informational
Standard 1
Ask and answer such questions as *who, what, where, when, why,* and *how* to demonstrate understanding of key details in a text.
Speaking and Listening
Standard 1
Participate in collaborative conversations about grade 2 topics and texts.

Core Practices

- Read Primary Source Material
- Synthesize Facts in Search of Deeper Meanings
- Jot Notes
- Collaborative Conversation

S: Well, if Nirvan hadn't come into the store that day, none of this would have happened.

T: Okay, can you tell us more about that? Why do you say that?

S: Caine didn't have any customers. Nirvan wanted to play and then he wanted to make a video.

T: So, if Nirvan hadn't come in . . .

S: The video wouldn't have been made and people wouldn't know about Caine's Arcade.

T: There was a bit of luck involved, then. If Nirvan hadn't come, if he hadn't tried out the arcade, if he hadn't thought of making a film, if he hadn't put it on the Internet, none of the other events would have followed. That's an interesting point. Can anyone piggyback off of this point?

S: But, if Caine hadn't built the arcade to begin with . . . that's really how it all got started.

S: However, he had to be discovered kinda like other stars.

T: What can we learn from all this? You might start with the words, "We can learn . . ."

S: We can learn it's good to do hard work.

T: Tell us more.

S: Caine worked hard to make the Arcade. He spent a lot of time and he used a lot of imagination and he was only nine!

T: He was nine years old, he worked hard, he used his imagination, so . . .

S: I'm eight. I could work hard and use my imagination and maybe make something.

T: Something that . . .

S: Something that would be fun.

S: Something that would inspire others like Caine did!

T: Okay, so to recap so far, we're thinking some luck played into the events. Nirvan was the perfect customer to come along. But, Caine was a hardworking, imaginative nine-year-old. Maybe we can do something fun and meaningful to impact others like Caine did. Anything else come to mind? Look at the notes you jotted down. Any idea might help push our thinking.

S: I remember how it showed in the film that Caine didn't have any customers and he still kept going to work every day, sweeping up, making new things, trying to talk people into playing.

T: That is important because . . .

S: Because he didn't give up. He waited a long time for a customer.

S: Yeah, sometimes things are hard!

T: So the point here is, it's good to stick to something you want to do, to not give up, even if it is hard. That is part of what it takes to pursue a goal or reach for a dream. Caine and Nirvan were both persistent and they both persevered.

S: I think another life lesson is it's important to help others.

T: What do you mean?

S: Well, Nirvan helped Caine, then the two of them helped inspire others to use their imaginations, and now they have the Cardboard Challenge.

T: How does the Cardboard Challenge help others, do you think?

S: It helps people make something out of their junk!

S: Yeah, it gets other people to use their imaginations. Who knows what they might make!

I sum up the additional points that have been made and close the conversation according to our norms.

Recap: Key Lesson Steps

1. Shared reading of Caine's updates from the website

2. Jot thinking about deeper meanings

3. Collaborative conversation

Wrap Up

In much nonfiction reading, there are real people, past and present, at the center of the information, driving information, so as we wrap up this lesson, I like to remind students of that. "I love how when we put our heads together, we can often find deeper meaning in facts and events. We came up with several points that might be considered life lessons. We thought about the personal qualities of Caine and his friend. If something new from our conversation caught your attention, take a moment to jot it in your think pad. You might want to use some of this thinking to close out your newspaper article, leaving your readers with something deeper to think about."

5

Companion
Writing
Lesson

Finish Draft, Peer Check, Teacher Conference, Publish!

Core Connections

Grade 2
Writing Standard 2
Write informative texts in which they introduce a topic, use facts and definitions to develop points, and provide a concluding statement or section.
Writing Standard 5
With guidance and support from adults and peers, focus on a topic and strengthen writing as needed by revising and editing.

Core Practices

- Incorporate Text Features Into the Writing
- Modeling
- Talk-It-Out Using Notes
- Draft, Revise, and Edit
- Peer Check
- Teacher Conference
- Final Publishing
- Publicize
- Distribute to Audience

Getting Ready

The materials:

- Drafts in progress
- Two-column notes (download a template at **www.corwin.com/thecommon corecompanion**)
- Think pads or other notes
- Peer checklist
- Document camera

Context of the Lesson

As we finish our drafts, students will engage in a peer check, then a teacher conference so they can publish their newspaper articles on the template. These processes may take two or three writing periods to complete.

The Lesson

"We'll start today with some modeling. First, I'll reread what I've already written. Notice, I may make revisions as I do this since writers are constantly rereading and revising as they draft. Then, I'll quickly talk out my second column of notes to prepare to write on, record my second heading, and start drafting. Watch as I work and be ready to tell me what you saw me do as a writer."

I model and think aloud, emphasizing critically rereading what I have, making changes, and then talking out my notes in sequential order. As I continue to draft, I'll record my second heading first, then go between my notes and my draft, rereading and making changes along the way.

"Okay, writers, what did you see me do?" After discussion, students follow the same process: rereading their own drafts, making changes, talking out their notes, and writing. I circulate, assist, and provide feedback. As students start to finish their drafts, I call the class together again.

"We need to talk about concluding our articles. Perhaps we can end this piece with a wise thought. We just had a conversation about deeper meanings behind all the facts we learned about Caine. Looking at my notes, I'm thinking I might end with something like, "Good thing Caine didn't give up on his dream, even when he had no customers! His hard work really paid off. We can all learn a lesson from Caine." When you look at your notes from our conversation, does anything come to mind for a closing sentence or two?" We share some examples aloud and I give students more time to write. If students are struggling, I may pull together a group to do more talking, note reviewing, and brainstorming conclusions together. (Again, this process may take a few sessions, so stop in a logical place and pick up where you left off during your next writing period.)

A few minutes later or to start our next writing session:

"We have some friends who are ready to do some final checks before publishing their newspaper articles. When you get to this point, I'd like you to find someone else who is also done and complete a peer check using this checklist. Then, sign up here for a teacher conference. (*I have a place on the board designated for this purpose.*) I'll meet with you briefly so we can polish things up a bit, if needed, then you can start publishing, on the template."

Since everyone in the class is publishing this piece, the teacher conference needs to be very focused and quick. I work down the sign up list, having the student read a bit to me, commenting on some positives, then helping the writer fix spelling and other errors.

As students begin to publish on the template, I model under the document camera so they see how to move from their draft to their finished piece. I emphasize where to write the title and headings and how to write the headings in bold to mimic what we've seen in our mentor articles. Further, we discuss what students might include in their pictures.

Finally, as we finish publishing, I pull four names out of a hat to read an announcement to publicize the release of our publications over the intercom. These four students rehearse the script for a few minutes the day before and the morning of the announcement (you might use shared or interactive writing to compose your own script or use the one provided below). Each student is responsible for reading a section of the announcement. I put up signs around the school the afternoon before the announcement to build excitement (another option is to invite early finishers to create advertising posters using digital resources). Just before the announcement the next morning, I set up the newspaper station outside the office, where students can come and pick up their copy!

Companion Website Resource

This checklist represents what we needed to focus on at the time in our process, but you should adapt it based on your instructional foci.

Available for download at www.corwin .com/thecommoncorecompanion

- If students are signed up waiting for a teacher conference, they can assist other peers who need to work through their checklists or work on other choice writing. I like to have a list of alternatives they might work on like these: add to your topics list, review your topics list and begin a piece of choice writing, continue to work on choice writing already in process, add to your writer's notebook, etc. The same is true if students finish publishing much ahead of their peers.

- Consider your audience and purpose when publishing. Does the final piece have to be 100 percent perfect? If so, more time will need to be spent in editing mode during the teacher conference. Parent or community volunteers can also be elicited to help (see A Snapshot of Using Volunteers to Help Students Prepare to Publish on page 227 for a volunteer protocol).

- If there are still errors present after a student has finished publishing, use white sticky-tape to cover the error and correct it. This way the student is not burdened with redoing a lot of work.

Sample Announcement Script

We'd like to share a little bit about a special kid with you. His name is Caine Monroy. At age 9, Caine made a cardboard arcade out of boxes and tape.

Luckily for him, a special customer came and made a video of Caine's Arcade. The video became very popular and tons of people came to play at the cardboard arcade.

Caine and some adults created "The Cardboard Challenge." Every October, kids around the world are challenged to make something creative out of old stuff. It's a lot of fun!

If you want to know more, google Caine's Arcade or The Cardboard Challenge. You can see Caine's videos and they will inspire you. Also, we have copies of newspaper articles we wrote about Caine. If you'd like a copy, pick one up from the table outside the office on the east side.

THANK YOU!

Recap: Key Lesson Steps

1. Model

2. Students reread, change (if needed), finish drafts

3. Complete peer checklist

4. Conference with students

5. Publish

6. Publicize and distribute newspaper articles

Wrap Up

I reflect with students on the processes we implemented to complete the task. What was the most difficult part? What was the easiest part? What have you learned that you would do again when composing other informative pieces? I ask them to write a short, informal list or paragraph in their think pads: What do you think is the most important thing or things you've learned about informative writing? (See Authentic Assessment on page 237 for a sample.) We share.

Also, we celebrate being published newspaper journalists by taking a class photo to put on our class Web page (students help me craft a caption). I ask a volunteer (partner or group of three) to write a short article about what we did for our class newsletter and Web page (using a well-crafted headline and headings, of course!).

A Snapshot of Using Volunteers to Help Students Prepare to Publish

Students should do much more informal writing than formal writing so they get plenty of practice, just as they do with reading. Informal writing can take many forms. It might be writing that takes place throughout the day in a think pad or notebook that is used for jotting about learning. It could include quick writes, writers' notebook entries, and learning logs. Students should be writing lots of pieces across genres and purposes, much of which is shared orally, in whole or in part, but not taken through all the steps of the "publishing" process.

When we do choose to publish something, one of the issues is the time it takes to revise and edit the writing so that it may be shared with an outside audience. We need to think, is this writing that needs to be perfect? If not, we may help students make corrections in a few focus areas, rather than focusing on the whole piece. Given the age we work with, some polishing, not perfection, might be the most appropriate goal.

Another way to cut down on the workload is to elicit the help of volunteers. This could be parents or people in the community. I get help when everyone in the class is publishing at the same time, as with the Caine's Arcade newspaper articles. I use the instruction sheet on the next page to guide volunteers as they interact with student-writers.

Naturally, we would only expect students *who are able* to go from a corrected copy to a published copy. Some students may enjoy typing their final product while others may like to rewrite it. Most second graders can easily handle this load as can many advanced first graders. For those who are unable, you may be able to get parent or community volunteers to type up their pieces.

Keep the extra work of publishing set aside for a few very important projects only. Don't let publishing get in the way of the high volume of writing work students should be doing every single day!

Notes

Instruction Sheet for Guiding Volunteers

Hello!

Thanks for helping! We couldn't do all this important writing work without the support of people like you. Here are the steps you should take when helping students revise and edit their writing as they prepare to publish:

1: Have the student read the piece to you. Comment on the content (not the grammar, spelling, or punctuation yet). Here are some suggestions for comments:

I see you've written about . . .

I like how you . . .

I see that you . . .

Why did you say . . . ?

Tell me more about . . .

I see you used this powerful word . . .

I see you used this powerful sentence . . .

Where might you add more details about . . . ?

I don't understand _____ about . . .

Tell me more ...

I have a question ...

This reminds me of ...

This is very descriptive ...

Maybe you could ...

Why don't you think about ...?

2: As you make positive comments, ask questions, and make suggestions, help the student make any changes he or she wishes to make. When finished, go back and reread *with* the student.

3: Make any spelling corrections by circling the incorrect word and writing the correct spelling above the word. Also, correct capitals, periods, and other mechanics.

4: Ask the student if he or she has any other questions or needs. If not, the student's ready to publish!

Again, thank you!

Source: Adapted from *Quick Start to Writing Workshop Success* by Janiel Wagstaff (New York, NY: Scholastic, 2011).

Available for download at www.corwin.com/thecommoncorecompanion

Kindergarten Adaptation

Core Connections

Kindergarten Writing Standard 2
Use a combination of drawing, dictating, and writing to compose informative/explanatory texts in which they name what they are writing about and supply some information about the topic.

Much of the writing we do in kindergarten and as we begin first grade is done as modeled then shared and as interactive writing, followed by independent writing time. Of course, we can push the envelope a bit more in both grades when we are working together. Keep this in mind when you look at the standards. For example, in a shared informative writing piece in kindergarten, we may push beyond what's expected in the standard by categorizing the information we supply under headings and including some type of closure.

Starting with visual stimuli catches kindergartners' attention and imaginations. This works well with informative writing. Though we started by reading an article about Caine in second grade then moved to watching the videos, I often flip this order in kindergarten settings. We view and closely study short video clips and photographs *first*, begin simple note-taking on these, then work with appropriate written sources to augment learning.

For the Caine's Arcade lesson sequence, we focus on just one question: Who is Caine Monroy? We view a *short segment* from Caine's Video 1 first, talk about what we learned, then rewatch, sketching and labeling some notes to answer our question. Then, we watch a *short segment* from the second video and follow the same process. Next, we scaffold moving into writing by talking it out. I model using my notes to talk about what we've learned about Caine then turn it over to the students (of course, this is only possible when students have had plenty of practice talking out their notes, if not, more modeling and guided practice is needed. See A Snapshot of the Talk-It-Out Strategy on page 30). After talking it out, we move to modeled and shared writing. Using chart paper, I model beginning to write, introducing the topic then adding some information from our notes. Then, I invite students to help add to the piece, working from their notes, to complete our piece about Caine. We read and reread as we go, making any changes needed. We also add a title and closing sentence.

Now, I have several choices. We might be done with the writing. I post our shared piece in the classroom for rereading. Or, I might decide to type our piece so every student can have a copy. We'll read it a few times together, and then I'll invite them to take it home to share. Or, if my students have had several prior experiences with informative writing, I might take the model away and ask them to write their own informative piece about Caine. As they write, I circulate, providing help and guidance, even 'sharing the pencil' (interactive writing) with students who need extra support. We might buddy up with another class so students can go in, find a partner and inform others about Caine.

For other experiences, there's plenty of grade-appropriate informational reading material we can draw from. If my kindergartners show an interest in butterflies, for example, I write down their questions and we pick one to investigate. We view photos and short video clips and take notes (whether through shared writing, on sticky notes, or in some kind of graphic organizer. Again, these could be "shared notes" we record together, or children can record their own, using our shared work as a guide). We read books about butterflies, focused on confirming the information we've learned to answer our question. Again, we use our notes to talk out what we're learning. At this point, I often differentiate. Those who are ready can go to their seats to write independently. They might choose to use a sentence frame, very simple paragraph frame, or other scaffold I provide.* Those who need more support work with me on the rug. I model then plug in shared or interactive writing, so we can complete a short piece together. After working as a group, I ask students to go back and write about butterflies on their own.

*Note: Here's an example. One spring, students were interested in how butterflies grow. We studied sources and took simple notes. Then, I provided this simple scaffold to support their informational writing (see the photo on the right).

You can see it has some key transitional words since we ended up learning about the life cycle of a butterfly. These words are color coded to match the steps in the cycle. Students used this scaffold to talk it out then write.

Below is a sample of independent kindergarten writing (retraced in pen for readability). You can see, this student relied on the scaffold. Since it was spring, the students had a multitude of informational writing experiences under their belts and most were able to write independently with ease.

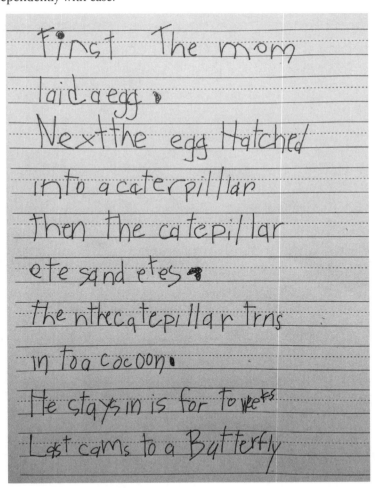

"First the mom laid an egg. Next the egg hatched into a caterpillar. Then the caterpillar eats and eats. Then the caterpillar turns into a cocoon. He stays in for two weeks. Last comes to a butterfly."

First-Grade Adaptation

Many of the strategies I use to adapt the work for kindergarten are useful in first grade, as well. Again, you can't beat modeling and shared and interactive writing as supports. Differentiating for students is a given. So, even if your whole class isn't ready to write informative pieces on their own, allow those who are to give it a go while you do shared writing with the others. However, even those who need the most support should have daily opportunities to write independently to grow. Make sure they get some time to work on their own pieces after they've engaged with the group.

I use more paragraph frames than sentence frames in first grade, though they are often quite simple, like the one below.

I learned about _____ (topic). _____ (topic) can _____

has

is

lives

eats

etc. (pick words that fit the topic and question(s) you've investigated.)

Possible conclusion starters:

I wonder _____

Maybe you could _____

I think (topic) is/are _____

Here's another example:

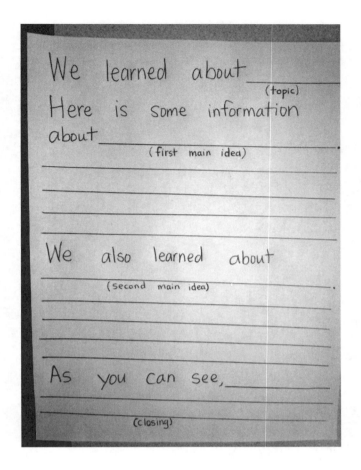

Scaffolds like the color-coded lists of transition words paired with color-coded key words are also useful for the explanatory writing included in Writing Standard 2 (see Kindergarten Adaptation on page 230). Students love writing the steps involved in making something or doing a favorite activity. Again, when I provide a scaffold like any of these, I always tell students they are free to use it, but they don't have to. I'm careful to model at a variety of levels: some more basic, mirroring the scaffold, and often more advanced, to push students' understanding of craft and structure and encourage them to take risks in their writing.

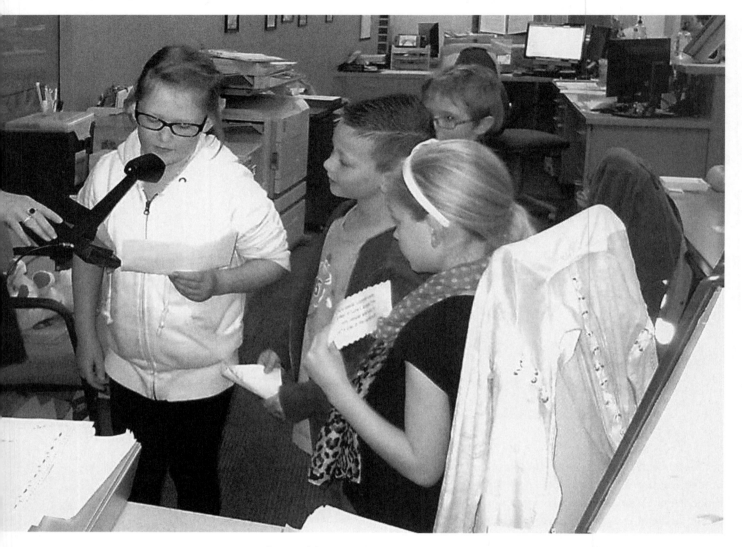

Going public! Students make an announcement on the office intercom to publicize the release of our newspaper articles!

What's ahead:

What Do I See?
A Student Sample of Informative Writing

Here's second grader Lily's published Caine's Arcade article:

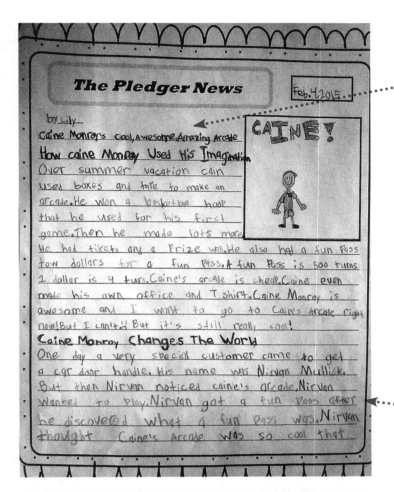

Lily easily meets all of the requirements of the standard. She introduces her topic in the title and first heading, includes several facts to develop her main points, and provides a concluding section. Her use of a variety of transitions that show temporal relationships is impressive. I would definitely point this out to other writers since it helps the organization and ease of reading of her article. I'm also impressed with how she logically weaves in so many details, especially in the second half of her article. It is evident based on her accuracy that Lily has taken detailed notes and referred to them consistently as she wrote. That takes effort!

Conferring Ideas: There is plenty to celebrate in Lily's article. One teaching point I might bring up is that she drifts off topic in the last three sentences under her first heading. I'd ask her to read that section again, then reread the last three sentences. "Do these feel like they fit here? Do they go with your heading? Where else might they belong in your article?"

Lily's conclusion is clever, pointing to the fact Caine was only nine years old. I love her voice here: "You can be any age. Go! Make something!" Her conclusion demonstrates she thought beyond the facts and was likely influenced by our collaborative conversation on deeper meanings.

What Do I See?
A Student Sample of Two-Column Notes

Involving students in all kinds of short, informal writing as you work toward a bigger goal is so important. It's a great way to get them continuously flexing their writing and thinking muscles, plus their samples can be used as ongoing formative checks. Intervening early when there is a misconception or problem is so much better than finding out later down the road after more work has been done. Here are the two-column notes Andy collected as we studied the sources on Caine.

Andy did a great job taking brief notes in the first column. He also clearly reread them as he worked to order them sequentially. I appreciate how he drew an arrow to remind himself where his sixth point belongs. Writers do this kind of thing a lot! Thinking is messy! A quick look at this column tells me he'll have plenty to fuel his writing and he'll likely cover the first writing target thoroughly.

A quick look at Andy's second column brought up a red flag. He only has notes on two important points about our second writing target and the notes are so brief, I worry he won't have enough information to do a thorough job. As I reviewed students' work, I found he was not alone. I needed to form a small group to talk, review content, and make additions to the notes so they would be successful when they talked it out and wrote.

Andy's piece also reminds me of how important it is to pause enough in our busy school day to listen, read, and notice what our readers and writers are doing, where they are in the journey. Andy's work and others is a reality check, underscoring that primary age students DO need "a lot of slow to grow" as Eve Merriam says.

Authentic Assessment:
Ideas for Evaluating Students' Learning

Here, let's look at how to evaluate students' work by inviting students to reflect on their learning. Self-reflection is a powerful tool. Students can self-assess their progress or outcome on a task; but they may also reflect on the process they underwent to complete a task. One of my favorite questions to ask is: "What do you think is (are) the most important thing (things) you've learned about _____ (in this case, informative writing)?" I often ask second graders to reflect in writing, using their think pads or a scratch paper to write a short, informal list or paragraph. When we share, the focus is on the processes learned and how they might be of assistance in the future. If students can name the steps, strategies, or processes they've undergone, great. If they can explain how these are helpful and when they'd use them in the future, that's even better. This sample is from second grader Ben. It shows his process reflection following the lesson sequence on Caine's Arcade.

Intresting topic
Be akurate
Check facts with more than 1 Source
This might take many days
organize your notes
    talk out the story
    Reread reread reread as you
write
REREAD!
Share with Someone
Does it make Sense?
It is a lot of work, but you
are an expert!

Yes, I offer these kinds of writing opportunities to kindergarten and first grade students. I want them to have the chance to put the pencil to the page. But, at these levels, most of our thinking comes together when we have conversations. Again, I might use shared writing to record a short list of highlights for future reference. This way, students see connections and learn how their prior experiences build their knowledge and understandings for success with future endeavors.

Peer Power:
Using Student Work as Mentor Texts

The writing that follows was composed by Isaac, a first grader. His class and I worked for about a week on informative writing on the topic of bats. We decided on two focus points to investigate: what are bats' bodies like and how do bats behave? We studied photographs and diagrams from the Internet then did some shared reading. We took notes in two columns. Students talked out their notes. Some used a paragraph frame to assist their independent writing.

According to the first-grade standard, students need to name a topic, supply some facts, and provide a sense of closure. Isaac's piece is a useful model, demonstrating all of the aspects of the standard. When I reviewed the class' work, I saw he elaborated on the facts more than other students. This makes his piece a useful model to share. Instead of simply stating that bats sleep during the day and hunt at night, like most students, Isaac added "Bats are nocturnal." We discussed this in our research, but didn't make a note about it. By including this vocabulary word, Isaac is doing a more complete job educating his reader. He does the same when he includes the fact, "Bats use echolocation" (though it would have been great if he defined what that meant). Again, this was discussed but not noted. I would definitely use Isaac's piece to celebrate his inclusion of academic vocabulary and encourage students to do the same in their future writing.

I'd also celebrate how Isaac added a detail to one of his sentences, using a carat. "Bats, eat lots of bugs ^and other things." This shows revision while drafting. Of course, I model this continuously, but always make a point of celebrating it when it shows up in student writing. As writers, we're always rereading, thinking if something needs to be said a different way or if something needs to be added or taken away. Obviously, Isaac was doing the hard thinking writers do! Yay for Isaac!

One more point comes to mind: how might I push first-grade writers like Isaac to craft their pieces in more interesting ways? Again, we don't want our writing to read like a list of facts, we want to engage readers and excite them. For example, during this investigation of bats, each student could have recorded three *ing* words (Hoyt, 2011) as we examined the photographs of bats in action, then used these words as an introduction or transition into the section on bats' behavior: "Hanging, swooping, hunting, get ready for some bat action!" I love it when students experiment with strategies like this and are surprised by the magic of their own words. Such experiences do much to "hook" writers for life! For more strategies on bringing informative writing to life see *Crafting Nonfiction Primary: Lessons on Writing Process, Traits, and Craft (Grades K–2)* by Linda Hoyt (FirstHand, Heinemann, 2011).

Again, students get excited when their writing has real purpose! These first graders shared their informative pieces with a kindergarten class. We showed a quick slideshow with photographs of bats that related to our two focus areas (accompanied by mystical music). Then, the first graders partnered with a kindergartner, read their writing, and entertained questions. It's fun to teach others! Go bat-writers, go!

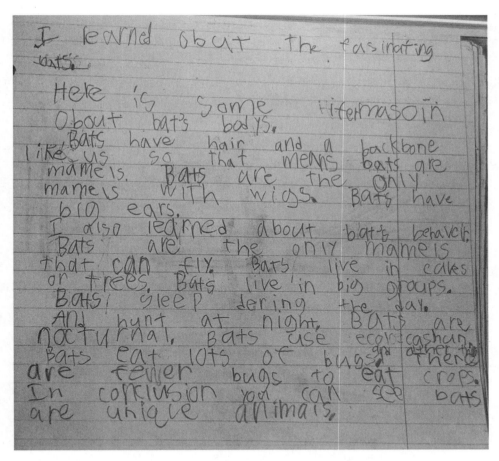

"I learned about the fascinating bats. Here is some information about bats' bodies. Bats have hair and a backbone like us, so that means bats are mammals. Bats are the only mammals with wings. Bats have big ears.

I also learned about bats' behavior. Bats are the only mammals that can fly. Bats live in caves or trees. Bats live in big groups.

Bats sleep in the day and hunt at night. Bats are nocturnal. Bats use echolocation. Bats eat lots of bugs and other things. There are fewer bugs to eat crops. In conclusion, you can see, bats are unique animals."

If/Then Chart

If students are having difficulty writing informative/explanatory pieces,	• Simplify. Work on just one or two aspects of the standard instead of everything at once. • Give them lots of oral practice. Inform one another about topics by investigating, writing some facts on sticky notes, organizing the notes, and sharing orally.* This is like a mini-version of the process. Once students feel comfortable doing this orally, they'll have more success in their writing. *Note: Since the standard includes explanatory writing, students can also list steps for explaining how to do something on sticky notes then share orally. Have them start with processes that are familiar to them like how to cross the monkey bars or how to skip rope. • Focus. Investigate just one question or focus area about a topic. Once students succeed at this, you can add more. • Guide students in taking notes. Keep the notes brief. If students are struggling to write the notes themselves, use shared writing to record them on a chart. • Guide students to talk out their notes before writing. If they have trouble, model this process sentence by sentence having them repeat as you go. • Differentiate. Pull a group and write a shared piece together. Then have students go back and write what they can about the topic independently. • Model, model, model. The focus of your modeling should be whatever aspect of the writing students currently need most. Think aloud explicitly about what you are doing and why. • Be sure to celebrate what they *are* doing well. Be specific. Show samples on the document camera for the sole purpose of celebration. Even small things count!
If students are having trouble organizing their informative/explanatory writing,	• Color-code the parts of your modeled writing samples. Label the parts (topic, main idea, details, main idea, details, closing). Work together to color-code and label students' examples. • Supply sentence or paragraph frames. There are several examples in this sequence.

If/Then Chart

If students are having trouble organizing their informative/explanatory writing, *(Continued)*	• Break it down. Give students one sentence frame to complete at a time. Model completing it first. Then, it's their turn. When they have it, move on to the next sentence. • Examine non-examples under the document camera. "Here's an informational piece about spiders written by a second grader I had a few years ago. It's confusing. He's mixing information about where spiders live with information about how spiders hunt. Let's work together to organize the information into categories and revise." Cut up the piece. Categorize the info. Talk about why you're doing what you're doing.
If students are having trouble writing conclusions,	• Create a chart with sentence frames. Build it over time with student input. Create the frames using the language from strong student examples and other mentor texts.
If motivation to write informative/explanatory pieces is waning,	• Investigate text features. Use mentor texts to study captions, bold print, headings, glossaries, and charts, for example. Compose short pieces that include some of these exciting elements. Have your students teach others about these features! • Give students more choice. If you've all focused on investigating one or two questions about a topic together, allow partners or individuals to investigate other questions related to the topic on their own. • Keep a running list of possible informative/explanatory topics and allow students to pick from these or develop their own. • Explore varied forms of informative/explanatory writing: brochures, pamphlets, how-tos, posters, flyers, guides, and blogs, for example. • Find ways to share students' informative/explanatory writing outside your classroom to make their work more meaningful. • Provide alternative ways to produce the writing. For example, students can create PowerPoint presentations or keynotes (on iPads) to share information or explain something.

(Continued)

If motivation to write informative/explanatory pieces is waning, *(Continued)*	• Move on to study another genre. While it's important to immerse students in a genre for a sustained period so they really become adept at that type of writing, if you see them losing interest, move on. In the weeks and months ahead, find logical places to work in more informative/explanatory writing.
If students are struggling with spelling,	• Build and use a Word Wall. Do this over time with your students. Make sure to include high frequency words as well as words with useful chunks to support spelling connections. Reference the Wall continually during modeled, shared, guided, and interactive writing. (See Integrating Foundational and Language Standards on page 251.) • Do "Challenge Words" lessons (see Integrating Foundational and Language Standards on page 251). These can even be done in small group for those in need, so you can give them words to attempt that are right on their level. Spend more time doing the steps of the routine *together* to provide heavier support. Bonus: This work will increase students' decoding skills, as well!
If, after much study, students still aren't including all the elements of informative writing for the grade-level standard,	• Show models with the elements color coded and labeled (e.g., the topic introduction is green, the first main idea with supporting details is yellow or, as is stated in the standard, "the facts and definitions to develop points for the first main idea are yellow"), the second main idea and details are orange, and the concluding statement or section is blue. • As students plan or prewrite, they color-code the elements, and then color-code them again in their drafts.
If students experience difficulty investigating topics independently,	• Have them work with a partner or group of three. • Have them investigate just one question or main idea about their topic. • Provide a simple graphic organizer to guide them.

If/Then Chart

If students are excelling,	• Allow them to investigate topics of their own choosing alone or with partners. • Provide them with more choice-writing time. • Up the ante with specific goals for the piece like: "Experiment with crafting a scene as an introduction" or "Craft an ending that goes beyond the facts to a deeper meaning." Of course, students will need some explicit strategies for achieving these goals and to be supported by examples in mentor texts.
If you have English language learners,	• Bring in related realia to support understanding informational topics. • Take notes through shared writing. • Limit the number of notes students work from. • Meet in small groups to support them as they talk out notes. Model turning one note into a sentence. Have students repeat your sentence. Continue one note at a time. • Use sentence frames to scaffold their speaking and writing. • Compose shared pieces together using sentence frames.

Mentor Texts

Actual Size by Steve Jenkins: From the smallest fish to the largest land animal, Steve Jenkins knows how to engage young readers in fascinating animal facts. With this book's focus on size, your reading will surely lead to active measuring and weighing. Don't miss the two-page spread of the giant squid's eye or the three-page foldout of the saltwater crocodile and goliath frog. As with all Steve Jenkin's books, you'll be sure to hear a bunch of *ews* and *ahs*. Guaranteed to motivate further investigation! (As you can tell, Steve Jenkins is another not-to-miss informational author-illustrator! Check out his numerous titles!)

An Egg Is Quiet by Dianna Aston: This book is a work of art in both its illustrations and its language. Aston follows the pattern: "An egg is . . ." followed by an adjective. She then gives fascinating factual information about why the adjective describes eggs. The illustrations compliment the information perfectly. Students are captivated! Aston examines several other topics in this same artistic way. Look for the other informational books in her series.

Beetle Bop by Denise Fleming: You can't go wrong with Denise Fleming! Her illustrations are so brilliant, one can't help but fall in love with the topic. Lyrical language adds to the allure. This book explores a variety of information about beetles. Often a close study of the illustrations leads to new information not shared in the text, eliciting more questions. Who knew there was so much to know about beetles? Check out her other informational books!

Lifetime by Lola Schaefer: Each two-page spread of this creative text showcases the number of times an animal performs a behavior or grows a feature in its lifetime with numbers from one to one thousand. Fun language and engaging illustrations are sure to get your students asking more questions about the animals featured or numbers in nature. Schaefer's kid-friendly prologue and academic notes in the back explain mathematical details, and she even poses some challenging math problems that mirror the structure of the book. Be sure to check out Schaefer's many other informational titles!

Over and Under the Snow by Kate Messner: This beautiful book tells the story of a father-child's day of adventure in the winter woods, including what they see, hear, and understand to be going on with animals over and under the snow. The beautiful language follows the pattern: "Over the snow . . . Under the snow . . ." The illustrations perfectly depict the varied subjects. You won't believe all that is happening over and under the snow! More facts about the subnivean zone are included in the Author's Notes at the end as is additional information on each animal. You'll also find further books to read and websites to explore. Surely this book will spark additional inquiry! *Up In the Garden, Down In The Dirt* and the forthcoming *Over and Under the Pond* follow the same pattern as this title and will make noteworthy additions to your informational resources.

Seed, Sprout, Pumpkin Pie by Jill Esbaum: Vibrant, real photographs and simple text depict the life cycle of pumpkins and how pumpkins can be used. Plenty of clear details enable teachers and students to easily follow these two subtopics about pumpkins. (I highly recommend the National Geographic for Kids books. The National Geographic Readers are leveled from prereader to Level 3 [fluent reader]). They all contain amazing photographs and text that is appropriate for K–2. As you go up the levels, the books contain the informative text features you want to highlight: table of contents, bold headings, vocabulary, diagrams, labels, charts, graphs, and glossaries, for example. The series is expertly done and perfect for the classroom!)

Stella and Class: Information Experts by Janiel Wagstaff: The students in Ms. Merkley's class become very interested in real chameleons while reading a narrative text with a chameleon character. Ms. M. works with the class to record their questions, investigate them, organize their notes, and write. Their shared piece comes out so well, they decide to publish it and put it in the library next to the narrative text. The book walks teachers and students through the steps they might follow to compose a lively and purposeful informational text!

What If You Had Animal Feet!? by Sandra Markle: Kids love this setup: on the left, you see real photographs of animals with fascinating foot facts, on the right there are fantasy scenarios featuring kids using those feet to accomplish amazing things. The illustrations are hilarious and the scenarios are fun to imagine. The real photographs include highlighted close-ups of the animal feet. This entertaining book has a text structure that begs to be imitated. Who's up for What If You Had Animal Eyes or Noses, for example. Don't miss Markles's other books in the series: *What If You Had Animal Teeth?* and *What If You Had Animal Hair?*

Who Would Win? Polar Bear vs. Grizzly Bear by Jerry Pallotta: This is one book in another series I highly recommend. Probably best for second grade and up, each book pits one animal against another. Readers explore various aspects of each animal through a combination of real photographs, amazing illustrations, and a mixture of text features. At the end, there is a fictional battle between the two animals to answer the question: Who would win? A final checklist encourages readers to review what they've learned.

Other K–2 Informational Staples

Anything by Seymour Simon

Anything by Gail Gibbons

Anything by Melvin Berger

Douglas Florian poetry

Joyce Sidman's poetry

Ranger Rick, Zoobooks, and other magazines

Websites

Beginning Reads http://textproject.org/classroom-materials/students/beginningreads/: From researcher Freddy Heibert and her team, leveled informative texts expressly designed for beginning readers. Levels from 1 (one word on a page) to 10 (three lines of text per page). These four-page reproducible books are also free.

FYI for Kids http://textproject.org/classroom-materials/students/fyi-for-kids: Researcher Freddy Heibert and her team provide one-page informational texts on a variety of science and social studies topics. The texts are leveled from first grade to fifth, and they include photographs. They are well written, kid friendly, and free to download and use.

Newsela https://newsela.com/articles/?category=kids: Up-to-date news articles covering topics of interest to kids. Printable and free. You can vary the Lexile level. Even at the lowest levels, many, but not all of these texts, are too difficult for K–2 readers, but they're great for read alouds and shared readings.

Other Notables

A Leaf Can Be by Lauria Purdie Salas: You won't believe all the useful things a leaf can be! Sure to spark questions and further investigation. This series is not to be missed! (Also see *Water Can Be*, and *A Rock Can Be* by Salas.)

The Egg (and other titles in the First Discoveries series) by Rene Mettler: This series is a real hit with students as concepts are brought to life with the inclusion of full-color transparency pages.

Feathers: Not Just for Flying by Melissa Stewart: The first sentence of the introduction on the book jacket sparked my students' attention. They couldn't wait to find out how birds use feathers like sunscreen, fancy jewelry, or a bullfighter's cape!

Fly Guy Presents: Sharks (and others in the series) by Tedd Arnold: Who doesn't want to learn from Fly Guy? Hugely engaging, great variety of text features. Fun!

I Am Earth (and others in the series) by Jean Marzollo: Great for kindergarten.

Favorite Explanatory/Procedural Texts

How to Babysit a Grandpa by Jean Reagan

How to Lose All Your Friends by Nancy Carlson

How to Read a Story by Kate Messner

How to Teach a Slug to Read by Susan Pearson

Extending the Work

As noted earlier, students would only be ready for the Caine's Arcade sequence after they've had extensive experience reading and writing informative texts. Experiences would build from the simple to the complex, and, in my view, the task in this sequence is quite advanced.

So, here are some questions I'd ask myself: Are my students in need of more intensive work writing informative texts? Are my (or most of my) students ready to work independently in this genre? Is there a purpose for this work? Should we turn our attention to explanatory tasks? Is it best to now, after all of the work that has been done, simply integrate smaller informative/explanatory writing tasks into the everyday curriculum where they naturally fit?

Let's say, for the purpose of extending this work, you'd like to spend some time building from the Caine's Arcade base, exploring other topics, and inviting students to report information for a class newspaper and class Web page.

Companion Website Resource

Planning Page for Newspaper or Web Page

Who's Ready to Report? Name(s): _____
_____

Topic: _____
_____

When and where did the event take place? _____

Who was involved? _____

What was the event? _____
_____

Why did this take place? What was the purpose? _____
_____

How did people react? _____
_____

What will happen next? _____
_____
_____

Headline: _____
_____

Features to include (refer to chart): _____
_____

Retrieved from the companion website for *The Common Core Companion: Booster Lessons, Grades K–2: Elevating Instruction Day by Day* by Janiel Wagstaff. Thousand Oaks, CA: Corwin, www.corwin.com. Copyright © 2016 by Janiel Wagstaff. All rights reserved. Reproduction authorized only for the local school site or nonprofit organization that has purchased this book.

Available for download at **www.corwin** **.com/thecommoncorecompanion**

LESSONS	READING Speaking and Listening	WRITING Speaking and Listening
6	**Lesson 6:** *Study Mentor Texts* • Shared read examples of class newspapers and class Web pages. • What features do these text types have? • What are these writers writing about?	**Lesson 6:** *Topic Generation* • Generate a list of possible topics for class newspaper and class Web page.
7	**Lesson 7:** *Study Mentor Texts* • Read *The Furry News* by Loreen Leedy. • Decide: Which of these how-to strategies would be useful to us in creating our own class newspaper and Web page?	**Lesson 7:** *Begin How-To Chart* • Create a list of how-to strategies based on *The Furry News*. • Brainstorm other strategies to add to the list.
8	**Lesson 8:** *Mine Mentor Texts* • Read other newspaper articles in pairs or small groups. Look for features to cut out to highlight on a chart (see next box).	**Lesson 8:** *Create Reference Chart of Features* • Label newspaper article features found while reading: What is the feature? What is its purpose? • Glue this to a chart: *Newspaper Article Features*
9	**Lesson 9:** *Brainstorm Class Event* • Discuss current class event that would be interesting to report in the newspaper or on the Web page. • What aspects of the event need to be included in an adequate report?	**Lesson 9:** *Detail Event and Write* • List aspects of event: who, when, where, what, why, how, reactions, further actions, for example.* • Cooperatively fill in the list based on earlier discussion about event. • Shared write short informative article about the event. ***Note:** This will become a planning sheet for students to use in the future.
10	**Lesson 10:** *Review Writing and Discuss* • Reread shared article composed yesterday. • Highlight and label aspects (elements) present in the article (who, when, where, etc.). • Engage in collaborative conversation: Is the shared piece effective? Why or why not? • What text features could be added to help readers build meaning?	**Lesson 10:** *Revise and Publish* • Make revisions to article based on analysis. • Pick volunteer(s) to type the article. • Pick volunteer(s) to create picture, chart, or graphic, if applicable. • Post the article on class Web page.

LESSONS	READING Speaking and Listening	WRITING Speaking and Listening

11	**Lesson 11:** *Prepare for Independent Reporting*
	
	• Reread and discuss the following:
	  ○ Possible class newspaper or Web page topics list
	  ○ How-To Strategy list
	  ○ Newspaper Article Features chart
	  ○ Who is ready to take on reporting on a topic?
		Lesson 11: *Plan Article*
		
		• Create working groups.
		
		• Students decide if they would like to report on a topic individually, with a partner or in a small group.
		
		• Groups or individuals list topic and begin to fill in the planning sheet (see **www.corwin.com/thecommoncorecompanion**).

12	**Lesson 12:** *Enjoy Another Mentor Text* • Read *Extra! Extra!: Fairy-Tale News from Hidden Forest* by Alma Flor Ada. • Collaborative Conversation: Are there any new aspects here that may inform our newspaper article or Web page writing? (If so, add to charts).	**Lesson 12:** *Draft Articles* • Students finish filling in planning sheet. • Students write short newspaper articles and create graphs, charts, pictures, photos, and graphics, when applicable.
13	**Lesson 13:** *Enjoy Another Mentor Text* • Read *Deadline!: From News to Newspaper* by Gail Gibbons • Collaborative Conversation: Is there new information here that informs our purpose? (If so, add to charts.)	**Lesson 13:** *Finish and Polish* • Finish writing. • Sign up for teacher conference. • Self-assess. • Begin new article or feature for class newspaper or Web page or work on other choice writing until teacher conference has occurred.
14		**Lesson 14:** *Publish* • Type article or feature. • Print for newspaper or post to Web page.
15	**Lesson 15:** *Collaborative Conversation* • How is this process going? Would we like to keep an ongoing class newspaper or Web page? • If so, how would this be managed? (This could be as simple as students writing their features during choice-writing time, then placing them in a folder labeled *Class Newspaper/Web Page*. As I have time or volunteers available, I take out an item in the file, conference with the student(s), and they publish. Additionally, if we add the option of oral reporting (see next box), students can indicate their desire to broadcast on the paper they put in the file.)	**Lesson 15:** *Who'd Like to Be a Newscaster?* • Open the option for students to orally report their news. • Those who are interested orally practice their report or feature (either from the planning sheet or a written piece). • A peer, the teacher, or a volunteer tapes the "newscast" and posts it to the class Web page.

Integrating Foundational and Language Standards

Foundational and Language Standards cover critical skills and strategies for our K–2 students. I chose not to cite them specifically in the sequences because they have a place in *all* our lessons (plus, if I had done so, this book would have doubled in size!). The speaking and listening, reading and writing we do are the contexts in which we apply what we're learning during foundational and language lessons. We explicitly teach the skills and strategies contained within these standards then reinforce them across the curriculum every day.

There are many fantastic, research-based instructional books written on the skills and strategies covered in the Foundational and Language Standards, and I'll recommend some of my favorite resources throughout the following section. So without further ado, here is a brief overview of the myriad of ways we can integrate these standards into students' everyday literacy activities.

Foundational Standards

Foundational Standard 1:
Print Concepts (Kindergarten and First Grade)

Teaching concepts of print is best done during shared reading and writing experiences and reinforced during guided and independent reading and writing time. As we read big books, charts, or text that is projected on the screen, we can repeatedly identify and label the directionality of print, word boundaries, spaces, and features of sentences. As students read and write, we prompt them: "begin pointing and reading here," or "remember to leave spaces between the words." Young students love to use pointers and show what they know. Thus, as these concepts are becoming solidified for learners, have volunteers come forward during shared reading and point them out for the class.

Here's an example of using shared reading/writing contexts to teach word boundaries: Before we begin reading a big book, I explain, "You can always tell a word by the spaces in between. Print has a pattern. It goes (*pointing*), 'word, space, word, space' Repeat that with me. *(Students: 'Word, space, word, space, word, space.')* We use that same pattern when we write. Let's look over at this chart we wrote together. Remember how we clapped and counted the words in our sentence, then had someone come up and hold two finger spaces between the words as we wrote? That's the same thing! If we don't leave spaces between words, our readers can't read what we've written. Look here (*I show a non-example, having rewritten the sentence from the same interactive writing chart without leaving spaces between the words*). Can you read this? *(No)* But, you just read it over here (*pointing to the chart*). What makes the difference? Share with your neighbor. *(After sharing)* See, that's how important it is to have spaces between words. Authors know this. And, that's why everything we read has spaces between the words. As we read our big book today, let's watch for this pattern: word, space, word, space. We'll stop on a few pages to check the pattern again and a volunteer can come forward and point it out using the pointer (*I point again to demonstrate*): 'word, space, word, space.'"

Another preferred context for these lessons is the Morning Message. I write a message every day to my class. They love it because it pertains to them and their day. As we read and discuss it, we'll often look for word boundaries, spaces, and sentence features.

Continual experiences like this solidify the concepts included in the standard. There are concepts of print assessments that can be used to test students' knowledge, but if you see them demonstrated in their reading and writing, you know students have them mastered. For example, it's not difficult to look for students following words from left to right and top to bottom as they read. Likewise, it's easy to see if students are spacing between words, starting the first words in sentences with capitals,* and using ending punctuation (first grade) when you examine their writing. When students are taking longer than their peers to master such concepts, meet with them in small groups for reinforcement, prompt them during guided and independent reading and writing, and continue to take a minute to identify these features during shared experiences.

*Note: Language Standard 2 for kindergarten includes "capitalizing the first word in a sentence."

Also included in the Print Concept Standard is recognizing all upper- and lowercase letters. In addition to the routines I have in place for explicitly teaching and reinforcing this knowledge (like starting with students' names and building and using a Name Wall; also see the Phonics and Word Recognition standards in this section), we continually review this skill during shared reading and writing. When we're writing on an interactive chart, we'll segment a word into sounds then identify the letters that represent those sounds. Though this process involves phonemic awareness and phonics, it also involves recognizing upper- and lowercase letters. Students' growing knowledge is thus used in purposeful ways, not just practiced to pass an isolated letter-identification assessment.

Foundational Standard 2:
Phonological Awareness (Kindergarten and First Grade)

We know phonological awareness abilities are huge predictors of reading and writing success. We also know as practitioners that if students don't understand what we mean by "sounds in words" or have the ability to segment words into sounds and blend sounds into words, they will be unable to progress through the developmental stages of decoding and spelling (though some take a sight-word approach, which is problematic when they need to figure out unknown words).

Research shows instruction in phonological awareness can be accomplished during brief periods of direct instruction (5 to 10 minutes) and should be well developed in students by the end of first grade. The best indicator of whether students are phonologically aware is whether they can sound out unknown words in grade-appropriate reading, and segment words into phonemes and represent them in their writing. Though using students' reading and writing as indicators of phonological awareness involves print and letter-sound correspondences, it also involves phonological awareness. Without phonological awareness, students cannot sound out to decode or use inventive spelling to write.

Most kindergarten and first-grade teachers rightly involve students in direct instruction of phonological awareness using oral language games and activities for rhyming; working with syllables; isolating, producing, and identifying "first, middle, and last" sounds in CVC (consonant-vowel-consonant) words; and blending and segmenting individual phonemes in single-syllable words. One of my favorite sources for hands-on activities is the Florida Center for Reading Research's website (www.fcrr.org). I also love to instruct these principles using students' names for sound play.

Since phonological and phonemic awareness always come up during interactive writing (we might "chunk" a word to spell it or work through all the phonemes), and is also in play when students sound out unknown words in their reading, I feel confident spending less time on whole-class direct activities once the majority of students are progressing beyond emergent levels in their reading and writing. However, time can always be spent working on larger words (two syllable, then multisyllabic words), orally blending, and segmenting, and identifying onsets, rimes, and syllables since these activities will support students as they work on reading and writing more difficult text.

Small group instruction definitely has its place. If, as the year goes on, you have students who don't seem to be getting it, who aren't reading and writing on par with the majority of the class, you can administer a phonological awareness assessment to pinpoint problem areas. Phonological awareness can be a sticking point that goes undetected, so it's helpful to take a closer look. Once problem areas are identified, intervening with concrete models can make a huge difference. Often students who struggle don't understand how sounds inside words work or what they are supposed to represent since they use words for meaning, not to focus on their sounds. Using three linked unifix cubes, I tell students to "watch a word come out of my mouth" then show them how to listen inside the word for beginning, middle, and ending sounds while separating the cubes from left to right. I have them watch in small mirrors how their mouths move with every sound (another way for them to distinguish sounds and get the overall idea). They also "see" how individual phonemes can be blended together as I demonstrate blending sounds by keeping my "motor running" (sustaining the sound of a phoneme as long as possible as I blend it into the next sound) as I push the unifix cubes back together. Plenty of hands-on practice helps students make progress. (For a host of other concrete models and innovative ideas, see *Using Name Walls to Teaching Reading and Writing*, Wagstaff, 2009.)

Pulling a word out of my mouth so it can be "seen" before I model segmenting it into phonemes by breaking the cubes apart.

Source: Reprinted from Wagstaff, 2009.

Favorite resources: The Florida Center for Reading Research website (www.fcrr.org), *Phonemic Awareness: Playing with Sounds to Strengthen Beginning Reading Skills* (Fitzpatrick, 2005), and *Phonemic Awareness Activities for Early Reading Success* (Blevins, 1999).

Foundational Standard 3:
Phonics and Word Recognition (K–2)

I've had phenomenal success using Word Walls to teach and reinforce phonics and word recognition. Once I teach a letter-sound correspondence, consonant digraph, or rime, it's posted on a Word Wall and referenced all year long during purposeful reading and writing. Students who need more time to master a phonics element get it because the reference never disappears.

As a bridge to automaticity with the phonics elements, I focus on teaching students to decode and encode by analogy. For example, when spelling an unknown word, a student might think, "I hear the /p/ sound at the beginning of the word *play*. That's the same sound I hear at the beginning of Paula's name, so I know I need the letter *p* just like /p/ /p/ /p/ Paula." Or, at a higher level, "I know the *ent* chunk in the word *tent*, so I know I need the letters *e-n-t* for the last chunk in the word *apartment*. They sound the same and end with the same chunk, so it's spelled the same." Likewise, when reading, "I see the letter *w* in this word I'm trying to read. Since I know 'Ms. Wag,' /w/ /w/ *wag*, I know I can begin to sound out this word with /w/." Or, at a higher level, "I see the chunk *o-c-k* in this word I'm trying to read. Since I know the word *sock* /ock/, I know this word is /r/ /ock/ /et/, *rocket*." When I teach an element (letter-sound, digraph, or rime), we work with that element all week during short review lessons (5 to 10 minutes) to build automaticity, then one key word containing that element is posted on the Word Wall on Friday. From then forward, for the rest of the year, we come back to those same key words repeatedly to make connections during modeled, shared, and interactive writing and during shared and guided reading, thus building in the repetitions needed for learning. I also prompt students to make analogies to solve words during independent reading and writing. Of course, once students know the element automatically, they no longer need to reference a Word Wall or make an analogy. (Common affixes [Grade 1 and 2]) can also be added to a Word Wall and referenced to read and write new words in this same manner.)

As you can tell, the focus of student learning is on mastering the elements and using them to read and write. My short phonics lessons have two purposes: (1) build automaticity, and (2) get students to use the elements strategically when reading and writing new words. This puts the teaching of phonics squarely in its place—it is simply a means to an end.

Research tells us a systematic approach to phonics teaching gets the best results. The standards outline what should be understood at the end of each grade level. Many teachers have a core reading program that has a scope and sequence so all elements are taught, retaught, and reinforced. Lessons should be brisk, to the point, clear, and easily comprehensible for students. They should also focus on automaticity and the use of elements in reading and writing. If putting a key word to represent each element on a Word Wall is not included, I highly recommend this extra step since it provides support for those who need it most and it makes repetition easier (each time we reference a

Word Wall to spell or decode a word, there's one more step toward moving a phonics element to long-term memory. Keep in mind, though, a Word Wall won't be used by students unless its use is constantly modeled and reinforced in real reading and writing).

I'd like to say a few more words about spelling. A key goal is to help students feel confident spelling unknown words independently in their everyday writing. Teachers know the issue well. Students begin writing and the first thing they ask is, "How do you spell . . . ?" Often, teachers respond to this query with "sound it out" or "spell it how it sounds." This simply isn't enough direction for K–2 students. They need to know what it really means to spell it how it sounds and how to be strategic in their approach. To this end, I provide my students with explicit, guided practice in using spelling strategies to spell unknown words accompanied by immediate feedback. I call these lessons *Challenge Words*. I explain that we all come to words we don't know how to spell as we write. But, we have to have strategies we can use to get those words down on paper, to give them our best shot, so we can use the words we choose (not just those we know how to spell) and get on with our writing rather than remaining stuck. I model and think aloud strategically connecting to words I know to help me spell new words or word parts. I use our Word Walls to make analogies. Then, I pose a word that I know will provide some challenge to students and tell everyone to give it a go on their papers using the same strategies I modeled. Everyone gives the word a try. I circulate and write down a few different attempts on the board. We then discuss each attempt: What is logical about this attempt? What did this speller do that works for this word? Students know the goal is not necessarily to get the word right, but instead, to give it a good, logical try using what we know.

For example, in fall in kindergarten, a challenge word might be *spot*. Student attempts might include: *s*, *s-t*, and *s-p-t*. I run my finger under each and give specific feedback. For *s*, "You can see this speller was able to listen inside the word *spot* to hear the first sound. He may have connected to /s/ /s/ *Sam* on the Name Wall or maybe he knew he needed the letter *s* for the /s/ /s/ sound. Good job! That's a start!" For *s-t*, "This speller was able to hear the beginning and ending sounds in the word *spot*. She has the letter *s* for /s/, and then heard that /t/ /t/ sound at the end, just like the word we know /t/ /t/ 'to.' Yep, the /t/ /t/ sound is represented by the letter *t*!" For *s-p-t*, "This speller was able to stretch the word even more /s/ /p/ /ot/. See how she started to spell *spot* with *s-p*? Let's all stretch the word slowly. See how our mouths moved from /sssss/ to /ppppp/? She knew she needed the letter *p* for that second sound. She has the ending sound, too. /Spt/ /spt/ *s-p-t*. That is a good attempt at the word *spot*. Now watch me." I model stretching the word orally, exaggerating my mouth movements, and writing a letter down for each sound. I always end the lesson by showing the correct spelling.

In fall in second grade, an appropriate Challenge Word might be *hiccup*. I teach students to clap the word to break it into syllables and write a line for each chunk (to remind them of each part they need to spell. They write the letters for the syllables on the lines). Then, they attack the spelling one small chunk at a time while making connections to words they know. Again, I circulate and write two or three different student attempts on the board. Then, I run my finger under each and provide feedback, thus reinforcing good spelling strategies. If one attempt is *hkup*, I might say, "I see this speller heard the beginning and ending sound in the first syllable, /h/ /k/ and connected to the right letters.

H-k is a good attempt for /hic/. But, we have to remember, *every* syllable, *every* chunk, has a vowel. Good attempt, though. For the last chunk she heard /up/ and spelled it just like the little word we all know *u-p*." If a different attempt is *hikup*, I respond, "This is another good attempt. *H-i-k* makes senses for /hic/, and this speller remembered the vowel /i/ /i/ /i/ like the word on our Wall *itch*. Usually the *ick* chunk is spelled i-c-k like *sick* or *trick*. He was also able to easily spell the ending chunk /up/ *u-p*. That makes good sense." I then model and think aloud, "I hear /hic/ (*drawing a line for that syllable*) and I'd probably try this chunk like other words I know with *h-i-c-k*. Then, the *up* chunk is easy, (*drawing a line for that syllable*) *u-p*. You know what? This word actually has an odd spelling. The first syllable is *h-i-c*, not *i-c-k* like most words and the second syllable is *c-u-p*; *h-i-c-c-u-p*. A writer could really get hung up on this word, but our attempts are logical and we'll get better and better as we practice!"

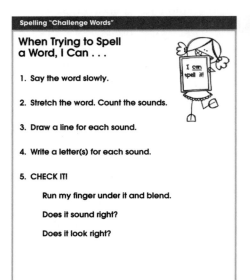

 Available for download at www.corwin.com/thecommoncorecompanion

Challenge Words should take only 7 to 10 minutes. We do these lessons right before writing workshop or independent writing. At the beginning of the year, I do them three times a week, then, as students' skills grow, I cut back to one or two. They also fit for small-group lessons so you can differentiate, giving students the types of words they need based on where they are. Additionally, I prompt students to use the same strategies we've practiced if they come to me for spelling help. For much more about Challenge Words and lessons like it, see Wagstaff, 1994, 2009, and 2011.

Note: The spelling strategies I've described help us address Language Standard 2 across the grade levels: "spell simple words phonetically . . ." (kindergarten); "use conventional spelling for words with common spelling patterns . . ." and "spell untaught words phonetically . . ." (first grade); and "generalize learned spelling patterns when writing words" and "consult reference materials as needed to check and correct spellings" (second grade).

Standard 3 also includes reading "common high-frequency words by sight" (kindergarten) and "recognizing and reading grade-appropriate irregularly spelled words" (first and second). Language Standard 2 addresses the spelling of these words: "use conventional spelling for . . . frequently occurring irregular words" (first grade). Working with high frequency words is a very common feature of reading/writing instruction in Grades K–2 as teachers know the critical nature of these words. Since they occur so frequently, and many of them are irregular, automaticity is essential. We don't want students slowing down to try to decode these words since they make up so much of what they read (plus irregularly spelled words aren't decodable, anyway). Furthermore, we don't want students constantly misspelling these words (like *sed* for *said*) since every time they do, the incorrect spelling is reinforced.

I teach the spelling and reading of these words in quick, explicit lessons. "Today we're learning to spell and read the word *the*. (*I hold up a card with the word boldly written on it.*) 'The' is always spelled the same way, *t-h-e*. Spell it with me. (*Students spell aloud as I point to each letter.*) It's important for you to be able to read the word *the* automatically, without trying to sound it out, because it is so common in everything we read. It is also important for you to spell the word *the* correctly each time you write it because it is not spelled like it sounds and it is a word we write so often. Let's look at the chart we were working on yesterday (*I point to an interactive writing chart*). How many times did we write the word *the*? (*We count.*) See? Can you believe how many *thes*? What if we spelled *the* wrong every time we wrote it? That would give our brains bad practice! We don't want to do that, so we'll practice *the* all week then add it to our Words We Know Wall* so we can be sure to spell it correctly each time we write it." After giving students guided practice in writing the word *the*, we continue to reinforce the word. "Let's highlight (using sticky highlighting tabs) every time we see the word *the* in this poem we are about to read (*I project a poem on the screen for shared reading*). This will help us recognize the word quickly but also remind us how important this word is to know since it comes up so frequently! (*After shared reading and highlighting*) Let's count how many times we read the word *the*."

*Note: I have a separate Word Wall for irregular high-frequency words. I want students to understand these words are different—you can't sound them out, you can't use them to make analogies, you just have to know them by heart. That's why we call it the Words We Know Wall. We interact with the Wall in a variety of ways to build automaticity (Wagstaff, 1999). I prompt students to slow down in their writing and refer to the Wall to make sure they "give their brains good practice" by spelling these words correctly. In first grade and beyond, if I see a word that's on the Wall misspelled in independent writing, I'll prompt the student to fix it. I do this orally if it's during a conference or, if I'm reviewing writing without the student present, I simply place a dot on the line in the writing in which the misspelling occurs. It then becomes the student's job to reread and find the word that needs fixing.

I'm not suggesting teachers go through these steps with every high-frequency word. But, it's useful for students to understand the importance of these words. Each needs to be taught directly, reinforced with guided practice for automaticity then referenced over and over again from a Word Wall and in real reading and writing so the correct spelling is mastered. As I mentioned earlier, one of my go-to contexts for reinforcement is the Morning Message. Once a high-frequency word is added to a Word Wall, we look for it in our Message. We'll practice identifying it within the message, and reading and spelling it. It takes just a minute to get a little practice in!

As you can tell, I don't separate teaching the reading (Foundational Skills Standard 3) and the spelling (Language Standard 2) of these words. Spelling facilitates reading, just as reading can reinforce spelling. You can bet if a student can spell the word automatically, he can read the word. Additionally, the tactile nature of writing helps move the word to long-term memory.

Favorite resources: The Florida Center for Reading Research website (www.fcrr.org), *Phonics for A to Z* (Blevins, 2006), *Teaching Reading and Writing with Word Walls* (Wagstaff, 1999), and *Using Name Walls to Teach Reading and Writing* (Wagstaff, 2009).

Foundational Standard 4: Fluency (K–2)

The kindergarten standard for fluency is different from the first and second grade, and rightly so, as students are just emerging as readers. The most important thing we can do to promote fluency at this level is to make sure students are experiencing tons of read alouds, and plenty of shared, guided, and independent reading with appropriate books, in addition to teaching the kindergarten reading standards. Kindergartners' fluency is also impacted by the work we do on quick and accurate recognition of high-frequency words.

As we promote reading "with sufficient accuracy and fluency to support comprehension" in first and second, we involve children in multiple repeated reading experiences for authentic purposes with engaging texts (readers' theater, radio reading, book talks which include reading text highlights, poetry readings, etc.). Our decoding and high-frequency word lessons promote accuracy as does plain ol' wide-reading. Another common practice to improve accuracy is to prompt students to self-correct when they make a mistake: "That didn't sound right. Can you fix it?" or "Go back and try that again" in an effort to aid students in developing the self-monitoring needed to self-correct. One trick I like to use is to have students read text on their level and tally on a sticky note any time they make an error. I prompt them to self-correct by rereading and we discuss the nature of the error (skipping word endings, omissions, etc.). Then, they read the text again, tallying errors, to see if their accuracy has improved.

One element of fluency instruction I often see missing in classrooms is the direct teaching of the characteristics of fluency along with why they are important. If we say fluent reading should be smooth and easy, what does that look and sound like? What does it *not* look and sound like? I model examples and non-examples so students hear the difference. We talk about why reading might sound choppy and what students can do if they have this problem (echo read with a more fluent reader, read an easier text, etc.). I often say, if the reading is smooth and easy, it is easier for your brain to understand because it sounds just like talking. Here's another example: If we say fluent readers read in phrases, what does that mean? What does that look like? Practicing lists of phrases may work for some students, but it's the ability to phrase in connected text that we're after. I model how we phrase as we talk to help students understand the nature of phrasing. I'll say something like, "Let's go to recess," emphasizing how we say 'let's go' together and 'to recess' together rather than talking word (pause) by (pause) word. I continually model "smushing" little words into bigger words "just like we do when we talk" during shared reading, and I "swoop" phrases by drawing a curved line under them to make it more concrete. Students practice swooping phrases in the texts they're reading. They come up to showcase their phrasing by reading aloud while showing their swooping examples under the document camera. Phrasing not only makes the reading smoother, but it also increases rate.

Similarly, we often tell students fluent readers pay attention to punctuation marks. But, why? How does this affect our understanding and the flow of the reading? I demonstrate by picking up a book from a desk, turning to a page, and reading all the words correctly while completely ignoring the punctuation (putting in random stops, pausing anywhere I please, and plowing through end mark punctuation). The result? I read every word correctly *but students can't understand what I read*. This really gets the message across. I say, "Now we see how important these little marks are. We have to read them very deliberately and accurately just like we read words." So, I continue to model and think aloud about reading expressively using punctuation as a guide. We'll practice reading with punctuation as a particular focus and talk about its effect on our reading, but I'm also *always on the lookout* for students doing what fluent readers do anytime we're reading. This way, I can stop the group, have a student model what she's doing well, and comment on what we're hearing. Thus, our focus on fluency is constant, not just something we attend to during fluency lessons.

Many states set specific grade level standards for fluency or use the Dibels Next correct-words-read-per-minute benchmarks (Good and Kaminski, 2011). As we work with students toward these goals it's important that (a) students know the goal and (b) students know where their performance is in relation to the goal. Research shows knowledge of a specific target like this can significantly increase achievement (Marzano, Pickering, & Pollock, 2001; Stiggins, 2014).

Share realistic options for students to improve their performance inside and outside of class. For instance, I tell students how, when I was a child, my favorite book was *Where the Wild Things Are* by Maurice Sendak. My spiel goes something like this: "I must have read that book one hundred times. I wanted my reading to sound entertaining, lively, and energetic, so I worked at it. Then, I read the book to my mom, I read it to my dad, I read it to my cat . . . anyone who would listen. I loved that book. It was a book I *could* read and I *loved* to read. Do you have any books like that? The more you read and reread them, the more fluent you'll become as you work to make the reading more lively and energetic!" I help students find books they love and that they want to practice. We do the same with favorite poems. Students often sign up to share their energetic reading of books and poems to the class. We end the school year with a "Poetry Jam," inviting family and friends to listen to our poetry readings.

You can see our fluency work is much more than repeated, timed readings and practicing high-frequency phrases in an effort to increase students' reading rates. The types of lessons described above are hallmarks of purposeful fluency instruction that makes a lasting impact.

Favorite resources: The Florida Center for Reading Research website (www.fcrr.org), *The Fluent Reader* (Rasinski, 2010), and *Building Fluency: Lessons and Strategies for Reading Success* (Blevins, 2002).

Language Standards

Language Standards 1, 2, and 3:
Conventions of Standard English (K–2)

If we want students to demonstrate command of conventions, grammar, and usage in speaking and writing, we have to teach and reinforce them within those contexts. I love the efficiency and purposefulness of explicitly teaching the skills in these Language Standards through the Morning Message. I take just a few minutes to explain a concept and why it is important, then we'll look for examples (or mistakes that we can fix) in the Message. As you can see in the photo below, I often create a visual to remind students of the concept. For this particular week in February in second grade, we were focused on linking verbs and capitalizing proper nouns. We fixed an improper linking verb in the first sentence and circled many examples of proper nouns. We listed a few of the proper nouns on our mini-chart (just an 8 × 11 piece of bright cardstock).

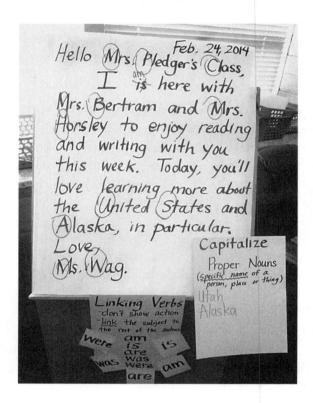

The next day, after we read and examined the Message, we used sentence strips and the sticky notes to link the subjects to the rest of the sentences (see below).

Each day, we review the concept in this manner. We look for examples to highlight in our shared reading. I also then connect what we're learning to writing by asking students to hunt in their writing for the targeted skills. If they find they have them and have used them correctly, they circle the examples, just like in the Morning Message! If they find a mistake, they fix it and circle it! Viola! Editing! (And real reinforcement of learning in appropriate contexts!)

Note: I use the process of "Circling Things We Know" in our writing (Wagstaff, 2011) continually. Once we've learned a grammar, usage, convention, or mechanics skill, I ask students to find examples and circle them in their everyday writing. (You can keep a running list or some other reference of the skills students should look for.) This way, they are always challenged to use what they know and they absolutely love looking back at their writing and congratulating themselves on all the things they've done well! We showcase their learning under the document camera. This is so simple and it really works—you'll find students using conventions like never before! If you have some students who have trouble with this, pair them with another student to look together at one piece of writing.

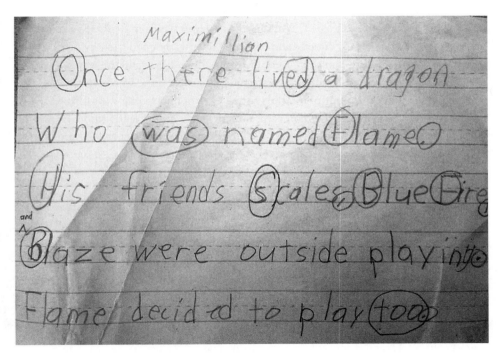

Here, first grader Maximillian "Circled Things We Know" in his story, including: capitals to start sentences, the inflectional ending *ed*, the irregularly spelled high-frequency word *was*, capitals for names, commas in a series, the homophone *too*, and periods to end his sentences! Notice, too, how when he went back to circle, he saw some mistakes and fixed them (lowercase *s* and *b* in the names). Wow! That's a lot of skill work applied in his writing. Great cause to celebrate! (This is an end-of-year sample.)

Research shows that sentence combing (or "*sentence play*" as we call it in K–2) is an effective way to work on grammar and usage, as well (Graham and Perin, 2007). Put two short sentences (or even phrases) on the board and have students play orally with putting them together in varied ways. For example, in second grade I may write "The dog barked." "The bark was loud." and ask students to put these together into one sentence, thus reinforcing adverbs. Likewise, in first grade, I may write, "Rex _____ a dog." "Rex is hairy." and ask students to orally fill in the right linking verb while combining the two sentences (thus reinforcing adjectives). Students enjoy the oral language play, especially when you use sentences with their names or that relate to them and what you're doing in class. As the year progresses, you might ask students to do some of this on paper, but do keep these lessons very short (5 minutes) and fun.

Language Standards 4, 5, and 6: Vocabulary Acquisition and Use (K–2)

One way I build students' vocabulary is by consistently using more complex words in my speech. I don't talk down to students; I "talk up." When students are immersed in mature language, they come to own and use it. I'm careful to include the academic language of the standards in my everyday speech, as you probably noticed as you read the sequences (some examples: identify, compare and contrast, support, text, events, text features, theme, etc.).

Research shows there are several keys to getting the most out of vocabulary instruction (Beck, McKeown, & Kucan, 2013). We must teach fewer words in depth (two or three per lesson), teach the words directly and explicitly by providing kid-friendly definitions, read the words in context, and share multiple examples of the use of the words. Plus, words taught must be kept in circulation so students can hear the words, speak the words, and see the words in print multiple times. One of my favorite ways to keep the words alive is to simply have them on cards and pick a card during transitions to act out, use in a sentence (a volunteer offers a sentence and the class repeats it), provide a derivation (e.g., choice, choose, chosen, chose), add an affix, or provide a synonym or antonym, for example.

When working on content-area writing, keep a short list of relevant vocabulary words. Then, watch for students using the vocabulary in their writing. Celebrate it under the document camera. Do the same with "mature" or "sophisticated" words; keep on the lookout for them in text, create an ongoing list, use them in your modelled writing, and call attention to them when they crop up in student writing!

The vocabulary standards emphasize teaching the use of context clues across grade levels. Using sticky tape or sticky notes, I cover one or two Tier II or Tier III words in shared reading. I teach students to use the words around the covered word to predict what the word might be. Even if they don't come up with the vocabulary word, they often come up with synonyms *and* they concretely see how context clues are helpful to determining word meanings. I also use this strategy to teach shades of meaning. I cover up an appropriate word like *peeked* and give students multiple related words to try in the sentence. We talk about how each changes the meaning and how some don't fit (for example, for *peeked*, we'd try *looked*, *glanced*, *stared*, and *glared*). Students love to act out how the words might look in the context. Then, we uncover the covered word and discuss why we think the author chose that particular word.

Favorite resources: The Florida Center for Reading Research website (www.fcrr.org), and *Teaching Vocabulary in the K–2 Classroom* (Kindle, 2008).

References

Adams, M. J. (1990). *Beginning to read: Thinking and learning about print.* Cambridge: MIT Press.

Adams, M. J., Foorman, B., Lundberg, I., & Beeler, T. (1997). *Phonemic awareness in young children: A classroom curriculum.* Baltimore, MD: Paul H. Brookes.

Allington, R. L. (2012). *What really matters for struggling readers: Designing research-based programs* (3rd ed.). Boston, MA: Allyn & Bacon.

Bear, D., Invernizzi, M., Templeton, S., & Johnston, F. (2011). *Words their way: Word study for phonics, vocabulary and spellings instruction* (5th ed.). Upper Saddle River, NJ: Pearson.

Beck, I. L, McKeown, M. G., & Kucan, L. (2013). *Bringing words to life robust vocabulary instruction* (2nd ed.). New York, NY: Guilford Press.

Blevins, W. (1999). *Phonemic awareness activities for early reading success.* New York, NY: Scholastic.

Blevins, W. (2002). *Building fluency: Lessons and strategies for reading success.* New York, NY: Scholastic.

Blevins, W. (2006). *Phonics from A to Z: A practical guide.* New York, NY: Scholastic.

Britton, J. N. (1970). *Language and learning.* Miami, FL: University of Miami Press.

Calkins, L. M. (1994). *The art of teaching writing.* Portsmouth, NH: Heinemann.

Cronin, D. (2011), *Click, clack, moo: Cows that type.* New York, NY: Little Simon.

Culham, R (2014). *The writing thief: Using mentor texts to teach the craft of writing.* Newark, DE: International Reading Association.

Daly, C. (2011). *Prudence wants a pet.* New York, NY: Roaring Brook Press.

Dowd, M. (2008). *Kevin knows the rules: Introduces classroom rules to kindergarten through third grade students.* Bloomington, IN: AuthorHouse.

Duke, N. (2014). *Inside information: Developing powerful readers and writers of informational text through project-based instruction.* New York, NY: Scholastic.

Duke, N., Caughlan, S., Juzwik, M., & Martin, N. (2011). *Reading and writing genre with purpose in K–8 classrooms.* Portsmouth, NH: Heinemann.

Fitzpatrick, J. (2005). *Phonemic awareness: Playing with sounds to strengthen beginning reading skills.* Cypress, CA: Creative Teaching Press.

Fisher, D. B., & Frey, N. (2015). *Text-dependent questions: Pathways to close and critical reading.* Thousand Oaks, CA: Corwin.

Fisher, D. B., Frey, N., & Lapp, D. (2012). *Teaching students to read like detectives.* Bloomington, IN: Solution Tree Press.

Gallagher, K. (2015). *In the best interest of students: Staying true to what works in the ELA classroom.* Portland, ME: Stenhouse.

Good, R. H. (III), & Kaminski, R. (2011). *Dibels next assessment manual.* Dallas, TX: Sopris West.

Graham, S., & Perin, D. (2007). *Writing next: Effective strategies to improve writing of adolescents in middle and high school.* New York, NY: Carnegie Corporation.

Graves, D. (1983). *Writing: Teachers and children at work.* Portsmouth, NH: Heinemann.

Graves, D. (1994). *A fresh look at writing.* Portsmouth, NH: Heinemann.

Hattie, J. (2009). *Visible learning: A synthesis of over 800 meta-analyses relating to achievement.* New York, NY: Routledge.

Hoyt, L. (2011) *Crafting nonfiction primary: Lessons on writing process, traits, and craft (grades K–2).* Portsmouth, NH: Heinemann.

Kindle, K. (2008). *Teaching vocabulary in the K–2 classroom.* New York, NY: Scholastic.

Marzano, R., Pickering, D., & Pollock, J. (2001). *Classroom instruction that works: Research-based strategies for increasing student achievement.* Alexandria, VA: ASCD.

McDonald, M. (1990). *Is this a house for hermit crab?* New York, NY: Orchard Books.

Miller, D. & Kelley, S. (2014). *Reading in the wild.* San Francisco, CA: Jossey-Bass.

Murray, D. M. (2003). *A writer teaches writing* (2nd ed.). Boston, MA: Wadsworth.

National Endowment for the Arts. (2007). *To read or not to read: A question of national consequence.* Washington, DC: Author.

Pearson, P. D., & Gallagher, M. C. (1983). The instruction of reading comprehension. *Contemporary Educational Psychology, 8,* 317–344.

Rasinski, T. (2010). *The fluent reader.* New York, NY: Scholastic.

Routman, R. (2005). *Writing essentials: Raising expectations and results while simplifying teaching.* Portsmouth, NH: Heinemann.

Routman, R. (2007). *Teaching essentials: Expecting the most and getting the best from every learner, K–8.* Portsmouth, NH: Heinemann.

Serravallo, J. (2015). *The reading strategies book: Your everything guide to developing skilled readers.* Portsmouth, NH: Heinemann.

Stiggins, R. (2014). *Revolutionize assessment: Empower students, inspire learning.* Thousand Oaks, CA: Corwin.

Spiegel, D. (2005). *Classroom discussion: Strategies for engaging all students, building higher-level thinking skills, and strengthening reading and writing across the curriculum.* New York, NY: Scholastic.

Taberski, S., & Burke, J. (2014). *The Common Core companion: The standards decoded.* Thousand Oaks, CA: Corwin.

Vygotsky, L. S. (1978). *Mind in society: The development of higher psychological processes.* Cambridge, MA: Harvard University Press.

Wagstaff, J. M. (1994). *Phonics that work: New strategies for the reading/writing classroom.* New York, NY: Scholastic.

Wagstaff, J. M. (1999). *Teaching reading and writing with word walls.* New York, NY: Scholastic.

Wagstaff, J. M. (2009). *Using name walls to teach reading and writing.* New York, NY: Scholastic.

Wagstaff, J. M. (2011). *Quick start to writing workshop success.* New York, NY: Scholastic.

Wagstaff, J. M. (2015a). *Stella tells her story.* Peterborough, NH: Staff Development for Educators.

Wagstaff, J. M. (2015b). *Stella writes an opinion.* Peterborough, NH: Staff Development for Educators.

Willems, M. (2004). *Knuffle bunny.* New York, NY: Hyperion.

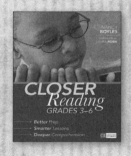

A SAGE Company

CORWIN HAS ONE MISSION: to enhance education through intentional professional learning.

We build long-term relationships with our authors, educators, clients, and associations who partner with us to develop and continuously improve the best evidence-based practices that establish and support lifelong learning.